T0397975

Christian Teachers in Second-Century Rome

Supplements
to
Vigiliae Christianae

TEXTS AND STUDIES OF EARLY CHRISTIAN LIFE AND LANGUAGE

The titles published in this series are listed at *brill.com/vcs*

Christian Teachers in Second-Century Rome

Schools and Students in the Ancient City

Edited by

H. Gregory Snyder

BRILL

LEIDEN | BOSTON

Library of Congress Cataloging-in-Publication Data

Names: Snyder, H. Gregory, 1959- editor.
Title: Christian teachers in second-century Rome : schools and students in the
    ancient city / edited by H. Gregory Snyder.
Description: Leiden ; Boston : Brill, 2020. | Series: Vigiliae Christianae,
    supplements, 0920-623X ; volume159 | Includes index.
Identifiers: LCCN 2020012729 (print) | LCCN 2020012730 (ebook) |
    ISBN 9789004422476 (hardback) | ISBN 9789004428010 (ebook)
Subjects: LCSH: Christian education–Italy–Rome–History–Early church, ca.
    30-600.
Classification: LCC BV1470.18 C47 2020 (print) | LCC BV1470.18 (ebook) |
    DDC 268.0937/63–dc23
LC record available at https://lccn.loc.gov/2020012729
LC ebook record available at https://lccn.loc.gov/2020012730

Typeface for the Latin, Greek, and Cyrillic scripts: "Brill". See and download: brill.com/brill-typeface.

ISSN 0920-623X
ISBN 978-90-04-42247-6 (hardback)
ISBN 978-90-04-42801-0 (e-book)

Contents

Figures

Notes on Contributors

Miguel Herrero de Jáuregui
is Associate Professor of Greek Philology at the Universidad Complutense de Madrid.

Robin M. Jensen
is Patrick O'Brien Professor of Theology at the University of Notre Dame.

Judith M. Lieu
is Lady Margaret's Professor Emerita of Divinity at Cambridge University.

Winrich Löhr
is Professor of Historical Theology at the University of Heidelberg.

Christoph Markschies
is Professor of Ancient Christianity at Humboldt University in Berlin and Director of the Greek Christian Writers Project at Berlin-Brandenburg Academy of Sciences and Humanities.

Fernando Rivas Rebaque
is on the Theology Faculty at the Universidad Pontificia Comillas (Madrid, Spain).

H. Gregory Snyder
is Professor of Religious Studies at Davidson College, Davidson, NC, USA.

Einar Thomassen
is Professor of Religion at the University of Bergen.

Heidi Wendt
is Associate Professor of Religions of the Greco-Roman World in the School of Religious Studies and the Department of History and Classical Studies at McGill University.

Introduction

Most of the essays in this volume were solicited for a workshop at the 2015 Oxford Patristics Conference on second-century teachers in Rome. Participants in the workshop all shared an interest in the ways that early Christian groups fit within the hyper-urban city of Rome and how they would have looked to contemporary eyes not blinkered by 2000 years of subsequent history. The institutions emerging from that history have not only controlled and constricted the available evidence, but more subtly, bequeathed to us the concepts, categories, and language with which we view what little evidence remains. It requires concerted intellectual effort to think outside of traditional categories. Contributors to this volume hope to have made progress in this regard.

Second, the essays gathered here touch in various ways on the larger context within which our understanding of Christian "schools" must be set, namely, that of other philosophical groups which were themselves quite heterogeneous and varied, not corresponding neatly to modern categories of "school." Many years ago, Peter Brown observed, "Small study-circles were the powerhouses of the Christian culture of the second and third century."[1] There is still plenty of room for comprehensive and comparative analysis of Christian groups that views them alongside other groups in Rome: medical sects, philosophical schools, cult groups, literary salons—wherever students are gathered around teachers. The editor and contributors hope to go some distance towards this goal by further enriching our understanding of the ways in which the variety of Christian teaching circles should be viewed among other philosophical, religious, and didactic groups. What points of continuity and discontinuity can be found between Christian teaching circles and philosophical groups when it comes to patterns of textual usage, or the ways in which they handle the balance between esoteric and exoteric instruction?

Finally, contributors to the volume all share, to varying degrees, a fascination with the city of Rome and its role as a noisy urban theater for groups of people calling themselves "Christians." In particular, it makes for a delightful starting point that three crucially important figures—Marcion, Valentinus, and Justin Martyr—were active in the city at various points under the Antonine emperors, living and teaching somewhere in its environs from roughly 130–160 CE. All three were Greek-speaking expatriates from the eastern Empire;

---

1 Brown 1982, 104.

all three gravitated to Rome as members of the new Christian movement; all three styled themselves as teachers and surrounded themselves with students and followers. All three of them were deeply committed to scripture and to the careful scrutiny of written texts. But all three of them held quite different ideas about what Christians should read, how they should, and how they should behave: Marcion dismissed the Hebrew Bible as useless, elevating the letters of Paul to scriptural status; likewise, Valentinus claimed Paul as a direct influence through a shadowy figure named Theudas. Justin, by contrast, never once mentions Paul in his extant writings and seems to know nothing about him. Marcion, the ethical rigorist, required celibacy of his followers and would have banned the practice of marriage; Valentinus and his followers, on the other hand, seem to have considered marriage as a fundamental concept for imagining divine-human relations, given their attachment to the enigmatic "bridal chamber" ritual. All three of these figures drew to themselves students, admirers, and patrons, all of them embedded in the social fabric of the city, residing in distinct neighborhoods, moving about, mixing and interacting with others.

On this point—mixing—the city of Rome stands alone in the ancient world for its population, its urban density, and its social complexity. Homi Bhabha's oft-quoted comment on the city environment seems especially *apropos* in this case: "it is the city which provides the space in which emergent identifications and new social movements of the people are played out."[2] The city environment thoroughly conditions the life of these groups: the patterns of movement imposed on the actors, the networks of patronage and ethnic connections, the possibilities for novel conflations of ideas, and the sheer concentration of people make for a wide range of possibilities where groups are concerned. We should expect that the range of groups identifying themselves as Christian will vary a great deal.

The idea of mixing relates to the volume as well. The seminar in Oxford brought together scholars from several different countries: Spain, the U.K., Germany, Norway, Italy, as well as the United States. Moreover, the authors represented in the volume cover a chronological spectrum, with essays from both senior and junior scholars in the field. And while the essays proceed mostly on the basis of literary sources, some of the papers (Jensen, Snyder) avail themselves of visual and archaeological evidence as well.

A word about the individual contributions and the connections they have to each other.

---

2   Bhabha 1990, 320.

Since Jews were present in Rome before Christians arrived, it makes sense to place Judith Lieu's essay at the beginning. Despite the paucity of evidence, she argues that when it comes to forms of life, Christian groups in Rome most likely followed in paths already trod by Jews. Rather than invoking the concept of "school," with its traditional connotations, she refers instead the "mixed economy" of "philosophical exchange and guidance." Within Jewish circles, reflection on the Septuagint is of central importance. After considering areas of strength and weakness in the evidence—rabbinic and epigraphic— she goes on to discuss lessons that might be learned from Justin's *Dialogue with Trypho*. Eschewing debates about audience or whether the *DT* represents an actual debate that took place in Ephesus, she rightly affirms that the *DT* surely portrays, "a world of argument about texts and meaning with distinctive techniques and terminology that was familiar." Moreover, regardless of the verbatim accuracy of the *DT*, Lieu suggests that "the Teachers" appearing throughout the DT carry echoes of actual debates and practices in Diaspora Judaism. Trypho is taken as a representative of such activities that may be independent of synagogue-based authorities. In this way, Jews are not fundamentally different than their Christian counterparts.

Einar Thomassen's essay follows naturally on Lieu's in light of its careful demurral when it comes to the use of "school," and moreover, when it comes to reflection on written texts. Beginning with a review of the senses of *scholê*, he marks out a skeptical position on the question, preferring the term *ekklesia* for Valentinian groups. In this regard, he differs from Markschies (this volume) and from scholars such as Ismo Dunderberg.[3] According to Thomassen, members of these groups sought salvation "through ritual acts and an attitude of faith," and so can rightly be characterized as "religious groups" rather than as schools analogous to pagan philosophical schools. But even though Thomassen wishes to maintain this distinction, he goes on to show that the nature of much Valentinian literature suggests that there is a good bit of school-like activity going on in these religious groups. Proper apprehension of the systematic treatises, exegetical works, and documents like *The Gospel of Philip* seem to presuppose a context in which a teacher is giving necessary background to students that would help them understand these difficult texts. Diatribal elements in *The Gospel of Philip*, for example, point directly towards this conclusion.

Christoph Markschies' essay makes an interesting point of comparison with that of Thomassen, given their disagreement on the whether the term "school" is rightly applied to "gnostic" groups. The term "apokrypha" serves as the start-

---

3 Dunderberg 2008, 3–4.

ing point of Markschies' paper, in particular, the *Apocryphon of John*. According to Markschies, this way of characterizing certain teaching—as secret, pointed at a select group of *cognoscenti*—suggests a structural likeness and perhaps even an organic connection between philosophical groups like Pythagoreans and Platonists and groups considered adherents of "Gnosis." The connection is clearer with the Sethian materials, but the author argues that the literary activity of Valentinian groups can also be understood in this way. The distinction between esoteric and exoteric teaching considered characteristic of Peripatetic groups also maps well over this landscape of public and private. If writings like Ptolemy's myth as described by Irenaeus should be considered as exoteric, rather than esoteric, a profound re-evaluation of Valentinian beliefs are in order. It would mean that what people like Tertullian and also modern scholars might have accepted as metaphysical truth claims about the existence and nature of certain "divine figures" is in fact, not propositional metaphysics at all, but rather something provisional, metaphorical, fictive, designed for an exoteric function, and that the real meaning of esoteric teaching lying behind this "artistic myth" needs to be re-thought. Markschies' essay thus treats the question of how written texts were used in school-like groups, but advances the inquiry by raising this question: what, exactly, does the extant shape and nature of the textual evidence we have tell us about the beliefs and practices of the groups from which they derive? If Markschies' claims have merit, then it may be necessary to re-evaluate how much we think we know about the beliefs current within these groups.

Robin Jensen's essay shifts the focus of attention from the beliefs and practices current within philosophical schools (broadly understood) to the ways in which philosophical figures would have been understood by their contemporaries. When discussing the Apologists, it is all too easy to rely solely on written sources, as if the teaching activity of these figures were primarily a written affair. But of course, the ways in which these figures were viewed is influenced by far more than what they themselves wrote or what was written about them. These teachers were approached and experienced by their contemporaries within the matrix of pre-existing ideas and expectations about who teachers typically were: what they looked like, their social patterns, and associations. A good percentage of these ideas and expectations were conditioned and captured by the visual evidence. It is vitally important, therefore, to include such evidence if we wish to understand how the figure of "teacher" within the Roman environment would have been understood by the students and onlookers that gathered around them. Jensen observes that the demand for portraits of philosophers and intellectuals shows a marked rise in the second and third century, during the Second Sophistic, suggesting, a deep connection between the ekphrastic impulse in rhetoric and the desire for visual portraiture. In some cases, the presence of such portraits might mirror the actual practice of learned activity, as in the case of Nigrinus, the philosopher that Lucian visits, standing with a book in his hand, surrounded by busts of ancient philosophers (*Nigr.* 3). But most of such portraiture probably served decorative purposes: commissioners of such pieces sought to project an image of "culture and refinement" by adorning their homes with images of learned men. Such a pattern suggests a widespread esteem for philosophical erudition, and many people with means were anxious to acquire the appearance (if not the reality) of such learning, by means of visual signals. Correspondingly, the cultural stock of teachers and philosophers must have run fairly high: high enough to enough to be deployed in the search for social capital, and high enough to draw the satirical eye of Lucian.

Because of its emphasis on the cultural environment of the Second Sophistic, Heidi Wendt's essay dovetails naturally with Jensen's. She builds on many of the results in her well-known book, *At the Temple Gates*, which examines the culture of free-lance religious experts in the Roman Empire, with particular emphasis on Rome. Characterized by a spirit of innovation and competition, such experts displayed their expertise with texts and traditions in order to persuade their hearers and readers and buttress claims to authority. Wendt sets the origins of gospel literature within this framework vision of intellectual literary activity. Gospel scholars have traditionally assumed that the four canonical gospels emerged from distinct communities, going by the name of their eponymous Gospel: the Matthean Community, the Johannine community, and so forth: remembrances of the historical Jesus and "sentiments of pious communities of early Christ believers." Recently, this way of thinking of gospel origins has come under spirited attack by Markus Vinzent among others, who prefers to assign the origins of Gospel literature to the second, rather than the first century. Wendt is willing to cautiously entertain these theories, bringing to the question her own considerable understanding of literary production and activity in the Second Century. Much of this literary activity is parasitic and competitive in nature, and this provides an intriguing stance from which to understand the Synoptic Gospels, say, Matthew's use of Mark, possible connections between the Gospels of Thomas and John, or Luke's claim in his preface, that having read a good many attempts to describe the growth of the Jesus movement, he might just be able to come up with something better. Such a claim sits naturally within the agonistic literary environment that Wendt so richly describes in her book. Along with William Arnal, Wendt subscribes to the idea that the origins of "Christianity" should be traced more to developments in the second century rather than the first: historical developments, but of course,

but intellectual ways of seeing, remembering, and claiming historical events in the formation of a new set of identities. Regardless of whether one adopts this new perspective wholesale, it is intriguing to consider that the formative process of gospel literature may well reflect the interests and inflections of rival literary figures. We should, claims Wendt, allow for the same "authorial interests and self-expression" in Gospel literature that we naturally assume for other intellectuals of the Early Empire. Justin's work as a teacher and exegete, as well as characters such as Theodotus the Cobbler, find a natural frame when seen from this perspective. *The Dialogue with Trypho* sits very comfortably here as well, as does Justin's public sparring with the Crescens, the Cynic philosopher. The Roman urban environment provided many "mechanisms and venues" for agonistic literary activity.

Sharing with Wendt's article an awareness of new work on Marcion, Winrich Löhr's essay turns the volume to the subject of individual teachers. Marcion and his work are the subject of lively debate in current scholarship, and Löhr gives a reliable synopsis of the state of affairs. He discusses perennial problems of the dating of Marcion and his identity as a shipowner (*nauclerus*) before moving on to his work as a teacher and textual expert. Did Marcion edit and amend the already-existing Gospel of Luke, or did he devise his own gospel that in turn led to the creation of what are now called the canonical gospels, as Markus Vinzent proposes? Were there "ur-gospels" in circulation that Marcion adopted and changed that eventually became the familiar canonical gospels, as Matthias Klinghardt, Jason BeDuhn and others maintain? And how are we to understand the relationship between and sequence of Marcion's *Antitheses* and his Gospel? Did *The Antitheses* offer a justification and program for the Gospel? Or was it an afterthought? Everything we thought we knew about Marcion is now up for negotiation and revision. Marcion the "proto-protestant," theologically dualist redactor of Luke, created by Irenaeus and Tertullian, and passed along by Harnack, is no longer satisfactory. In this review article, Löhr does not pretend to offer answers to these sweeping questions, though he does usefully discriminate the ways that Vinzent and Klinghardt relate Marcion's *Antitheses* and his Gospel. For Vinzent, the two are tightly coupled, the former giving rise to the latter; for Klinghardt, *The Antitheses* are a later defense against polemic stirred up by his Gospel. Characterizing the general state of affairs, Löhr speaks of the "splitting" of Marcion into different figures: Marcion the author/editor and Marcion the teacher. While this fragmented situation is hardly satisfying, it may for the moment be necessary, as problems with Marcion the user, editor, and disseminator of texts are worked out. Based on these results and a plausible construal of the shape of Marcion's literary activity, then it will be possible to see how this literary activity dovetails with his activity as a Roman teacher.

Moving to Justin Martyr, Fernando Rivas Rebaque helpfully invokes Antonio Gramsci's concept of the "organic intellectual." Bearing the socially approved marks of pedigree and education, the "traditional intellectual" serves as a spokesperson for the prevailing ideology (either knowingly or unknowingly). In contemporary society, the "traditional intellectual" comes bearing a Ph.D. or an equivalent, along with social involvements recognized by the hegemonic, bourgeois culture within which the traditional intellectual lives and moves. The "organic intellectual" arises from within communities outside of and oppressed by the hegemonic culture. The "organic intellectual" does not come armored with an advanced degree. He or she articulates the needs and agendas of the group that gave birth to them. The organic intellectual crystallizes the alternative discourse of such a community, giving voice and structure to its thoughts and needs. At a first level of approximation, one might supply Malcolm x as a modern example of an organic intellectual. According to Rebaque, Justin and his work fit into this taxonomy of intellectuals, even if somewhat imperfectly. Here the term "as" in the title of the article seems to me, critical. It is better to say that in certain respects, Justin functioned "as" an organic intellectual, rather than to say that he "is" (or was) an organic intellectual. Considered from the point of his origins, Justin presents himself as a traditional intellectual, one who has studied with a succession of philosophers: first a Stoic, then a Peripatetic, then finally a Platonist—though he confesses to falling short when quizzed by a Pythagorean about his acquaintance with music, geometry, and mathematics (*Dialogue with Trypho* 2). Moreover, his mode of dress, intentionally and recognizably that of a philosopher, indicates his own sense of placement. But his affiliation with the Christians places him within a different context, in which he becomes a spokesperson for a subaltern group and adopts its discourse.

Justin functions as an organic intellectual in his role as a defender of Christianity over against the hegemonic regime (both politically and philosophically) of the Roman Empire. This outsider status makes him bold enough to address the emperor as a fellow philosopher, and also insouciant enough to make demands ("we demand that charges against the Christians be investigated"), even to scold dismissively ("you are without excuse"), as he does at the beginning of his *First Apology*. On such occasions, Justin definitely stands outside the role of the "traditional intellectual." Justin's role as an organic intellectual equips him for discussion and debate with outsiders like Crescens as well. The organic intellectual also faces inwards to the Christian community, when it comes to the policing of borders, adjudication of beliefs (accepted *versus* heretical) and relations with other groups such as Jews. The title bears comparison with Wendt's use of "religious specialist," though there are important differences: the authority of the organic intellectual grows up out of the group of which he or she is a member; on Wendt's account, "religious specialists" stage themselves as authoritative practitioners, based on their facility with texts or traditions. But there are similarities too: the organic intellectual mediates a relationship between such texts/traditions and those who desire to access them—individuals standing outside traditional elite categories. Moreover, the work of the organic intellectual and the independent religious specialist is marked by strife and competition, both with the dominant structures of society and with other intellectuals and specialists.

Following in the wake of Justin is his student Tatian, the subject of Miguel Herrero's essay. Noting and then sidestepping Tatian's reputation for disagreeableness, Herrero examines the ways in which Tatian deploys certain key philosophical concepts: *mimesis, thauma, pathos,* and the significance of being *autodidaktos.* In light of his Platonic ancestry, Tatian subscribes to a general skepticism about mimesis: imitation is always imperfect: copies are liable to introduce corruption, and copies of copies, corruption on top of corruption. For Tatian, only one source escapes the inevitable degradation connected with *mimesis,* namely, the Scriptures, which convey the very teaching of God and the Logos. Only the word as found in Scripture is exempt from the loss mechanisms that typify *mimesis.* In a particularly bold move, Tatian likens his own teaching to that of the Logos, implicitly making the claim that in his exposition of Scripture, Tatian, like the Logos, is not subject to loss (it is no wonder, perhaps, that a man who boldly likens himself to the Logos should be an insufferable person) Herrero goes on to highlight what must surely be consciously drawn contrasts between the philosophical conversion of Heraclitus who claimed to be "self-taught" (*autodidaktos*) and Tatian the "God-taught" (*theodidaktos*). Among the many fine observations in this essay, two in particular stand out: first, Tatian's deliberate way of situating himself within the cultural field of the Second Sophistic, with its emphasis on the charismatic and inspired speaker. Second, Herrero makes a good case for the way in which Tatian's philosophical commitment to Scripture as a teacher dovetails with his authorship of *The Diatessaron.*

The next essay in the volume touches on a figure whose image cuts across many of the categories encountered so far: Theodotus the Cobbler, a character who in some respects, answers to Rebaque's description of the "organic intellectual," but perhaps more so to Heidi Wendt's figure of the religious expert/entrepreneur. Hitherto, Theodotus has been noted chiefly for his place in the history of doctrine, as a poster child for the heresy of adoptionism. This paper takes a different angle, exploring the curious phrase "learned cobbler." I argue that this label is part of Theodotus' self-definition as a working philosopher: by deploying it, Theodotus invokes the cachet of Simon the Cobbler, who has a long history in Platonist and Cynic literature. It also owes something to the example of the Apostle Paul, whom Acts describes as a tentmaker. In this respect, Theodotus is an example of a different kind of teacher than Justin, Marcion, or Valentinus, expanding the spectrum of possibility for what Roman teachers looked like and where they might have been active.

With Theodotus, we find ourselves at the end of the second century. The essay ends on a spatial note, depositing the reader on the streets of Rome, the Vicus Sandaliarius, which makes for a fitting ending for the volume, as well as an opening to future progress when it comes to thinking about schools, study-circles, literary salons, and cult groups. It is difficult to be precise and conclusive when it comes to situating these people and their groups, given the fragmentary state of the surviving evidence. I have argued elsewhere that Justin Martyr's "school" can with modest confidence be situated outside the Porta Capena near the "bi-via," the fork of the Via Appia and the Via Latina.[4] And I believe it highly likely that Christians of a Valentinian persuasion were located in a suburban villa along the Via Latina.[5] Yet even in the absence of high confidence about precise locations, it should be possible to furnish our imaginations with examples of the kinds of spaces in which the teaching activities mentioned in this volume would have taken place: an apartment above a bath? A cramped tenement room on the third floor, or a more generous *medianum* flat on the piano nobile, facing a palaestra? A suburban villa? An urban *domus*? Either of the latter two might be site for a salon like that of Marcellina, where, it seems, images of Jesus, Plato, Pythagoras, were on display, playing a role in the group's rituals:

> Among these was Marcellina, who came to Rome under Anicetus and, with this teaching, she destroyed many. They call themselves Gnostics. They also possess images, some of which are paintings (*imagines*), some made of other materials, saying that Christ's image was copied by Pilate at the time Jesus lived among men. They put garlands on these images and exhibit them along with the images of the philosophers of the world, images of Pythagoras, Plato, Aristotle, and the rest. Toward these [images] they practice other rites like those of the nations.[6]

---

4   Snyder 2007.
5   Snyder 2014.
6   *Haer.* 1.25.6. The translation given here is from Unger 1992, 89–90, with a few minor changes. For a recent discussion, see Peppard 2015, 239–240 and Snyder 2017.

The garlanding mentioned suggests ritual action, and that the images in question were not confined to a lararium, but standing busts in a room, as in the home of the Platonist philosopher Nigrinus, whom Lucian finds with "a book in his hands and many busts of ancient philosophers (εἰκόνες παλαιῶν φιλοσόφων) standing round about (*Nigr.* 3)."

Imagining the settings and spaces for these groups, populating them with the kinds of people who would have inhabited them, we can think in more detailed, granular ways about their particular forms of life. What kind of advantages and constraints do physical locations and spatial environments impose on school activities and social patterns? If indeed Justin's domicile/school is located within a stone's throw of the Mutatorium Caesaris, one of the main points of entry to the city, what are the consequences for networking and ease of access? What kind of neighborhood is this? Who passes through it? What ties, if any, bind its inhabitants? What are the streets and venues where a person like Justin might hold a public disputation with an opponent like Crescens? Justin sets his *Dialogue with Trypho* in "the walks of the Xystus" in Ephesus; are there analogous spaces in his neighborhood in Rome? Where else in the city might he travel and how easy would that be? To what lengths would he go to find an audience, and to what lengths would prospective hearers and students go to reach him? The same questions can be asked of Christians living in a suburban villa in the outskirts of Rome, with all the development in play under Trajan and Hadrian. Questions such as these, and imagined answers to them, disciplined by knowledge about urban social and spatial dynamics, can help us conceive of different kinds of schools, student-teacher circles, philosophical salons, and cult groups in appropriately nuanced ways. This volume endeavors to make a step in that direction.

In conclusion, I would like to express my gratitude to Davidson College student Emily Privott, who proofread all the essays and helped to regularize the many inconsistencies between essays. When it came to the task of publication, Dirk Bakker was a thoughtful and thorough editor, and it was a pleasure to work with him.

Bibliography

Bhabha, Homi. 1990. "DissemiNation." Pages 291–322 in *Nation and Narration*. Edited by Homi Bhabha. London: Routledge.

Brown, Peter. 1982. *The Body and Society: Men, Women, and Sexual Renunciation in Early Christianity*. New York: Columbia University Press.

Dunderberg, Ismo. 2008. *Beyond Gnosticism: Myth, Lifestyle, and Society in the School of Valentinus*. New York: Columbia University Press.

Peppard, Michael. 2015. "Was the Presence of Christ in Statues? The Challenge of Divine Media for a Jewish Roman God." Pages 225–269 in *The Art of Empire; Christian Art in Its Imperial Context*. Edited by Lee Jefferson and Robin Jensen. Minneapolis, Minn.: Fortress Press.

Snyder, H. Gregory. 2007. "'Above the Bath of Myrtinus'; Justin Martyr's 'School' in the City of Rome." *Harvard Theological Review* 100:335–362.

Snyder, H. Gregory. 2014. "The Discovery and Interpretation of the Flavia Sophe Inscription; New Results." *Vigiliae Christianae* 68:1–59.

Snyder, H. Gregory. 2017. "'She Destroyed Multitudes': Marcellina's Group in Rome." Pages 39–61 in *Women and Knowledge in Early Christianity*. Edited by Ulla Terva-hauta, Ivan Miroshnikov, Outi Lehtipuu, and Ismo Dunderberg. Leiden: Brill.

Unger, Dominic. 1992. *Irenaeus of Lyons,* Against the Heresies. Vol. 1. Ancient Christian Writers 55. New York: Paulist Press.

CHAPTER 1

Jewish Teachers in Rome?

Judith M. Lieu

This paper will argue that the broader context for locating Christian teachers in Rome must also include Jewish teachers. That Jews engaged with the intellectual practices associated with "schools" has been well-established for Alexandria for which we do have direct evidence. In the case of Rome, Jewish voices are largely refracted through those of others. However, including them in the picture may help reconfigure some of the binary oppositions with which discussions both of Jewish identity and of the development of Christian thought operate.

The emergence of Christian schools, most evidently in Alexandria but also, as in other contributions to this volume, in Rome, has sometimes been associated with the move of the "Jesus movement" from its original Jewish setting to that of the intellectual life of the Greco-Roman city. In an older terminology, it belongs to the "Hellenization" of early Christianity. Despite the fact that any simplistic contrast between "Jewish" and "Hellenistic" has long been relegated to the false dichotomies of the past, the assumption that each represents a differentiated set of structures and intellectual *modus operandi* continues to cast a long shadow.[1] Here it will be argued not only that, as in so many other aspects of diaspora existence, Christian communities may have been following a path already taken by Jewish ones, but also that Jewish teachers and schools were part of the mixed economy of what may be broadly termed philosophical exchange and guidance, not least in Rome.

1   The Puzzle of Diaspora Judaism

That there was a substantial Jewish community at Rome is clear, but reconstructing the structures and life of that community, particularly in the early

---

1   This is implicitly the model with which the influential study of Roman Christianity by Peter Lampe (2003) works, with its contrast between "synagogal tradition" associated with Jewish Christians and the "pagan" philosophical environment of someone like Justin (e.g. pp. 75–79, 283–284, 353–355).

Empire, is far from easy.[2] As a starting point, it might be assumed that the conclusions that have been drawn more generally about diaspora Judaism would also apply to that at Rome. On the basis of the available evidence, which outside first century Alexandria is predominantly archaeological and epigraphic, most attention has been paid to questions such as the nature of the "synagogue," however defined, to the degree of integration within the civic context, and to comparison with other city-based institutions, namely the *collegia*.[3] While the debate continues as to how far Diaspora Judaism was a relatively cohesive and uniform phenomenon, as may be suggested in part by commonalities in titles given to functionaries and in architectural styles where available (although not in Rome), or how far it was unpredictably diverse, perhaps responding to specific local circumstances (as at Dura Europos), the overall consensus has been to mark the difference from rabbinic Judaism as it developed initially in the Land of Israel during the early Empire. Hence in the context of the present topic the broad consensus is that Diaspora Judaism was not under the sway of rabbinic Judaism, at least before the fourth century, and that it is illegitimate to use rabbinic sources as representing anything that might have been done, practiced, or taught in Diaspora communities.

This liberation of Greek-speaking Judaism from the shadow of rabbinic literature has been seen as largely positive, in particular because rabbinic literature can present itself as alien and impenetrable, not just in language but also in the epistemology it takes for granted. For our purposes it would be inappropriate to project upon Diaspora Judaism the self-sufficient, solipsistic, world-view of the rabbis, nor need we be concerned about the vigorous debates in scholarship as to whether the symbolic universe projected by that literature was nothing more than an intellectual construct of a relatively powerless, self-selecting minority, or whether it had actual social expression among the majority non-rabbinic population. On the other hand, given the massive volume of rabbinic literature and the paucity of literature from the Diaspora (other than epigraphic material), this considerably constrains our ability to say very much at all with confidence about the life, and particularly the intellectual life, of Diaspora Jews, including those in Rome. Yet a paucity of evidence does not necessarily mean a paucity of activity and substance; the apparent disappearance, with few exceptions, of Hellenistic Jewish literature from the record after the end of the first century remains a puzzle, but it is likely to be due to the fact that Christian circles had little reason to preserve it as they did the earlier material which they

---

2 Yet more can be said than regarding many other cities: see Barclay 1996, 282–319; Rutgers 1995; Cappelletti 2006.

3 The literature is now extensive; see Trebilco 1991; Barclay 1996.

could interpret for their own purposes, while it lay outside the textual tradition which formed the core of the eventual survivors within rabbinic Judaism.[4] Nonetheless, in recent years a more positive approach has endeavored to move beyond a picture of Diaspora Judaism that starts from two "deficiency" principles, namely, first, of being defined negatively as non-rabbinic, and, secondly, of a primary focus on the responses by a minority group of separation, accommodation, or assimilation over against the dominant culture. Of particular significance among new insights has been the emphasis on the importance of the Septuagint and of its consequent effect for life and also for study in Diaspora Judaism, both initially and continuing well beyond the period when according to older accounts it was expropriated by Christians and hence dropped by Jewish communities (see Rajak 2009).

2   Scripture and Law among the Jews of Rome

Within this broader setting the specific political situation of Rome, as well as the distinctive character of the surviving evidence, may stimulate a somewhat richer set of possibilities. References in classical sources indicate the presence of Jews in Rome from the second century BCE, but the influx of prisoners after Pompey's campaigns in 63 BCE and especially after the Roman victory in 70 CE would have had particular impact. Estimates of the size of the Jewish population in Rome range between twenty and sixty thousand for the first century CE. (Noy 2000, 257). However, other than generally hostile comments by Roman authors, and references in Josephus and Philo, both of whom spent time in Rome but are surprisingly uninformative about the community there,[5] the primary direct evidence is epigraphic, almost exclusively from the catacombs, of which there is indeed an abundance.[6] Although the oldest parts of the Jewish catacombs may be dated to the second, and even to the first century, much of the substantive evidence begins in the third-fourth centuries and is of a later date than our concern; even so, it is sufficiently consistent to allow for some conclusions regarding the previous period. For example, a number of synagogues are mentioned, with which some of those buried are identified; in contrast to the organization of the Jews in Alexandria, the evidence suggests

---

4   Recently a growing interest in Jewish educational structures, including in Hellenistic Jewish sources, has emerged: see *inter alia*, Brooke and Smithuis 2017; Zurawski and Boccaccini 2017.

5   See also Acts 28:16–31.

6   Rajak 1994; Rutgers 1995.

that these various congregations largely acted independently without any over-arching ruling Council.[7] It is probably no coincidence that a similar absence of central organization and cohesive structure also seems to be true of the early Christian communities in Rome, as indeed of other "foreign groups." It follows that it cannot be assumed that all communities were identical in their practices or pattern of organization, neither can we be sure how association with a particular synagogue effected the inclinations and attitudes of their members.

In a recent study Tal Ilan has observed that we know nothing about the language or Bible of the early Jews at Rome or even whether the style of Judaism they practiced was "associated with the Hellenistic brand" familiar from Alexandrian sources or was closer to that "developed in the Land of Israel" (2009, 364). The cautionary tone is valuable but just as the stark alternative in the second clause may be over-simple, so too the first claim may be overly negative. In a study of the evidence for groups of foreigners at Rome, David Noy acknowledges that the spoken languages of family and internal community life are inevitably hidden from us, but he also notes the extent to which the use of Greek predominates in written, including epigraphic, remains (Noy 2000, 169–178, 264). Certainly, knowledge of Hebrew or Aramaic cannot be excluded, particularly after each influx of prisoners from Judaea;[8] later, from the fourth century, there is more consistent evidence of its reintroduction, as is also the case elsewhere in the Diaspora. Nonetheless, over three-quarters of the Jewish epitaphs are in Greek, the rest being for the most part in Latin;[9] despite an increasing use of Latin, following a pattern also found among some other groups, Greek continues to predominate, leading Noy to conclude that it formed an "in-group" language for the community. Echoes of scripture are very rare, the most persuasive being three allusions to Prov 10:7, all dated to the third-fourth century, two closer to Aquila and one to the Septuagint (*JIWE* 2, 112, 276, 307). The fact that *1 Clement*, written from Rome, draws heavily on the Septuagint may suggest that the Old Greek was also the version available in Jewish synagogues or archives, as will be argued further below.

Yet the paucity of scriptural references (and indeed of scriptural artistic representation) is likely to be a matter of epigraphic practice and not of disinterest.

---

7 Against Williams 1998, who argues for an over-seeing council, but without conclusive evidence.

8 However, *JIWE* 2 (= Noy 1995) 112, dedicated to "Macedonis the Hebrew from Caesarea in Palestine," is in Greek and alludes to Prov 10:7 (Aquila). The numbers in references to *JIWE* 2 refer to the text numbers, whereas any general discussion by the editor is referenced as Noy 1995, with page number.

9 Precise figures vary according to how bilingual inscriptions, those with a word or phrase in Hebrew, and those whose Jewishness is disputed, are counted; see Rutgers 1995, 176–191.

With reference to the catacombs Rutgers has noted how, when it comes to design, technology, and artifacts, Jewish practice followed the same patterns and development as their non-Jewish (including Christian) neighbors, while at the same time the iconography displays an over-riding preference for Jewish themes (1995, 92–95). Most important among these is the menorah, along with other symbols with liturgical associations, lulabs, ethrogs, shofar, and perhaps a couple of representations of huts for the Feast of Tabernacles (*JIWE* 2, 246, 588 [on a glass]); however, representations of a Torah shrine, often containing scriptural rolls, are also to be found (Williams 2011, 332–334, 346–349).

Further, the specific importance of scripture and of the law is demonstrated epigraphically by the number of epithets given to individuals which in some way relate to these: so, for example, in addition to the conventional "lover of mother/father/child/husband," we encounter "lover of the commandment" (φιλέντολος) four times, twice applied to women—Crispina, who is also described as "zealous," and Victorina, praised in Latin also as "righteous and holy";[10] the other two individuals so-described also held some role or status in the synagogue and are given further epithets, Priscus, possibly an "archon," as "lover of the people and lover of the poor," and Pancharius, a "father of the synagogue," as "lover of the people." Together these confirm the centrality of the commands in the value system of the community (*JIWE* 2, 240, 281, 564, 576). Similar epithets include "lover of the law" (φιλόνομος), used of a child but also of someone who holds the roles of scribe and psalm-singer (*JIWE* 2, 212, 502); "disciple of the law" (νομομαθής, four times), including a certain Eusebius who is also described as "teacher" (*JIWE* 2, 68; also 270, 374, 390); "teacher of the law (νομοδιδάσκαλος)" of an individual whose name is lost; and a certain Mnaseas labelled "disciple of the wise" while also being "father of synagogues" (*JIWE* 2, 307, 544). To a large extent all these epithets are absent, rare, or very late in the literary record—and mainly confined to Christian sources—, and so may constitute an "in-group" vocabulary mimicking but consciously different from contemporary honorifics.[11]

Equally striking is the frequency of the designation "scribe" (γραμματεύς), represented almost thirty times, including four in Latin,[12] and outnumbered

---

10   *JIWE* 2, 564, "*dicea osia filentolia.*"

11   Elsewhere in Greek literature "Philolaos" and "Philonomos" primarily occur as proper names, while "lover of the command" [commandment] as well as "disciple of the law" and "teacher of the law" are mainly restricted to later Christian sources (other than "teacher of the law" in Luke 5:17, Acts 5:34; 1 Tim. 1:7, and quotations). Noy 1995, 536, 538 lists the last two as "Jewish titles" and the others as "epithets," but it is not clear that this distinction can be made.

12   Including two references to a "scribe designate" (μελλογραμματεύς).

only by the somewhat unspecific "ruler."[13] Noy suggests that this role was similar to that also found in *collegia*, "an office which was apparently functional and relatively low in the internal hierarchy" (1995, 10), but it is far from obvious that this is correct: those commissioning the epitaphs felt it worthy of record, either of themselves or of the deceased, and in one case of both (*JIWE* 2, 223). Certainly, on several occasions a scribe is associated with a specific synagogue, and no doubt community life would have demanded a number of literate activities (*JIWE* 2, 1, 114, 428, 436(?), 452). Undoubtedly this was a role that demanded a certain level of education, not shared by many of his (*sic*) compatriots.[14] Indeed, Martin Goodman has argued more generally that within a Jewish context the status of "scribes" may have been based on their role in copying texts, and their responsibility for their accuracy—something not shared with most other *collegia* (2007, 88–90).[15] Admittedly, the presence of three children, aged 5, 6 and 12 (Latin), described as "scribe" may give some pause for thought (*JIWE* 2, 255, 256, 547), and they contribute to a broader debate as to how far any such titles were (primarily) "honorific." In one case it would appear that a certain Rufus, who was an "archon," made dedications to his father (aged 70) and to his son (aged 6), both of whom were "scribes" (*JIWE* 2, 256 and 257), although that there was a family tradition of service and of seeking the appropriate education is not unlikely.[16] In all this it is important to note how Jewish funerary practice both followed that of wider society, drawing attention to virtues, status and titles, while shaping it to their own distinctive values and to status-roles within the synagogue or community—ruler, ruler of the synagogue, *gerousiarch*, father or mother of the synagogue.

If the epigraphic record suggests that the importance of scripture and law was recognized in a distinctively Roman way, considerable debate has surrounded the repeated anecdotal evidence from rabbinic sources of links between the rabbinic community and Rome, unparalleled for elsewhere in the Diaspora. There are a number of reports of visits to Rome by leading rabbis, particularly in the second century; while these reports may have considerable legendary elements, such visits are not intrinsically unlikely, whether they had a

---

13   "Scribe" is not common in Jewish epitaphs outside of Rome: Williams 2011, 340, n. 69.

14   Williams suggests that the obscure symbol on the plaque dedicated to Castricius is a ruling-board (Williams 2011, 341).

15   Although primarily addressing Judaea, Goodman 2007 cites the frequency of the term at Rome.

16   Williams notes that the ascription to children of virtues associated with adults is found elsewhere in Roman practice (Williams 2011, 343–344). The term "rabbi" appears in inscriptions from Italy from the fourth century although its precise reference is debated. Similarly, Patristic sources refer to "sapientes" or σοφοί among the Jews.

political purpose or a desire to see "the sights," and in particular the spoils taken from Jerusalem (Noy 2007). The primary interest in these reports is how these rabbis negotiated maintaining observance of food and ritual purity in that alien context, or engaged in internal halakhic debate about it; they give few hints of any contact with Jewish groups or communities, although it seems unlikely that they would not have attempted some (*b. Betzah 23a; y. Moed Qatan* 3.1).

An exception is provided by references to exegetical debates between rabbis engaged on an embassy to Rome—in one account to try to persuade the Roman authorities to annul decrees against Jewish observance—and a certain Matthiah ben Heresh who lived there (*b. Yoma* 53b, 57a, 86a; *b. Me'ilah* 17a); elsewhere, a catalogue of teachers whom would-be disciples are urged to search out and follow includes "following Matthiah (b. Heresh) to Rome" (*b. Sanhedrin* 32b). These references consistently locate this Matthiah in the second century, but that they, together with other references to various halakhic judgements made by him, provide evidence that he established a respected Rabbinic academy or Beit haMidrash in Rome, as has often been claimed, may be over-credulous.[17] David Noy's conclusion that "This perhaps implies an interest among the Jews of Rome in being kept up to date with the latest theological thinking" surely overstates the case, but that visiting teachers would provide the opportunity for theological or halakhic debate is not unlikely.[18] The suggestion that some accounts of Matthiah's exegesis, wherever formulated, indicate that it was in conscious challenge to Christian teaching, however, has no explicit support in the sources, and, like other similar arguments about the identity of the implied opponents of some rabbinic debates, relies on prior assumptions about the dynamics between the two groups.[19]

Another particularly provocative set of rabbinic traditions centers on a certain Todos or Theodoros, who might be dated any time in the first century BCE–CE, and who reportedly taught the Jews at Rome to eat a whole roast lamb at Passover, provoking rabbinic ire but not a ban (*t. Yom Tov* 2.15; *y. Pes.* 7.1; *b. Betzah* 23a).[20] Although the conclusion is sometimes drawn that Todos was a leader of the Roman community, the sources say nothing of this, or of which or how many Jews he may have taught—although the question of celebration of the Passover in the Diaspora and after the destruction of the Temple was

---

17   Cappelletti 2006, 8–9.

18   Noy 2007, 377; see Rutgers 1995, 203–204.

19   Segal 1992, questioned by Ilan 2009, 389 on the grounds of the late date of the sources. See also *Exod. Rabbah* 30.9 where the rabbinic visitors to Rome debate with a sectarian (*min*) over God's failure to observe the Sabbath.

20   Bokser 1984, 103–104.

evidently a significant issue.[21] Further, that Matthiah and Todos operated in Hebrew or Aramaic, as often has been assumed, cannot be determined. Even so, such accounts do act as a reminder that contacts between Rome and the provinces, or between rabbinic centers and the capital, might be expected, but their perspective remains that of the Palestinian rabbis, and confirms a lack of interest on their part in the forms of practice and teaching outside the Land of Israel. While it may be possible to surmise that their hermeneutical and halakhic concerns were not totally unprecedented in Rome, there remains little to build on from these sources regarding the local intellectual dynamics in the Jewish Roman context.

While the evidence examined so far has focused on the internal scholarly and scriptural activity of Jews in Rome, the interest in this paper is on their participation in the wider intellectual currents of the period—although the former is surely the precondition of the latter. It is true that Roman authors tend to portray Jews as belonging to the lower classes, numbered among the beggars, while the onomastic evidence of the epitaphs suggests that "Jews had much in common with the non-Jewish urban masses" (Rutgers 1995, 169). Nonetheless, at least in the first century, some Jews undoubtedly belonged to more influential networks, especially through the Herodian family and through Agrippa. Josephus' own experience, and his literary and social contacts, probably point to the continuing presence of more educated circles. It has even been suggested that there may have been a library or archive where he could have accessed some of the sources he used when writing the *Antiquities* (Ilan 2009, 366). Reference has already been made to the body of, and the disappearance of, Hellenistic Jewish literature, whose main thrust Tessa Rajak has described as "outward, towards making connections. The main challenge for its authors was from the beginning to generate new forms of fusion of their two received literary heritages, themselves subject to continual reinterpretation" (2009, 250). Unfortunately, few of these can be associated specifically with the Roman Jewish community, although the historian Eupolemus is probably to be identified with the ambassador sent to Rome by Judas Maccabee in the mid-second century BCE (1 Macc 8:17–20); his work, along with that of others, was collected and epitomized by the prolific and encyclopaedic author, Alexander Polyhistor, in Rome in the first century BCE; if the latter did not find it in existing archives, then he introduced it through his own extensive collection (Ilan 2009, 366–367;

---

21 The story in *y. Pes.* 7.1 ascribes the restraint of the rabbis to the support lent to them by Todos, an etymology of his name. The only other tradition associated with Todos is a haggadic explanation of the willingness of the three in the fiery furnace to die (*b. Pes.* 53b).

Adler 2011, 230–232, 238). Philo of Alexandria visited Rome in the mid-first century seeking an audience with Caligula following the conflicts in Alexandria. As shall be seen further below, it has been argued that he wrote his *Exposition* for a Roman audience, following the model of other ambassadors to Rome who engaged in literary activity. Maren Niehoff has proposed that while there he radically changed his approach and adopted a historical mode more suitable to a Roman audience than that of Commentary, and also that he came to be more overtly influenced by Stoic ideas (Niehoff 2011a; 2016). However, there appears to be no certain further evidence of literary Roman Jews until perhaps the fourth century. Leonard Rutgers has made a very strong case that the so-called *Collatio Legum Mosaicarum et Romanarum*, a comparison between Pentateuchal law and Roman law, composed in Latin and dated to the fourth century, is to be ascribed to a Jewish author and not to a Christian one, as had become the conventional view (1995, 210–253).[22] He makes a similar and credible case for the *Letter from Anna(s) to Seneca* (1995, 253–259). Perhaps less persuasive is the further attempt by Tal Ilan to argue that the Latin *Biblical Antiquities* ("Pseudo-Philo") also originated in the Roman Jewish community in the third-fourth century—possibly along with a translation of the scriptures into Latin which lies behind the Vetus Latina—and further that it helps provide a picture of Roman interpretation of Torah as having a stronger haggadic than halakhic interest (2009, 376–381).[23]

3   "Schools" and Jewish Study of Scripture and Tradition

That Jews participated in the sort of intellectual enquiry and literary activity that might be identified with "schools" as loosely defined in second century contexts is evident, even if they did so within the framework of their own traditions and sacred texts. Indeed, recent scholarship has begun to portray the "rabbinic movement" in our period as constituted not as a single cohesive system but much more as a number of sages or teachers, each with their own circle of disciples, who would discuss their interpretations of the classic texts (i.e. the Scriptures) and hand them down. While the methods of analysis and treatment of texts would have differed from those of their Greek contemporaries elsewhere, as a social form and mentality there is more in common.[24] Further,

---

22   This continues to be debated: see Frakes 2011, 129–149, who defends Christian authorship.
23   The suggestion that a Jewish translation lies behind the Vetus Latina as it survives in Christian sources has had few supporters in comparison with a similar claim for the Old Syriac.
24   See Samely 2017.

although representing a very small minority of traditions, there are accounts of rabbis debating with non-Jews, and even of acknowledging other bases for argument than the characteristic rabbinic appeal to the authority of scriptural revelation and rabbinic tradition (see Labendz 2013). Without claiming historical authenticity for any of the encounters described, the narratives do at least betray an awareness of living within a wider intellectual universe. Indeed, there is other evidence of rabbinic knowledge of Graeco-Roman education (Hezser 2010, 42–44). To give a specific example, in third century Palestine, the interactions between Origen and the rabbis have been described as following "in some respects, the patterns of disputes of popular philosophers in late antiquity" (Blowers 1988, 115).

If this was true in the Land of Israel, then it would have been even more likely the case where Jewish communities received and studied the scriptures in Greek. Although initially associated with Alexandria, the general dependence on the Old Greek or Septuagint by Christian authors already in the first century CE is evidence of its wide dissemination, even if that does not mean that every community would have had scrolls of the whole of the Greek Scriptures. As has already been noted, Tessa Rajak has made a particularly strong and largely persuasive case that the central role of the Septuagint for Hellenistic Jewish communities continued well into the period when the Christians were also claiming it for themselves (Rajak 2009). While Rajak is cautious about overplaying the parallel between the status of Homer for those with a Greek education and that of the Greek Bible for Jews (2009, 239–257), others have gone further in arguing that at least in Alexandria some of the techniques developed in Homeric scholarship were applied to the Jewish Scriptures both by Philo and by his predecessors (Niehoff 2007, 2011b; Sterling 2017). According to Eusebius, Aristobulus addressed questions or "investigations" to the Scriptures, particularly identifying the contrast between the natural and allegorical meaning (*P.E.* VIII.10). Philo adopts, among other techniques, the question and answer style as well as the technical vocabulary of Graeco-Roman analysis, but he also attacks others within the Jewish community whose methods or conclusions he rejects (Niehoff 2008). Although Niehoff has argued that he changed tack when he travelled to Rome for the sake of his outreach to non-Jews (see above), that need not mean that exegetical debate with others who adopted their own analyses of texts would have been alien there.

Indeed, that Jews (like Christians) could be perceived in terms of a philosophical school is shown by Galen who criticized their tendency to rely on faith and miracle rather than on logical proof, and yet who even so applied to them the language of the schools: "as if one had entered the school (διατριβή) of Moses and Christ" (*De Puls. Diff.* II.4; cf. also III.3).[25] We may imagine that when he differentiated the Mosaic understanding of the Creator (demiurge) from that of Plato (*De Usu Partium* XI.14), he had encountered the former in a school context; that this was during his sojourn in Rome (where he may also have encountered Christians) is as likely as anywhere.[26]

4   Jewish and Christian Scriptural Encounters at Rome

If Galen did encounter "the school of Moses and Christ" in Rome, it was probably not long after the death of Justin Martyr (c. 165/166 CE). Justin himself undoubtedly belongs firmly within the "teacher/school" model, which has been identified as a seminal form of Christian activity in second century Rome.[27] Whatever judgement is made about the historicity of the *Martyrdom of Justin*, its presentation of him as welcoming to his "meeting place" above the baths of Myrtinus(?) those seeking "the words of truth" strikes an authentic note; those arrested with him explain that, although converted to or born into Christianity elsewhere, they have come to him for teaching (*Mart. Just.* A. 3–4). In the *Dialogue* he describes his own journey through a sequence of philosophical teachers, culminating with a Platonist, before his conversion to the true philosophy conveyed by the prophets; that this mimics a highly stereotyped *topos* does not detract from its value in locating Justin in the world of philosophical competition (*Dial.* 2–3). Yet while his continued debt to Platonic modes of thought is unquestionable, it is thoroughly mediated through his interpretation of the Jewish Scriptures in Greek. Thus, his fundamental definition remains that God is "That which always continues the same and in the same manner and is the cause of the existence of everything else," and "the one who is not moved, being unconfinable in place, even in the whole universe" (*Dial.* 3.5; 127.2); but this definition acquires traction when addressed to the Scriptures. His philosophical principles make it self-evident—not even "one with the smallest mind" would disagree—that "the maker and father of everything[28] [would not] leave the all that is above heaven to make an appearance on some small portion of earth,"

---

25   The conventional translation "school" is probably best when followed by the names of "founders" (cf. Lucian, *Alex.* 5), although elsewhere a looser sense of "discourse," "treatment" is possible. The extent to which Galen differentiated Christians from Jews is a matter of debate.

26   See now Flemming 2017, who does not limit Galen's encounters with Christians to Rome.

27   Pouderon 1998; Löhr 2016.

28   ὁ ποιητὴς τῶν ὅλων καὶ πατέρα; cf. Plato, *Tim.* 28c.

but for him this is a point of contention not with regard to Greek myth but to the scriptural account. Thus, if the scriptural accounts do describe one who can be called "God" so appearing, for example in the burning bush or in conversation with Jacob or with Abraham, then evidently, they must refer to some other who can still be so named (*Dial.* 60).

That these examples come from his account of his encounter and debate with a Jew, Trypho, is important. The scene is set not long after the Bar Kochba revolt, from which Trypho is a fugitive, and now living mostly in Greece, in fact in Corinth. The language is heavily redolent of philosophical (school) debate, confirmed by Trypho's greeting "Hail, philosopher" (*Dial.* 1.1). Although scholars debate whether it took place in Ephesus as claimed by Eusebius (*Hist. eccl.* IV.18.6) or somewhere further east, the failure of the text to be any more precise is surely deliberate; the encounter happens in appropriate philosophical mode as Justin was walking "in the colonnades of the arcade" or "gymnasium" (ἐν τοῖς τοῦ ξυστοῦ περιπάτοις). Justin expects his readers to recognize the genre and its rules, and to have no difficulty in projecting them into their own situation. The *Dialogue* was composed as a treatise (80.3) some twenty or more years later, probably in Rome, during the last decade of Justin's life. Whether or not there was an actual encounter and, if there was, regardless of whether Justin had kept any records of it, the arguments must surely have been rehearsed more than once, presumably in the wider context of Justin's own activity of teaching and debating. Recognition of this is more important than the unresolved discussion as to who was the intended audience of the *Dialogue*.[29] That pagans would not have waded their way through the finer points of long scriptural quotations and that Jews would have found the denigration and polemic unacceptable is less important than that Justin is portraying a world of argument about texts and meaning, with distinctive techniques and terminology, that was familiar.

In the opening gambit both protagonists agree that the prime task of philosophy involves investigations (ζητήσεις) concerning divine monarchy and foreknowledge (1.3, cf. Plato, *Tim.* 47a), and what follows in the debate over the scriptures is presented as a series of such questions or investigations. Justin both acknowledges Trypho's right to examine carefully (ἐξετάζω) all that had been discussed, and yet insists on plying him with yet more questions (ἀνερωτάω), and he gets impatient when Trypho refuses to admit matters that have yet to be the subject of investigation, such as whether or not there is anyone other than the one father (68.3–4). As the debate develops, Justin's impatience increases:

---

29   See Lieu 1996, 103–109; Rajak 1999; den Dulk 2018.

If we had not undertaken a lengthy discussion about these things, I would have begun to doubt whether you are asking this because you do not understand something; but since we have engaged in the analysis (ζητήμα) with demonstration (ἀποδείξις) and conviction (συγκατάθεσις) I do not think you can be ignorant of what has already been said or are being disputatious ... (123.7).

Trypho is represented as responding in a similar vein:

Give your proof ... for we are not prepared for any such hazardous answers (ἀποκρίσεις), since we have never before heard someone searching or investigating or demonstrating such things (56.16).

From Justin's perspective, Trypho is posing unnecessary "problems" (πρόβλημα: 65.3).[30]

While this vocabulary is ubiquitous in philosophical literature, Justin's method anticipates the influential and long lasting genre of "Questions and Answers" (*erotapokriseis*) or "Investigations and Solutions," a literary form which probably reflects the practices of instruction in the philosophical schools of late antiquity, and which had already been adopted by Philo and perhaps by Aristobulus (Jacob 2004; Papadoyannakis 2006). Although rooted in the pedagogical relationship between teacher and pupil, this approach could easily become a means of articulating and reinforcing a "correct" reading of the matter or text.

In the *Dialogue* the central issue may be about the singleness of God (see above), but it is anchored in a dispute over a supposedly shared text: Trypho continues the protest quoted earlier, "For we would not have put up with your speaking if you had not related everything to the scriptures. For you are keen to draw all your demonstrations from them, and you do not present anyone as God above the maker of all"; this is indeed what Justin does, subjecting even phrases (λέξις) to investigation for the purposes of demonstration (56.16; 71.1). Again, contention over the true meaning of the authoritative text, and indeed over its original form, was fundamental to the activity of the second-century schools (Sedley 1989). Justin would not be alone in starting from a conviction that there cannot be contradictions in scripture (65.3).

---

30   Justin's disciple Tatian, while at Rome, is credited with composing "Problems" regarding what was "uncertain or hidden in the divine scriptures" which were addressed by Rhodon with his "Solutions" (Eusebius, *Hist. eccl.* v.13.8); see Lieu 2015, 308–309.

Yet what is striking is that the *Dialogue* does not set Justin over against Trypho in the interpretation of the text but over against "the teachers." In contrast to Justin's *Apologies*, where "teacher" and "teaching" are primarily associated with Christ and Christian experience,[31] in the *Dialogue* these terms are overwhelmingly used of the Jewish authorities who stand behind Trypho. For both Justin and Trypho it is from start to finish a matter of whether or not to be persuaded (πείθω) by these teachers and their understanding of the scriptures (*Dial.* 9.1; 38.2; 142.2). Indeed, according to Justin, the teachers go so far as to impugn the interpretation (or translation: ἐξήγησις) made by "your seventy elders," and dare to offer their own; even so, he finds himself forced to restrict his own investigations and the proofs he offers (ζητήσις, ἀποδείξις) to that on which both sides agree (68.7; 71.1). These disagreements extend to the wording of the text, with "the teachers" insisting that "young woman" (νεᾶνις) rather than "virgin" (παρθένος) was to be read at Isa 7:14, and then interpreting the text as if it referred to "your king Hezekiah" (43.8; cf. 120.4–5).[32] He even charges the teachers with excising from the scriptures passages on which the Christians rely, and which he asserts were an authentic part of the interpretation or translation (ἐξηγέομαι) of the seventy (71.1–73.4; 120.5)—although in most cases it would appear to be Justin's version which shows signs of secondary adaption for Christian purposes.[33] As well as changing key passages from scripture they offer alternative—on his account faulty—interpretations (62.2; 83.1; 112.2). Yet what is at stake is also the underlying principles of interpretation, whether the mundane words of scripture might carry powerful symbols, or which passages are to be deemed worthy of investigation (112.2, 4; 114.3; 134.1–2).

Although the conflict comes to a head primarily over Justin's Christological reading of scripture—for example of Psalm 45 or 110 (38.1; 83.1; cf. 110 on Micah 4:1–7 which Justin interprets of a future coming of Christ in glory)—it also touches on matters that were debated more widely. Justin pays careful attention to the first person plural, "Let us make," at Gen 1:26, referring to the specific position adopted by "the teachers" of a Jewish ("your") school or sect (αἵρεσις) which took it to refer to the angels, as responsible perhaps for the creation of the human body (62.2–3).[34] Equally problematic was the meaning of scriptural anthropomorphisms and theophanies (114.3), whether God was consistent, or

---

31   Jesus is teacher in *Dial.* 76.3; 108.2.

32   νεᾶνις is read by Aquila, against the παρθένος of the Septuagint.

33   It would appear that Justin's version of the Greek Bible varied from the one he knew was used by Jewish teachers: see Lieu 1996, 125–129.

34   The philosophical rather than religious ("heresy") meaning of αἵρεσις is to be understood here.

acted from foreknowledge and justly (92.5), or, more obscurely, the absence of female camels at Gen 32:15 (112.4). In addition, there are disagreements which suggest a more immediate contemporary application: the teachers interpret Malachi 1:11 of the Jewish diaspora, although Justin denies that this extends to such a universal range as do the Christians (117.4). However, he also accuses the teachers of interfering more directly; they instruct people like Trypho to avoid any engagement in debate with Justin as he carries out his interpretation (ἡμῶν ἐξηγουμένων ... μηδὲ εἰς κοινωνίαν λόγων ἐλθεῖν: 112.4; cf. 38.1):[35] this charge should not be assimilated to Justin's claim that Christians were cursed in the synagogues, or to the debate about the so called "heretic benediction," but points to contexts where exegetical debate could be pursued.[36] Justin's awareness that this was a competitive contest is clear when he claims a small victory when one of Trypho's companions finds Justin's explanation more persuasive than the weak answers he had got from the teachers (94.4).

Justin does little to clarify the identity and location of these teachers. While he identifies "the synagogues" as the places where the Jews ("you") curse Christ and those who believe in him, he does not hold the teachers responsible for this (16.4; 47.4; 96.2).[37] The one exception is the much-quoted passage: "Do not unite in reviling the son of God nor, as persuaded by Pharisees, teachers, denigrate the King of Israel then, in the ways that your rulers of the synagogue teach you (to do) after the prayer" (137.2); however, the idiosyncratic vocabulary and strange phrasing of the injunction provide no grounds for identifying the teachers as synagogue authorities.[38] Rather, since Justin asserts that copies of the scriptures which have not yet been subject to excision by the teachers might still be found "in the synagogues of the Jews," he may present the teachers as to some extent independent of the latter settings (72.3). Elsewhere Justin refers in general terms to the scriptures as in "your" possession, and as read daily "by you" (32.2; 55.3); in the *Apology* he had merely claimed that the Greek translation was to be found "until now among the Egyptians and exists everywhere among the Jews who do not understand what is said" (*1Apol.* 31.5). That copies may have been held in a more public, school, context or in accessible archives cannot be excluded: it is striking that Ignatius uses the term ἀρχεῖα,

---

35 Commentators regularly compare *b. Avodah Zarah* 17a where Eliezer admits to having been seduced by an interpretation offered by a *min*, and the ruling mentioned in *b. Avodah Zarah* 27b that no-one should have dealings with *minim*; cf. *t. Hull.* 2.20–24. These are set within the Land of Israel.

36 See generally Horbury 1982.

37 See also *Dial.* 93.4; 95.4; 108.17; 123.6; 133.6, without reference to the synagogue.

38 Justin does introduce "teachers" alongside the Pharisees and scribes as those responsible for Jesus' death, but only within a self-contained exegesis of Psalm 22 (102.5; 103.2, 9).

usually taken as adopted from his opponents, as a reference to the Jewish scriptures and then reapplied to the Christian message (*Philad.* 8.2). Certainly, such more public availability would facilitate Justin's efforts to compare the Jewish copies with those with which he was familiar in a Christian context. On the other hand, since study and teaching were integral to the conceptualization of the scriptures, it may have extended from being a synagogue-based activity across to other contemporary social and intellectual models.[39]

The ubiquitous presence of the teachers renders inadequate the scholarly debate as to whether Trypho is but a "straw man," a stooge scripted for failure. He represents the possibility that the objections and alternative ways of interpreting the scriptures emanating from the teachers might be listened to and found persuasive. If the imaginative world inhabited by the *Dialogue* is one frequented by teachers, and if this is presented as a persuasive setting for Roman readers, then it is likely that they were also at home in the real intellectual world.

In support of this conclusion is that a number of the interpretive issues raised in this debate are attested elsewhere, including among Jewish exegetes, in particular Philo and Aristobulus, as well as later in rabbinic or targumic tradition. The first-person plural in Gen 1:26 is discussed by Philo (*Opif.* 72–75) and in rabbinic sources (*Genesis Rabbah* 8.3–9), while the theophanies provoked a range of reactions from those anxious about an anthropomorphic understanding of the divine.[40] It is true that Marcion in particular has been associated with drawing attention to the "problems" of the representation of God in the scriptures, and with using them to question that God's status; indeed, some have argued that Justin's *Dialogue* is in fact either directed against Marcionism or draws heavily on an earlier treatise against him.[41] Yet this is to fail to see how securely Marcion fits in his context; even if his radical conclusions mark him out, in the questions he asked he was in good company in the second century.[42] No doubt in different forms these debates about how the scriptures were to be read and interpreted were not characteristic only of one city or one intellectual and philosophical tradition. So, too, many of the objections that Celsus raised a

---

39   How central "the synagogue" was in the life of many members of the Jewish community, or how it should be imagined, remains a matter of debate. In *de Spec. Leg.* II.62 Philo speaks of myriads of "schools (διδασκαλεῖα) of understanding" which are open every sabbath, while in *Moses* II.216 he uses the same language of their "prayer houses" (προσευκτήρια).

40   Niehoff 2008; Bucur 2014.

41   So den Dulk 2018.

42   Cf. Lieu 2015, 357–366. See above n. 30 on Tatian's "Problems" and Rhodon's "Solutions," composed at Rome.

little later have their counterparts in the writings of Philo. Although some have concluded from this that Celsus should be located in Alexandria, others have supposed he must have had some knowledge of the Roman context because of his references to Marcionite ideas. Moreover, in ethos such *aporiae* echo the debates that in other "schools" would have centered on the interpretation of Homer, namely as to how such a classic might be understood within the norms of a Platonic understanding of the divine. Admittedly, those who attended to the Greek classics rarely debated the Jewish Scriptures and vice versa: only a few could move in both worlds, and then only to a limited extent—Justin himself and perhaps Numenius.[43] But this need not exclude a larger number who did at least sit in the audience or who reacted critically to the claims that Jewish Scriptures could be treated on a par with Greek classics. Much has been made of the preference voiced by the author of *On the Sublime* IX.9 for the account of God by "the legislator of the Jews" over the Homeric accounts which must either be allegory or utterly impious. More common may have been the response of Celsus who, by contrast, rejected the possibility of applying allegory to the Christian scriptures (Origen, *Cels.* IV.48–51). The breadth of contexts in which such debates are reflected means that they cannot be limited to private or church-based polemics.

If Christians have been brought out of the ghetto into which scholarship has often confined them, and have been located among the philosophical school encounters of second century Rome, then so too should be Jews—only presuppositions about the self-exclusion of Jewish communities can refuse them entry. Yet, if this is so, we should not see the Christian engagement with philosophical debate as a consequence of, and as coterminous with, their emancipation from their Jewish roots, but as part of a shared venture and shared assertion of the place of the Scriptures in the intellectual marketplace.

Bibliography

Adler, William. 2011. "Alexander Polyhistor's *Peri Ioudaiōn* and Literary Culture in Republican Rome." Pages 225–240 in *Reconsidering Eusebius: Collected Papers on Literary, Historical, and Theological Issues*. Edited by Sabrina Inowlocki and Claudio Zamagni. Leiden: Brill.

Barclay, John. 1996. *Jews in the Mediterranean Diaspora*. Edinburgh: T&T Clark.

Blowers, Paul. 1988. "Origen, the Rabbis and the Bible: Towards a Picture of Judaism

---

43   See Lieu 2015, 313–315.

and Christianity in Third Century Caesarea." Pages 96–116 in *Origen of Alexandria: His World and His Legacy*. Edited by Charles Kannengiesser and William L. Petersen. Notre Dame, Ind.: University of Notre Dame Press.

Bokser, Baruch M. 1984. *The Origins of the Seder*. Berkeley: University of California Press.

Brooke, George and Renate Smithuis, eds. 2017. *Jewish Education from Antiquity to the Middle Ages: Studies in Honour of Philip S. Alexander*. Leiden: Brill.

Bucur, Bogdan. 2014. "Justin Martyr's Exegesis of Biblical Theophanies and the Parting of the Ways between Christianity and Judaism." *Theological Studies* 75:34–51.

Cappelletti, Sylvia. 2006. *The Jewish Community of Rome: from the Second Century B.C. to the Third Century C.E.* Leiden: Brill.

den Dulk, Matthijs. 2018. *Between Jews and Heretics: Refiguring Justin Martyr's Dialogue with Trypho*. London: Routledge.

Flemming, Rebecca. 2017. "Galen and the Christians: Texts and Authority in the Second Century AD." Pages 171–187 in *Christianity in the Second Century: Themes and Developments*. Edited by James Carleton Paget and Judith Lieu. Cambridge: Cambridge University Press.

Frakes, Robert. 2011. *Compiling the* Collatio Legum Mosaicarum et Romanarum *in Late Antiquity*. Oxford: Oxford University Press.

Goodman, Martin. 2007. "Texts, Scribes and Power in Roman Judea." Pages 69–90 in *Judaism in the Roman World*. Leiden: Brill.

Heszer, Catherine. 2010. "The Graeco-Roman Context of Jewish Daily Life in Palestine." Pages 28–47 in *The Oxford Handbook of Jewish Daily Life in Palestine*. Oxford: Oxford University Press.

Horbury, William. 1982. "The Benediction of the *Minim* and Early Jewish-Christian Controversy." *Journal of Theological Studies* 33:19–61.

Ilan, Tal. 2009. "The Torah of the Jews of Ancient Rome." *Jewish Studies Quarterly* 16:363–395.

Jacob, Christian. 2004. "Questions sur les questions: Archéologie d'une Pratique Intellectualle et d'une forme discursive." Pages 25–54 in *Erotapokriseis: Early Christian Question and Answer Literature in Context*. Edited by Annelie Volgers and Claudio Zamageni. Leuven: Peeters.

Labendz, Jenny. 2013. *Socratic Torah: Non-Jews in Rabbinic Intellectual Culture*. New York: Oxford University Press.

Lampe, Peter. 2003. *From Paul to Valentinus: Christians at Rome in the First Two Centuries*. Translated by Michael Steinhauser. Edited by Marshall Johnson. Minneapolis: Fortress.

Lieu, Judith M. 1996. *Image and Reality: The Jews in the World of the Christians in the Second Century*. Edinburgh: T&T Clark.

Lieu, Judith M. 2015. *Marcion and the Making of a Heretic*. Cambridge: Cambridge University Press.

Löhr, Winrich. 2016. "Editors and Commentators: Some Observations on the Craft of Second Century Theologians." Pages 65–84 in *Pascha Nostrum Christus*. Edited by P.F. Beatrice and B. Pouderon. Paris: Beauchesne.

Niehoff, Maren. 2007. "Homeric Scholarship and Bible Exegesis in Ancient Alexandria: Evidence from Philo's 'Quarrelsome' Colleagues." *Classical Quarterly* 57:166–182.

Niehoff, Maren. 2008. "Questions and Answers in Philo and *Genesis Rabbah*." *Journal for the Study of Judaism in the Persian, Hellenistic, and Roman Periods* 39:337–366.

Niehoff, Maren. 2011a. "Philo's Exposition in a Roman Context." *Studia Philonica Annual* 23:1–21.

Niehoff, Maren. 2011b. *Jewish Exegesis and Homeric Scholarship in Alexandria*. Cambridge: Cambridge University Press.

Niehoff, Maren. 2016. "Justin's *Timaeus* in the Light of Philo's *Timaeus*." *Studia Philonica Annual* 28:375–392.

Noy, David. 2000. *Foreigners at Rome: Citizens and Strangers*. London: Duckworth.

Noy, David. 2007. "A Jewish Pilgrimage in Reverse?" Pages 373–385 in *Pilgrimage in Graeco-Roman and Early Christian Antiquity: Seeing the Gods*. Edited by Jas Elsner and Ian Rutherford. Oxford: Oxford University Press.

Noy, David. 1995. *Jewish Inscriptions of Western Europe*. Vol. 2. Cambridge: Cambridge University Press.

Papadoyannakis, Yannis. 2006. "Instruction by Question and Answer: The Case of Late Antique and Byzantine *Erotapokriseis*." Pages 91–106 in *Greek Literature in Late Antiquity: Dynamism, Didacticism, Classicism*. Edited by Scott Johnson. Aldershot: Ashgate.

Pouderon, B. 1998. "Réflexions sur la formation d'une elite intellectuelle chrétienne au IIe siècle: les 'écoles' d'Athènes, de Rome et d'Alexandrie." Pages 237–269 in *Apologistes chrétiens et la culture grecque*. Edited by B. Pouderon and Joseph Doré. Paris: Beauchesne.

Rajak, Tessa. 1994. "Inscription and Context: Reading the Jewish Catacombs of Rome." Pages in 226–241 *Studies in Early Jewish Epigraphy*. Edited by Jan Willem van Henten and Pieter Willem van der Horst. Leiden: Brill.

Rajak, Tessa. 1999. "Talking at Trypho: Christian Apologetic as Anti-Judaism in Justin's *Dialogue with Trypho the Jew*." Pages 58–80 in *Apologetics in the Roman Empire: Pagans, Jews and Christians*. Edited by Mark Edwards, Martin Goodman, Simon Price and Christopher Rowland. Oxford: Oxford University Press.

Rajak, Tessa. 2009. *Translation and Survival: The Greek Bible of the Ancient Jewish Diaspora*. Oxford: Oxford University Press.

Rutgers, Leonard V. 1995. *The Jews in Late Antique Rome: Evidence of Cultural Interaction in the Roman Diaspora*. Leiden: Brill.

Samely, Alexander. 2017. "Educational Features in Ancient Jewish Literature: An Overview of Unknowns." Pages 147–200 in *Jewish Education from Antiquity to the Middle*

Ages: Studies in Honour of Philip S. Alexander. Edited by George J. Brooke and Renate Smithuis. Leiden: Brill.

Sedley, David. 1989. "Philosophical Allegiance in the Greco-Roman World." Pages 97–119 in *Philosophia Togata: Essays on Philosophy and Roman Society*. Edited by M. Griffin and J. Barnes. Oxford: Clarendon.

Segal, Lester A. 1992. "R. Matiah ben Heresh of Rome on Religious Duties and Redemption: Reaction to Sectarian Teaching." *Proceedings of the American Academy of Jewish Research* 58:221–241.

Sterling, Gregory. 2017. "The School of Moses in Alexandria: An Attempt to Reconstruct the School of Philo." Pages 141–166 in *Second Temple Jewish "Paideia" in Context*. Edited by Jason M. Zurawski and Gabriele Boccaccini. Berlin: De Gruyter.

Trebilco, Paul. 1991. *Jewish Communities in Asia Minor*. Cambridge: Cambridge University Press.

Williams, Margaret. 1998. "The Structure of the Jewish Community in Rome." Pages 215–228 in *Jews in a Greco-Roman World*. Edited by Martin Goodman. Oxford: Clarendon.

Williams, Margaret. 2011. "Image and Text in the Jewish Epitaphs of Late Ancient Rome." *Journal for the Study of Judaism in the Persian, Hellenistic, and Roman Periods* 42:328–350.

Zurawski, Jason M. and Gabriele Boccaccini, eds. 2017. *Second Temple Jewish "Paideia" in Context*. Berlin: De Gruyter.

CHAPTER 2

Were There Valentinian Schools?

Einar Thomassen

It has been usual to speak about the ancient Gnostics as forming "schools." The habit goes back to antiquity. Irenaeus, for example, spoke about the σχολή of Valentinus.[1] So did Clement of Alexandria, Hippolytus and others.[2] But what precisely did these authors mean by the word? Were they referring to a school in the sense of an educational establishment, with a teacher, students and regular classes, or did they use the word more loosely, just as today we may speak of a "school of thought"? The Greek word σχολή does in fact often refer to a school in the sense of an educational institution. In his book about Antiochus and the Late Academy, John Glucker made a study of the relevant vocabulary and came to the conclusion that whereas αἵρεσις always means a school of thought, and is never used with reference to an actual institution, or to teaching as an activity, almost the opposite is the case with σχολή, which normally implies the existence of an educational institution.[3] When the word is used with reference to philosophical schools, it is with the implicit assumption that such schools exist as organised educational realities. Glucker found this usage to be consistent in Hellenistic Greek, and, at least as far as the philosophical schools are concerned, in Late Antiquity as well. However, Glucker did not study how this terminology was used by Christian writers, and it remains to be seen whether the distinction between σχολή and αἵρεσις is equally valid there. My impression is that this is not the case.

1 "School" as a Heresiological Term

As a matter of fact, when Christian authors use the word σχολή to refer to a certain historical figure as being the founder of a "school," or describe a particular person as belonging to somebody's "school," it is less than obvious that they have an organised educational enterprise in mind. A quick survey of the

---

1 Irenaeus, *Haer.* 1. *praef.* 2; 1.30.14; 2.19.8.
2 Clement of Alexandria, *Strom.* 3.92.1; 4.71.1; [Hippolytus] *Haer.* 6.29.1, 37.9, 42.2, 55.1, 55.3; 10.13.1, 13.4; Eusebius, *HE* 4.30.3.
3 Glucker 1978, 159–192. See also the summary in Le Boulluec 1985, 41–48.

passages where the word appears in the heresiological works gives the impression that its usage may be sorted into three categories. First, a σχολή may be a "school of thought," encompassing all such persons as (in the eyes of the heresiologist) adhere to a specific type of doctrine or set of opinions. For example, the author of the *Refutation of All Heresies*[4] speaks about how the Christology of Theodotus of Byzantium differs from that of the "school" of the Gnostics, Cerinthus and Ebion ([Hipp.] *Haer.* 7.35.1). Secondly, the word may refer to a distinct party, or a faction, as such, without reference to a common doctrine as the unifying factor. Thus, the *Refutatio* refers to the party of Callistus, the author's rival as bishop of Rome, as a σχολή ([Hipp.] *Haer.* 9.12.20). In both these cases, σχολή is practically synonymous with αἵρεσις. Thirdly, and probably most importantly, the school as an institution may be used as a metaphor: such words as "teacher," "teaching," "disciples" and "successors" seem to be freely used in order to postulate a doctrinal affinity between the views of certain individuals, without necessarily implying an institutional context for this affinity in the sense of personal contact and instruction. It seems clear that this set of metaphors is modelled on the institutional reality of the philosophical schools and the descriptions commonly made of the operations of such schools in doxographical literature. An important heresiological purpose behind the use of these metaphors is evidently to construe an analogy between those schools of pagan thought and the doctrines and activities of the persons to whom those metaphors are applied.

The use of such metaphors is clearly not neutral. It must be noted that the heresiologists invariably use them to characterise *deviant* opinions and groups. They never apply them to the type of institutions to which they belong themselves, which are, instead, normally referred to by the name ἐκκλησία and are by definition assumed to be the repositories of sound, apostolic doctrine.[5] σχολή is a word that is used in order to deny one's opponents the right to call themselves an ἐκκλησία; it situates them outside the Church as a pagan type of institution or as a deviant faction with illegitimate claims. σχολή is not a term those excluded groups ever apply to themselves. The Valentinians are the group that most frequently gets this school terminology attached to them, but σχολή never appears as a self-designation in our sources.[6] What we invariably find instead

---

4　The attribution of this work to Hippolytus of Rome has now been generally abandoned; see, most recently, Litwa 2016, xxxii–ilii.

5　Cf. Brent, *Hippolytus*, 423–424.

6　*Pace*, e.g. Dunderberg 2008, esp. 3–4. It is true that Valentinian sources describe the material world as a "school" (Irenaeus, *Haer.* 1.6.1; *Tri. Trac.* 104:18–25, 123:11–16; *Val. Exp.* 37:28–31). This idea forms part of a theory about the divine economy of salvation that provides a theodi-

is in fact the word ἐκκλησία.[7] Those who still want to speak about "the school of Valentinus" are thus perpetuating a pejorative heresiological terminology that was originally designed to exclude certain groups and individuals from the community of Christians.

2   Religious Communities, Not Schools

Our sources offer a certain amount of information about the practical aspects of Valentinianism. We know that the performance of rituals was essential, in particular an initiation ritual which included water baptism and anointing and was considered to effect "redemption" and the eschatological entry into "the bridal chamber."[8] Valentinians also convened for regular services, during which they sang hymns, listened to sermons, celebrated eucharistic meals, and experienced the gifts of the Spirit through outbursts of prophetic speech.[9] Thus, they had a rich program of distinctly religious activities. There is not much in these activities that resembles the normal operations of a philosophical school in the later part of Antiquity, which typically included lectures on and discussions of authoritative texts or specific topics given by a teacher before a group of students.[10]

---

cal justification for the fall of the last aeon, the subsequent creation of the cosmos, and the presence of the spirit in the material world: the Father's children needed to experience imperfection in order to learn the nature of perfection. The theme of the Saviour as a teacher (*Gos. Truth* 19:10–34; *Interp. Know.* 9:17–27) should be seen in this context as well. These ideas do not imply that the Valentinian community itself was conceived of as a school or had the structure of an educational institution.

7   Irenaeus *Haer.* 1.5.6; *Exc. Theod.* 41.2; *Tri. Trac.* 125:4–5, cf. 121:31.37, 123:17–18; *Interp. Know.* 5:33.35, 9:18, etc.

8   Thomassen 2006, part IV; Thomassen 2011.

9   Thomassen 2013.

10   For a general presentation of how philosophical schools operated in Antiquity, see, e.g., Pierre Hadot's admirable *What is Ancient Philosophy*. Naturally, the degree of institutionalisation varied between the different schools and over time. Platonism and Aristotelianism tended to have more regular programmes of instruction and greater continuity than other traditions, though even there the individual teacher and his personality were a decisive factor. See the balanced and well-informed remarks in Lössl 2016, esp. 38 n. 3, 45–48, with good references to the relevant literature. I am not of course arguing that the teaching of philosophy had no religious aspects, or that religious rituals could not on occasion include components of a didactic nature. The point is that teaching and religious worship were generally considered and institutionalised as two distinct forms of activity both in Greco-Roman culture generally and in Christianity ("catechetical schools") and Judaism (*bet ha-midrash*, etc.) specifically.

Nonetheless, assertions continues to be made that, "… the Valentinian movement had the character of a philosophical school, or network of schools, rather than a distinct religious sect";[11] and, "the closest parallel to Christian gnostic teachers … is provided by the masters of pagan philosophy."[12] Such assertions are curious, considering that teaching activities resembling those of the philosophical schools are not in fact described in our sources, in either first-hand Valentinian documents or the heresiological reports. The descriptions we do have of their activities suggest on the contrary that the Valentinian groups were religious communities concerned above all with procuring the eternal salvation of their members by means of ritual performances, and not philosophical teaching institutions.

3 School Activities within the Framework of a Religious Community?

An objection might be raised at this point: this is all very well, but does the one necessarily exclude the other? After all, teachers did exist in early Christianity—people like Justin Martyr in Rome and the heads of the so-called catechetical school of Alexandria, from Pantaenus to Origen, who offered more or less formalized programs of intellectual instruction as a supplement to the regular ritual activities of the Christian communities.[13] Is it not possible that a similar situation may have obtained among the Valentinians? Perhaps the so-called Valentinian teachers did in fact teach?

In what follows I shall try to argue that this may in fact well have been the case, though I have to warn that the argument to be presented is still rather tentative, and even speculative. We have, as was said above, no direct evidence for Valentinian teaching activity. The argument therefore has to be indirect, based on what may be inferred from the nature of the sources themselves, in particular, their genres.

Looking at the literary forms produced by the Valentinians, we find impressive diversity. We have hymns, prayers, homilies, letters, systematic treatises, exegetical works and collections of brief comments on various topics. In what kinds of contexts were these diverse textual forms used? The question to be

---

11   Layton 1982, 267.

12   Löhr 2012, 351.

13   The basic study remains Neymeyr 1989. See also Markschies 2007, esp. 88–109. The precise nature of Justin's "school" continues to be debated, see, most recently, Georges 2012 and Ulrich 2012. The long debate about the "catechetical school" in Alexandria is succinctly summed up in Ashwin-Siejkowski 2015, 86–87.

asked in particular for our purposes is whether any of these genres may betray signs of teaching activity. Hymns and prayers are of course genres that belong in the context of religious services.[14] The same may be said about homilies (*Gos. Truth*, *Interp. Know.*), though such addresses may also have been delivered on other occasions than those of communal worship.

Letters are a more problematic category with regard to the question of institutional context, since there exists a tradition for the public reading of letters in Christian services. The Valentinian examples (Valentinus' letters, frags. 1– 3, Ptolemy's *Flora*, *Treat. Res.*), are however best regarded as didactic epistles resembling those written by philosophical masters to their students. They evidently presuppose some sort of teacher-pupil relationship, but it is difficult to say whether the texts may reflect the kind of discussion a Valentinian teacher would have conducted orally before a group of students.

In the present contribution I shall be more concerned with the remaining three categories: the systematic treatises, exegetical works and the collections of comments on various topics.

4   Systematic Treatises

As is well known, Valentinian theologians wrote relatively lengthy texts expounding in a systematic manner the nature of god, the emanation of the spiritual realm, the creation of the cosmos and of humanity, the mission of the Savior and the ultimate redemption of the human spirit. A number of such treatises have been preserved; they share distinct family resemblances, but none of them are identical.[15] Unfortunately, we are never told how these treatises were actually used. Were they just literary creations, or did they perform a function in the context of teaching activities? The Valentinian Ptolemy may give us a

---

14   Valentinus produced a psalm-book (Muratorian Canon, lines 81–85; [Hipp.], *Haer.* 6.37.7; Orig. *Enarr. in Job* 21.12 [PG 17.80]), which seems to have been regarded as having something resembling canonical authority among the Valentinians (Tert. *Carn.* 17.1). Prayers are found in liturgical contexts in Iren. *Haer.* 1.13 and 1.21, and in NHC XI,2a–c; *Pr. Paul* (NHC I,1) may have been used by Valentinians.

15   The most completely preserved versions of the system are 1) Iren. *Haer.* 1.1–8; 2) [Hipp.] *Haer.* 6.29–36; 3) *The Tripartite Tractate* (NHC I,5); 4) *The Valentinian Exposition* (NHC XI,1); 5) Iren. *Haer.* 1.11.1 ("Valentinus"); 6) Iren. *Haer.* 1.14 (the *Sige* of Marcus); 7) Epiph. *Pan.* 31.5–6 (the Valentinian *Lehrbrief*). In addition, numerous other variants of the system are attested in a more fragmentary fashion, especially in the *Excerpts from Theodotus* and in Irenaeus, *Haer.* 1.11–12, as well as in the supplementary remarks that are interspersed in Irenaeus' exposition of his main source in *Haer.* 1.1–8.

hint in his *Letter to Flora*. In that letter, Ptolemy explains the origins and nature of the Jewish laws and argues that these laws derive neither from the highest god, nor from the devil, but from a third, intermediate figure who is neither evil nor entirely good. Towards the end of the letter, Ptolemy promises Flora that once she becomes worthy, she will be taught about the origins of this intermediate figure, who is the Demiurge and the Lawgiver, as well as about all other related matters.[16] It is plausible to infer that the instruction Ptolemy holds out for Flora is precisely the sort of subject matter that is expounded in the various Valentinian systematic treatises.

Several peculiar features of these system texts do in fact point in the direction of a classroom setting. The fact that each Valentinian teacher appears to have composed his own version of the system suggests in itself a situation that highlights the independent authority of the individual teacher vis-à-vis his students. But how were these texts actually used? Were they, perhaps, classroom texts that were not only read out to the students but were also commented on and explained by the master? It is clear that important features of the Valentinian system are barely comprehensible simply on the basis of the texts themselves. This is the case in particular with the philosophical underpinnings of the system, which are borrowed from Neopythagorean philosophy. The Valentinian system texts regularly employ a distinct set of technical terms—"extension," "spreading out," "withdrawal," "division," "limit," "audacity," "otherness" and "movement"—which are all firmly rooted in contemporary Neopythagorean theories about the generation of the Dyad from a single first principle, and which can also be detected in Plotinus.[17] In the Valentinian treatises these terms are so consistently used in the narratives about Sophia that a deliberate intention to assimilate the figure of the errant aeon to the Pythagorean Dyad must be assumed. In some cases, this vocabulary is also used at a higher level in the system, to describe how the second principle, the Son, emerged from the Father. The underlying motive for using this vocabulary is to explain theoretically how duality and plurality may be generated from the undivided oneness of the eternal Father.

This philosophical theory of first beginnings is thus embedded as a deeper level of signification within the mythological narrative of the treatises. In fact, the myth can be seen as a deliberate allegory of the Neopythagorean theories: Sophia is motivated by audacity, *tólme*, a desire for otherness; she spreads or

---

16 "If God permit, you will learn in the future about their origin and generation, when you are counted worthy of the apostolic tradition which we as well have received by succession ..." (Epiph. *Pan.* 33.7.9).

17 Thomassen 2006, esp. 269–307.

stretches outward in a disorderly movement into infinity before she is eventually cut off and Limit is imposed; the rest of the Pleroma withdraws from her. Later, Sophia is "converted," which means that she becomes a soul that turns upwards, opening herself to the formative action of the Savior-Logos that will be sent down to her. Here we have the two movements of extension and return which are familiar from philosophical theories of emanation. This deeper, philosophical significance of the myth is not obvious, however, at the surface level of the narrative, even though it is consistently present in all the versions of the myth. It must have been conveyed by other means than just by reading the texts themselves. Most likely it was transmitted orally, by a teacher commenting on the text and divulging its more abstract meaning to students.

In a more general perspective it may be observed that this kind of covert interrelationship between a surface meaning and a deeper level of significance is a typical and constitutive feature of Valentinian discourse in general. The student is expected to grasp not only that the dramatic story of Sophia entails an explanation of the generation of matter and the inferior world, but that it is also homologous with the narrative of the passion of the Savior: his descent into the material world, his being nailed to a cross, with his limbs extended, spread out, with the cross representing matter as well as the restraining action of the Limit; and the eventual separation of his spirit from his body as he expires on the cross and withdraws to the place he came from. Finally, the student is also expected to understand how these remarkable correspondences between the Sophia narrative, philosophical physical theory and Christian soteriology correspond to indications given in the gospels and the letters of Paul, where all these things are being hinted at: the apostasy of the twelfth apostle signifies the fall of Sophia, the twelfth aeon; her passion is indicated by the woman who suffered from a hemorrhage for twelve years, and so on (Iren. *Haer.* 1.3.3, etc.). Perceiving how all these things hang together in a consistent web of significations is not something one is likely to achieve just from reading the texts themselves. Attaining this holistic vision of physics, soteriology and scriptural exegesis requires the guidance of a teacher who can help the student to see the underlying unity of apparently disparate phenomena. Such a coherent vision seems precisely what the systematic treatises, supplemented by oral instruction, are designed to produce.

5   Scriptural Exegesis

In addition to being used as proof-texts supporting the systematic exposition of doctrine, scripture could also be an object of study in its own right, as we see in the case of Heracleon's commentary on the gospel of John and the commentary on John's prologue in Iren. *Haer.* 1.8.5. Did these commentaries originate in the classroom? There is no reason to assume otherwise. Commenting on authoritative texts was a normal form of school activity in Antiquity, not least in the philosophical schools. Moreover, Heracleon's commentary is described by Origen as ὑπομνήματα, a term that suggests notes for use in a teaching context.[18] It is also to be noted that Heracleon's so-called commentary is not a verse-by-verse commentary as one might expect from a literary commentary (such as that of Origen, for example), but only treats selected passages that are of particular interest for illustrating Valentinian doctrine. Here again we may discern a teaching situation in which the student is led to discover a deeper meaning in the materials put forward for scrutiny and to understand how they resonate with the global vision of reality offered by the teacher.

6 Collections of Comments on Various Topics

By this category I have in mind in particular the somewhat enigmatic document called the *Gospel of Philip*, to which may be added, perhaps, some of the materials used by Clement of Alexandria in his *Excerpts from Theodotus. Gos. Phil.*, I would suggest, has features that align it with the style of the diatribe known from the classrooms of the philosophers.[19] Consider, for example, the following passage discussing opposing views on the resurrection:

> I also find fault with those[20] who say that it [i.e. the flesh] will not arise.
> —Really?[21] Are both parties wrong, then?
> You say that the flesh will not arise. Then tell me what it is that will arise, and we shall praise you.[22]
> You say: "The Spirit."
> —In the flesh!

18 Wucherpfennig 2002, 34: "Aus Origens Bezeichnung ὑπομνήματα und der Gestalt der Fragmente Herakleons lässt sich daher schließen, dass die vorliegende Schrift vermutlich für eine Art gelehrten Unterricht zum Johannesevangelium gedacht war"; cf. *ib.* 385, 387.

19 For the classroom setting of the diatribe cf. Stowers 1981; id. 1988, esp. 74–75.

20 ⲁⲛⲟⲕ ϯⲟⲛ ⲁⲣⲓⲕⲉ ⲁⲛⲕⲟⲟⲩⲉ: I take "also ... those" to be the meaning of ⲛⲕⲟⲟⲩⲉ here, which would seem to give a solution to the problem raised by Schenke, 1997, 235. As Schenke notes, a contrast is intended with "some are afraid ..." in 56:26–27.

21 Accepting Schenke's interpretation of ⲉⲓⲧⲉ 57:10 as = εἶτα (1997, 236).

22 Cf. Epict. *Diatr.* 3.23.24 δίδαξόν με καὶ ἐπαινέσω.

And then (you say) this: "It is light."
—In the flesh!
"It is a *logos*."
—That, too, is in the flesh!
Thus, whatever you say, nothing you mention is outside the flesh. It is necessary to arise in this flesh, since all is in it.

57:9–19

The imaginary dialogue is a typical feature of the diatribe, as is the elliptical style (which has caused considerable problems to modern translators).[23] The passage even contains a phrase that has a direct parallel in Epictetus. Considering *Gos. Phil.* as a whole I find it not impossible that what we have here is the record of the teaching of a Valentinian master written down by one of his pupils, similar to Arrian's record of the *diatribai* of Epictetus. A number of disparate topics are commented on, several of them, one may imagine, having been raised by the students themselves. What unites them is the method by which these topics are treated, that is, the search for a hidden significance beneath the surface, no matter what the subject is: social and ethnic categories, husband and wife, the significance of names, biblical narratives, the Jerusalem temple, agriculture and crafts. The treatment is often paradoxical, as if to force the student to see below the surface and realise that the world itself is to be read like a book, filled with signs that point towards a higher reality of which the world that we see is but an inferior image. This must be part, at least, of what is meant by the idea that the world itself is a "school, such as exists in the regions that have been so fashioned as to provide it with the likeness of the images and the archetypes in the manner of a mirror" (*Tri. Trac.* 123:12–16).[24] The world itself provides the teaching materials, as do the names that are generated in the world (*Gos. Phil.* 54:13–18) and the texts of scripture, but these materials need to be explained and elucidated, which is obviously the task of the Valentinian teacher, whose task it is to bring out their hidden meanings.

---

23   For further instances of diatribe in *Gos. Phil.* detected by Schenke, cf. 60:34–61:5 (Schenke 1997, 297–298), 62:26–35 (ib. 320), 66:23–29 (ib. 368), 67:14–18 (ib. 375), 69:4–8 (ib. 401), 69:8–14 (ib. 402), 76:17–22 (ib. 466), 80:4–8 (ib. 488).
24   Cf. *Tri. Trac.* 104:18–25; Iren. *Haer.* 1.6.1.

7   Conclusion

In the absence of any solid evidence for organized teaching activities among the Valentinians, this paper has asked the question whether such activities may be inferred from some of the literary forms they employed, and it has been argued that the systematic treatise, the commentary and the diatribal discourse of the *Gospel of Philip* may all be understood as texts emerging from a situation of oral instruction. It is inherently probable that such instruction was taking place: Valentinian leaders presumably did not restrict their activities to delivering homilies during the Sunday services and to write texts intended for private study. They very likely spent some of their time together with students as well.

This does not, however, make Valentinian communities "schools." Teaching activities took place in the context of what the Valentinians themselves regarded as an *ekklesia*, a Christian congregation whose purpose was the salvation of its members obtained through ritual acts and an attitude of faith.[25] Instruction was carried out in the service of redemption, which was effected through the ritual of initiation and was regularly celebrated in congregational worship.

Was there a program of teaching designed to make the student progress from elementary to more advanced stages of *gnosis*? We are left to speculation. There clearly existed a kind of teaching which was pre-baptismal and catechetical: the famous words of the *Excerpts of Theodotus* (78.2), that knowledge about "who we were, what we have become, where we were, where we have been put, where we are going, from what we are redeemed, what birth is, and what rebirth" is necessary for baptism to be efficient, suggest that the kind of information supplied by the systematic treatises was imparted to the candidates before they were admitted to baptismal initiation. Tertullian says that the Valentinians subject their candidates to a catechetical instruction lasting five years (*Val.* 1). Were they rehearsing the system of the local master during all that time, or were they studying other materials as well?

Texts such as Heracleon's commentary on John and the kind of symbolical comments on diverse topics that we find in the *Gospel of Philip* seem on the other hand to presuppose that the students have already acquired familiarity with the Valentinian system. The purpose of these texts seems to be to deepen the appreciation of the system as a universal key to understanding biblical texts and the world in general. This kind of teaching therefore appears to be more

---

25   Cf. the importance of faith vis-à-vis intellectual understanding in the opening passages of *Treat. Res.* and *Interp. Know.*

suitable for advanced students who have already been initiated, but aspire to make further progress towards gnostic understanding. The suggestion that *Gos. Phil.* addresses catechumens[26] I find unpersuasive: a novice must have found the argument of the text discomfortingly confusing. It is therefore likely that Valentinian teachers offered two types of instruction: one pre-baptismal and catechetical, and another for advanced students.

In conclusion, then, Valentinian communities were as such not schools, but teaching activities did take place in them. Moreover, teaching was soteriologically important, not only because it provided, through the Valentinian system, the self-knowledge necessary for redemption, but also because it aimed to produce in the student the particular symbol-oriented frame of mind that enabled him or her, in sudden flashes of insight, to acquire a holistic vision of reality through which everything made sense by means of a complex web of mutually reinforcing symbolic correspondences. That vision surely contributed to a sense of self, of being "one who knows," someone who, unlike the untrained person, has penetrated beneath the surface of both words and things and understood how everything hangs together at a deeper level of significations. By thus building up the sense of being a *gnostikós*, creating the self-awareness of being a spiritual person, teaching surely played an indispensable role in the operation of the Valentinian community as a vehicle for salvation. Certainly, this is not dissimilar to the ambitions the philosophical schools had for the training of their students; there as well, a unitary vision of reality was the aim which would lead the students to a sense of being masters of the world.[27] The important difference is that for the Valentinians, intellectual teaching was inextricably linked to religious practice. If *gnosis* is necessary for baptism to be effective, as the *Excerpts from Theodotus* tells us, the opposite is surely also the case: without the ritual of *apolytrosis*, redemption cannot be attained.

Bibliography

Ashwin-Siejkowski, Piotr. 2015. "Clement of Alexandria." Pages 84–97 in *The Wiley Blackwell Companion to Patristics*. Edited by K. Parry. Hoboken: Wiley.

Brent, Allen. 1995. *Hippolytus and the Roman Church in the Third Century: Communities in Tension before the Emergence of a Monarch-Bishop*. Vigiliae Christianae Supplements 31. Leiden: Brill.

---

26   E.g. Isenberg 1968, id. 1989; Van Os 2007; cf. Schmid 2007, 44–50.
27   See Hadot 2002, who highlights this theme, especially in his accounts of Hellenistic and Imperial philosophy.

Dunderberg, Ismo. 2008. *Beyond Gnosticism: Myth, Lifestyle, and Society in the School of Valentinus*. New York: Columbia University Press.

Georges, Tobias. 2012. "Justin's School in Rome—Reflections on Early Christian 'Schools.'" *Zeitschrift für Antikes Christentum* 16:75–87.

Glucker, John. 1978. *Antiochus and the Late Academy*. Hypomnemata 56. Göttingen: Vandenhoeck & Ruprecht.

Hadot, Pierre. 2002. *What is Ancient Philosophy*. Cambridge, Mass.: Harvard University Press.

Isenberg, Wesley W. 1968. "The Coptic Gospel According to Philip." Ph.D. diss. University of Chicago.

Isenberg, Wesley W. 1989. "Introduction." Pages 1, 131–139 in B. Layton (ed.), *Nag Hammadi Codex II, 2–7 Together with XIII,2*, Brit. Lib. Or. 4926 (1), and P. Oxy. 1, 654, 655*. Edited by Bentley Layton. Nag Hammadi Studies 20–21. Leiden: Brill.

Layton, Bentley. 1987. *The Gnostic Scriptures*. Garden City, N.Y./London: Doubleday.

Le Boulluec, Alain. 1985. *La notion d'hérésie dans la littérature grecque: IIᵉ–IIIᵉ siècles*. 2 vols. Paris: Études Augustiniennes.

Litwa, M. David. 2016. *Refutation of All Heresies*. Writings from the Greco-Roman World 40. Atlanta: SBL Press.

Löhr, Winrich. 2012. "Christian Gnostics and Greek Philosophy in the Second Century." *Early Christianity* 3:349–377.

Lössl, Josef. 2016. "Theology as Academic Discourse in Greco-Roman Late Antiquity." *Journal for Late Antique Religion and Culture* 10:38–72.

Markschies, Christoph. 2007. *Kaiserzeitliche christliche Theologie und ihre Institutionen*. Tübingen: Mohr Siebeck.

Neymeyr, Ulrich. 1989. *Die christlichen Lehrer im zweiten Jahrhundert: Ihre Lehrtätigkeit, ihr Selbstverständnis und ihre Geschichte*. Vigiliae Christianae Supplements 4. Leiden: Brill.

Schenke, Hans-Martin. 1997. *Das Philippus-Evangelium (Nag Hammadi-Codex II,3)*. Texte und Untersuchungen zur Geschichte der altchristlichen Literatur 143. Berlin: Akademie Verlag.

Schmid, Herbert. 2007. *Die Eucharistie ist Jesus: Anfänge einer Theorie des Sakraments im koptischen Philippusevangelium (NHC II 3)*. Vigiliae Christianae Supplements 88. Leiden: Brill.

Stowers, Stanley K. 1981. *The Diatribe and Paul's Letter to the Romans*. SBL Dissertation Series 57. Chico, Calif.: Scholars Press.

Stowers, Stanley K. 1988. "The Diatribe." Pages 71–83 in *Greco-Roman Literature and the New Testament*. Edited by D.A. Aune. SBL Sources for Biblical Study 21; Atlanta: Scholars Press.

Thomassen, Einar. 2006. *The Spiritual Seed: The Church of the "Valentinians."* Nag Hammadi and Manichaean Studies 60. Leiden: Brill.

Thomassen, Einar. 2011. "Baptism Among the Valentinians." Pages 895–915 in *Ablution, Initiation, and Baptism: Late Antiquity, Early Judaism, and Early Christianity*. Edited by David Hellholm et al. Vol. 2. Beihefte zur Zeitschrift für die neutestamentliche Wissenschaft 176. Berlin: De Gruyter.

Thomassen, Einar. 2013. "Going to Church with the Valentinians." Pages 183–197 in *Practicing Gnosis: Ritual, Magic, Theurgy and Liturgy in Nag Hammadi, Manichaean and Other Ancient Literature. Essays in Honor of Birger A. Pearson*. Edited by A.D. DeConick et al. Nag Hammadi and Manichaean Studies 85. Leiden: Brill.

Ulrich, Jörg. 2012. "What Do We Know about Justin's 'School' in Rome?" *Zeitschrift für Antikes Christentum* 16:62–74.

Van Os, Bas. 2007. "Baptism in the Bridal Chamber: The Gospel of Philip as a Valentinian Baptismal Instruction." Ph.D. diss. University of Groningen.

Wucherpfennig, Ansgar. 2002. *Heracleon Philologus: Gnostische Johannesexegese im zweiten Jahrhundert*. Wissenschaftliche Untersuchungen zum Neuen Testament 142. Tübingen: Mohr Siebeck.

CHAPTER 3

Esoteric Knowledge in Platonism and in Christian Gnosis

Christoph Markschies

Exactly what "Gnosis" actually meant in the ancient world has always been a matter of controversy and is once again the focus of much discussion at the present time.[1] Despite all the differences in the research literature, however, which disagrees on so many aspects of the "Gnosis" phenomenon, one does find several characteristic features of the movement that are used by nearly everyone when describing "Gnosis." In the present, most extensive exposition available on the German-language market and written by Marburg religious scholar, Kurt Rudolph, Gnostic cosmology and anthropology are presented in line with one of the tractates from the Gnostic codices found at Nag Hammadi, which the author introduces without much ado as the "Secret Book of John" ("The Apocryphon of John").[2] As such, Rudolph translated the Coptic title formed using Greek loanwords of a Gnostic text from Roman imperial times that was handed down in four revised versions, which, translated very literally, is known as the "Apocryphon of John" (NHC III,*1*: ⲡⲁⲡⲟⲕⲣⲩⲫⲟⲛ ⲛ̄ ⲓ̈ⲱ̄ⲅⲁⲛⲛⲏⲥ) or, based even more strictly on the titles of the gospels that became canonical, the "Apocryphon according to John" (NHC II,*1* and IV,*1*: ⲕⲁⲧⲁ ⲓ̈ⲱ̄ⲅⲁⲛⲛⲏⲛ ⲛ̄ⲁⲡⲟⲕⲣⲩⲫⲟⲛ).[3] Clearly, this text, which Rudolph holds to be characteristic of the "nature and structure" of Gnosis, both secret and revealed—as the beginning of the unabridged version of the text shows—is secret knowledge. In this version, the text begins with: "The teaching of the savior, and the revelation of the mysteries and the things hidden in silence, even these things which he

---

1 The following lecture was given at the "Second Dahlem Seminar on the History of Science in Antiquity: Esoteric Knowledge in Ancient Sciences" under the auspices of my colleagues Prof. Dres. Mark Geller and Klaus Geus on 10 January 2012; a few footnotes were added to it for this publication.

2 Rudolph 1994, 89, 120.

3 In NHC III,*1* one finds the title ⲡⲁⲡⲟⲕⲣⲩⲡⲏⲟⲛ ⲛ̄ ⲓ̈ⲱ̄ⲅⲁⲛⲛⲏⲥ on the flyleaf at the end of the text; BG 2, NHC II,*1* and IV,*1* (in the form ⲕⲁⲧⲁ ⲓ̈ⲱ̄ⲏⲛ [= ⲓ̈ⲱ̄ⲅⲁⲛⲛⲏⲛ] ⲛ̄ⲁⲡⲟⲕⲣⲩⲫⲟⲛ) only bring (cf. the German version) the title as *subscriptio*. See Waldstein and Wisse 1995, 12, 176–177.

taught John, his disciple" (NHC II,*1* 1.1–4). In Rudolph, a summary section about the Gnostic communities, cults and modes of conduct comes after the afore-mentioned lecture about Gnostic teachings. In the first main section "Nature and Structure" ("Wesen und Struktur"), Rudolph continues that, nowadays, one still knows of

> … admission ceremonies and "sacraments" in various Gnostic communi-ties, which render them similar to the secret societies. The obligation in these "secret societies" to maintain secrecy about certain teachings and practices was just as inherent to Gnosticism as were various degrees of knowledge and intelligence of the "secrets" (pneumatics or spirituals, psy-chics).[4]

At another place, the author writes, "… the Gnostics practiced a more or less strict obligation to maintain secrecy (the so-called Arcane Discipline)."[5] So much for the view expounded by Kurt Rudolph.

The most recent English-language publication about "The Gnostics," written by David Brakke of Indiana University, also refers to the so-called "Apocryphon of John," which he terms as "the *Secret Book*." The author points out that, in the secret writings, one can read in several places the phrase, "It is not the way Moses wrote and you heard" (the German version speaks of "Protestexegese")[6] and, as such, in such Gnostic texts, a secret knowledge is actually revealed, which leads to a different, namely critical, attitude towards previous religious bodies of knowledge. My American colleague Brakke links up this Gnostic self-presentation in the so-called "Apocryphon of John" (or, as it were, in the "Secret Book According to John") with the majority church polemics, as they are found, for example, in the work of the Gallic Bishop Irenaeus of Lyons, who origi-nally came from Asia Minor. In his anti-Gnostic work "Exposure and Refutation of "Knowledge" Falsely So-Called," written at the end of the second century, Irenaeus speaks of "arcane mysteries" (*recondita mysteria*, in Greek perhaps ἀπόκρυφα μυστήρια), "which they teach only to the pneumatics in secret and

---

4   Rudolph 1994, 232: "[...] dass wir von verschiedenen gnostischen Gemeinden Eintrittszere-monien und 'Sakramente' kennen, die sie den Mysterienvereinen ähnlich machen. Die in diesen 'Mysterien' gepflegte Geheimhaltungspflicht über bestimmte Lehren und Vorgänge ist der Gnosis ebenso eigen gewesen wie verschiedene Grade des Wissens und der Einsicht in die 'Geheimnisse' (Pneumatiker bzw. Vollkommene, Psychiker)."

5   Rudolph 1994, 224–225: "… übten doch die Gnostiker eine mehr oder weniger strenge Geheim-haltungspflicht (sogenannte Arkandisziplin)."

6   Brakke 2010, 71: NHC II,*1* 22.22–23; see also 13.19–21 and 29.6–7.

[keep] hidden from the others" (*seorsum et latenter ab reliquiis perfectos doce-bant*).[7] Irenaeus refers to such knowledge unceremoniously as "drivel" (*ab his deliratur*).[8]

So much for my very brief informational outline of one characteristic element found in many descriptions of the Gnostic movement—despite all the differences, most authors agree that knowledge imparted in the Gnostic groups, which was designated "secret," was only accessible to a small selection of especially qualified persons and in some places corrected, in some places confirmed, and in some places complemented, the Biblical teachings of the Christian majority church. What I aim to do in this article, on the *one* hand, is to ask whether we really are dealing with a form of presenting and imparting knowledge that is characteristic for the Gnosticism of the ancient world *in its entirety* (whose sheer irreducible plurality we have come to appreciate much better in the past years). On the *other* hand, I am also interested in other explanations from the ancient world of this mode of presenting and conveying knowledge and, as my title indicates, I would *ultimately* like to present some conventions in this series of explanations that were taken from ancient Platonism which might be seen as a possible role model for Gnostic types (types of Gnosticism). My article ends with a consideration of the consequences these observations have for the interpretation of Gnostic writings, in particular, writings from what is referred to as Valentinian Gnosis.[9]

One of the first indications of possible backgrounds in the history of thought for the Gnostic way of presenting knowledge as secret and something only to be passed on to a selected elite, is reflected in the title of the already much-mentioned "Apocryphon according to John" which, in fact, is characteristic of a certain current stream within the Gnostic movement (so-called Sethianism) and which might originate in its contemporary, fourfold Coptic form from the third century, but perhaps also did not emerge until the fourth century. It traces back, however, to the formation of systems and perhaps also to an original text, which we can date to the end of the second century. The key word ἀπόκρυφον is used in the title. The Greek word ἀπόκρυφος means first and foremost "concealed," "cryptic," "secret."[10] It is a favourite word used by ancient astrologers

---

7   Iren., *Haer.* 3.3.1 (ed. Rousseau and Doutreleau, SC 211, 30.7–8); see Brakke 2010, 121.
8   Iren., *Haer.* 3.3.1 (ed. Rousseau and Doutreleau, SC 211, 30.6).
9   Markschies 2002.
10   Oepke 1938, 962 with documentary evidence. Also on this matter: DiTommaso, 2001, 113–115 (definition and classification). In the following sections, I paraphrase from my main introduction to Markschies and Schröter 2012, 18–21.

and in ancient grimoires, but is also used in the Greek translation of the Old Testament, in some places quite profanely, for example, to describe "hidden treasures" (1 Macc 1:23), but on the other hand also when speaking of the "hidden things" that only God can reveal: "He declareth the things that are past, and the things that are to come, and revealeth the traces of hidden things" (Sir 42:19: ἀποκαλύπτων ἴχνη ἀποκρύφων). The Theodotianic text of the prophet Daniel, a Greek translation of the Hebraic Old Testament that differs from the Septuagint, even states when speaking of God: "He reveals deep and hidden things" (Daniel TH 2:22: αὐτὸς ἀποκαλύπτει βαθέα καὶ ἀπόκρυφα). However, even pagan Greeks liked to use this expression in religious contexts, for example, when referring to the Egyptian religion.[11] In the Hymn to Isis from the Cyclades island of Andros, which originates from the first century BCE, the goddess says: "I have found the clever Hermes' hidden signs of the tables (ἀπόκρυφα σύνβολα δέλτων) and inscribed them with styles with which I have indicated the sacred doctrine which infuses the initiate with pious awe."[12] Also to be understood in this same context are efforts to trace Greek philosophy back to secret oriental books, which were referred to as ἀπόκρυφα βιβλία:[13] Pherecydes, the teacher of Pythagoras, did not himself have a teacher, but gained his education from studying the "secret books" of the Phoenicians. Thus, the great Leyden magical papyrus prefaces the revelation of the "great Uphor-charm" with the instruction: ἔχε ἐν ἀποκρύφῳ ὡς μεγαλομυστήριον. Κρύβε, κρύβε ("So keep this in a secret place as a great mystery. Hide it, hide it!").[14]

The book title Ἀπόκρυφον (about the authenticity of which we admittedly know nothing) therefore signalled to a group of readers of or listeners to this Gnostic text that it was revealing secret religious knowledge founded on divine

---

11   Bardy 1950.

12   Peek 1930, 15, line 10 = Totti 1985, 5, no. 2, line 10. In his commentary, Peek points out the obvious reference to hieroglyphics: "what is meant rather, is that Isis has discovered the graphic characters which had long since been invented by Hermes, but kept secret, 'hidden' by him, and has made these available to the public." (1930, 33: "gemeint ist vielmehr, dass Isis die von Hermes längst erfundenen, aber geheimgehaltenen, 'versteckten,' Schriftzeichen aufgefunden und den Menschen zugänglich gemacht hat").

13   Suda Φ 214, s.v. Φερεκύδης (ed. Adler *Lexicographi Graeci* 1.4, 713.16 = Diels and Kranz, *Fragmente der Vorsokratiker* 2, 199.25).

14   Papyri Graecae magicae XII 322 (ed. K. Preisendanz, vol. 2, 79). Further sections in Bardy 1950, 517; Papyri Graecae magicae IV 1115; XIII 343–344, 731, 1059; *Catalogus Codicum Astrologorum Graecorum* 8.4: *Codices Parisini*, Codicum Parisinorum partem quartam descripsit P. Boudreaux, edidit appendice suppleta F. Cumont (Brussels: Lamertin, 1922), 176.16–17 (Cod. Astr. Graec. Paris. 82 = Paris. Graec. 2425, fol. 112ᵛ–116ʳ: ... ἔμπειροι γίνονται, ... ἀποκρύφων βίβλων ... πολυΐστορες).

authority. The respective terminology was widely disseminated among Jews, Christians and members of pagan religions, so that the title of the "secret writings" and their introduction in the long version say little at first glance about who the intended readers and/or listeners were; while Jews and Christians at least were targeted, so almost certainly were people who were interested in these religions but had not yet become members of them. The "Apocryphon according to John" was by no means the only "Apocryphon" in the Gnostic movement. According to Clement of Alexandria, who was active in Alexandria at the turn of the second to the third century, various Gnostics refer to βίβλοι ἀπόκρυφοι (as does the Essene community: Josephus, *War* 2.142), and works from these circles bearing the corresponding incipits have survived.[15] In addition to the very popular "Apocryphon of John," which has been handed down several times and in different forms (NHC III,*1*/BG 2/NHC II,*1*/NHC IV,*1*), in which this title simply means "secret writings of John," we must also mention the Gospel of Judas, which was critically edited for the first time only recently and whose Coptic *incipit* is "The secret account of the revelation that Jesus spoke in conversation with Judas Iscariot ..." (Codex Tchacos 3, p. 33.1–4; reconstructed in Greek by the editor: λόγος ἀπόκρυφος),[16] and ultimately, the famous Gospel of Thomas, whose *incipit* states: "These are the secret sayings (λόγοι ἀπόκρυφοι) that the living Jesus spoke and Didymus Judas Thomas recorded" (NHC II/2, p. 32.10–11). The term ἀπόκρυφος was obviously supposed to describe especially important secret books for certain Gnostic groups; far more evidence to this end could be provided.[17]

---

15   Clement of Alexandria, *Strom.* 1.69.6 (ed. Stählin/Früchtel/Treu, vol. 2, 44.5–6). Referred to here are sacred books of Zoroaster (see also NHC II,2 19.8–10), owned by "the Group surrounding Prodicus"; for more on this group, whose teachings allude to the teachings of the so-called Sethians and Valentinians, see Hilgenfeld 1963, 552–553 and Van Den Broek 2005.

16   See Kasser and Wurst 2007, 177–252, there 179. See also the coming text edition: Jenott 2011.

17   See, for example, the beginning of the so-called First Book of Jeu from the Oxford Bruce Codex, more of an *incipit*: "This is the book of the gnosis of the invisible God, by means of the hidden mysteries which show the way to the chosen race, leading in refreshment to the life of the Father" (based on the German translation in GCS Koptisch-gnostische Schriften 1, 257.5–8 ed. Schmidt and Till), see also from the Second Book, chap. 43 (ed. Schmidt and Till 304.6–13). Naturally, not all Gnostic writings that are titled "Apocryphon" today are titled or subtitled as such in manuscript: The "Apocryphal Epistle" of Jacob (*EpJac*) has neither an *incipit* nor a *subscriptio*, beginning simply with the usual introductory greeting, "From Jacob to ..." (NHC I,2 1.1; this beginning has also been lost). Nevertheless, *EpJac* NHC I,2 29–31 refers to secret teachings that the Apostle transcribed in "Hebraic lettering": "Endeavor earnestly and take care not to rehearse this text to many—this that the Savior did not wish to tell to all of us, his twelve disciples."

It is very obvious that the idea that Gnostics characterized their knowledge as a secret knowledge of religious revelation is therefore not merely polemic spread by critics from the majority church, but is indeed a self-representation created by the Christian groups in question from their beginnings in the second century CE.

While these observations bring us to a popular understanding of the term "esoteric knowledge" that is currently widespread no matter where you look, we still have not looked at the ancient term ἐσωτερικός and how it was used when talking about knowledge or bodies of knowledge in ancient, or even Gnostic texts. As we know, the term first appears in its actual meaning in the works of satirist Lucian of Samosata who, in his satirical work about the *Sale of Creeds* caricatures a "beautiful Peripatetic": "He is temperate, good-natured, easy to get on with; and his strong point is, that he is twins." In response to the question put by the buyer who is puzzling about what this means, Hermes answers: "Why, he is one creed outside, and another inside. So remember, if you buy him, one of him is called Esoteric, and the other Exoteric."[18] It was clear to those readers with a well-founded knowledge of the classics that Lucian was alluding to the term ἐξωτερικοὶ λόγοι here, which appears eight times in the teachings of Aristotle and, what is more, by itself complements the obvious antonym in Greek ἐσωτερικός.[19] If one holds with Konrad Gaiser, who attempted forty years ago to present the meaning of this word pair and the original meaning of ἐξωτερικοὶ λόγοι for the philosophical *œuvre* of Aristotle in a summarized form, then there are *three* possible interpretations of the meaning: ἐξωτερικοὶ λόγοι refers to *either* the literary, published dialogues as opposed to the strictly philosophical treatises of the school (the esoteric writings)—this first interpretation is advocated by Cicero (perhaps taken on by Antiochus of Ascalon), Plutarch and most of the ancient commentators of Aristotle—*or* to teaching exercises that were propaedeutic in nature, and which were publicly available for a larger circle of listeners with rhetorical-political interests. This second interpretation was accepted by Gaiser himself, but also by Wolfgang Wieland and Franz Dirlmeier. At this point, I do not want to go into the traditional point of view of these two interpretations to be found in Jakob Bernays und Werner Jaeger (Bernays and Jaeger based the distinction on the difference between literary works and lectures for teaching purposes), because this would embroil

---

18   Lucian., *Vit. Auct.* 26.533–535 (ed. Itzkowitz, Bibliotheca Teubneriana): (ΕΡ.) ἄλλος μὲν ὁ ἔκτοσθεν φαινόμενος, ἄλλος δὲ ὁ ἔντοσθεν εἶναι δοκεῖ· ὥστε ἢν πρίῃ αὐτόν, μέμνησο τὸν μὲν ἐξωτερικὸν τὸν δὲ ἐσωτερικὸν καλεῖν.

19   Evidence in Gaiser 1972, 866 note 1.

us in questions of the philology of Aristotle. Furthermore, four years before his death in 1988, Gaiser himself revised his uncompromising opinion from 1972, arguing in favour of distinguishing between the *written* texts (ἐξωτερικοὶ λόγοι) of the Stagirite and his *unwritten* statements (the same as ἐσωτερικοὶ λόγοι) based purely on the status of their readability.[20] More interesting for our purposes is the fact that Lucian and Galen obviously applied the classical Greek duality ἐξωτερικός—ἐσωτερικός to the similarly classical Aristotelian term ἐξωτερικοὶ λόγοι, thereby accepting both the duality "public/not public" and the second duality "of-the-discipline/extra-disciplinary" in their interpretation of Aristotle. There is also no need to deal in this article with the questions posed by Gaiser[21] and others concerning whether the interpretation of the teachings and works passed down by Plato should be examined with the help of this duality or not (which has generally been the case, at least since Schleiermacher.)[22] It is certain that a distinction between two different levels of openness and two scholarly levels, which is reflected in the conceptual pair ἐξωτερικός—ἐσωτερικός as it were, was already "closely related with the notion—rooted in the Pythagorean tradition—of deliberately keeping certain teachings secret"[23] in the second century.

This act of assigning to our conceptual pair ἐξωτερικός—ἐσωτερικός the idea of maintaining secrecy about certain teachings becomes especially clear when we look at the Christian theologian Titus Flavius Clemens from Alexandria, who was highly versed in the works of Plato and whom I already dealt with above. Clemens describes the act of keeping writings secret as usual practice in philosophy:

> It was not only the Pythagoreans and Plato then, that concealed many things; but the Epicureans too say that they have things that may not be uttered, and do not allow all to peruse those writings. The Stoics also say that by the first Zeno things were written which they do not readily allow disciples to read, without their first giving proof whether or not they are genuine philosophers. And the disciples of Aristotle say that some of their treatises are esoteric (only meant for the closest followers: τῶν συγγραμμάτων αὐτοῦ), and others common and exoteric (also understandable for outsiders: κοινά τε καὶ ἐξωτερικά). Further, those who instituted the mys-

20   Gaiser 1984, 100–101.
21   Gaiser 1988.
22   F. Schleiermacher, *Platons Werke* ¹1804, Introduction, quoted by Gaiser 1972, 866.
23   Gaiser 1972, 866: "Die so vorgenommene Unterscheidung konnte mit dem in der pythagoreischen Tradition verwurzelten Gedanken an eine bewusste Geheimhaltung bestimmter Lehren verquickt werden."

teries, being philosophers (οἱ τὰ μυστήρια θέμενοι, φιλόσοφοι ὄντες), buried their doctrines in myths, so as not to be obvious to all.[24]

Clement of Alexandria refers to the concealment of esoteric writings which, in his opinion, was usual among philosophers, with some degree of sympathy—the section quoted here closes with the rhetorical question: "and was it not more beneficial for the holy and blessed contemplation of realities to be concealed?"[25] And in the following line of argumentation in his *Stromateis*, Clement attempts to show that maintaining secrecy concerning the authentic philosophical teachings is an apostolic and therefore Christian practice. To do so, he uses Biblical quotes, for example, from the Epistle to the Ephesians, which is today considered to be deutero-Pauline: "Rightly, therefore, the divine apostle says, 'By revelation the mystery was made known to me (as I wrote before in brief, in accordance with which, when ye read, ye may understand my knowledge in the mystery of Christ), which in other ages was not made known to the sons of men, as it is now revealed to His holy apostles and prophets.'"[26]

In the further course of his argumentation, Clement leaves no doubt about the fact that the real and true knowledge—he uses the Greek term γνῶσις—according to both the pagan-philosophical and Christian interpretation is meant purely for the initiated, who have been introduced beforehand to the secrets and that only the appearance of Jesus Christ in the flesh increased the circle of potential initiates extraordinarily. The convergence of Plato and Paul is something that Clement repeatedly emphasizes in his *Stromateis*:

> Rightly then, Plato, in the Epistles, treating of God, says: "We must speak in enigmas that should the tablet come by any mischance on its leaves either by sea or land, he who reads may remain ignorant." For the God of the universe, who is above all speech, all conception, all thought, can never be committed to writing, being inexpressible even by His own power. [...] Akin to this is what the holy Apostle Paul says, preserving the prophetic and truly ancient secret from which the teachings that were good were derived by the Greeks: "Howbeit we speak wisdom among

---

24   Clem. Al., *Strom.* 5.58.1–4 (ed. Stählin et al., 2.365.6–15).
25   Clem. Al., *Strom.* 5.58.5 (ed. Stählin et al., 2.365.16–17): ... τὴν δὲ τῶν ὄντων ὄντως ἁγίαν καὶ μακαρίαν θεωρίαν οὐ παντὸς μᾶλλον ἐπικεκρύφθαι συνέφερεν.
26   Clem. Al., *Strom.* 5.60.1 (ed. Stählin et al., 2.366,18–367,3). On this topic, see also: Wyrwa 1983, 290–297.

them who are perfect; but not the wisdom of this world, or of the princes of this world, that come to nought; but we speak the wisdom of God hidden in a mystery."[27]

At this point, I would like to briefly explore the intriguing question of how assigning Pythagorean notions of the secrecy of esoteric knowledge to the duality ἐξωτερικός—ἐσωτερικός actually responds to the traditions which hold that Pythagoras and Plato were initiated in the secret teachings of Zoroaster. Both traditions, which Matthias Baltes has lucidly presented and intelligently commented upon in the "Platonica Maiora," are supported by evidence among early Christian authors—Hippolytus at the beginning of the third century and Eusebius in the fourth.[28] In fact, one could say that the assignment of the duality "exoteric/esoteric," as it was understood in terms of the degree of publicity and level of knowledge in the early Roman Empire, stood at least in connection with a historical understanding (or in any case conjecture and debate) of how foreign secret knowledge was received in Plato's philosophy.

It appears to me that the Gnostic practice of reserving secret knowledge for a highly qualified elite is an exact parallel to this reported philosophical tradition (and, incidentally, it shows that the old Berlin connection between Christian Gnosis and ancient philosophy, as once supported by Harnack and since revived, for example, in John Whittaker's dictum of Gnosis as a "watered down Platonism," certainly has a *particula veri*, to put it mildly.)[29] We recognize this, for one thing, by the fact that the differentiation among various levels of expertise of a given proclamation expressed in the duality ἐξωτερικός—ἐσωτερικός is imparted not just by Clement, but also by Gnostic groups. Irenaeus reports of the urban Roman or Gallic Gnostics, that they would adapt "their teachings to the mental capacities of their audience and their answers to the expectations of the questioner" (*fecerunt doctrinam secundum audientium capacitatem et responsiones secundum interrogantium suspiciones*).[30] Irenaeus sees this as hypocritical, while happily noting that the Gnostics claimed merely to be copying the practice of the apostles.[31] The "accommodation theory" presented here is surprisingly similar to that proposed by Clement of Alexandria and once again documents the fact that the "Christian Gnosis" of the major-

---

27   Clem. Al., *Strom.* 5.65.1–5 (ed. Stählin et al. 2.369,24–370,8).
28   Dörrie 1990, modules 67 and 68, particularly 67.1 and 68.2.
29   Cf. Whittaker 1980 and Markschies 1994.
30   Iren., *Haer.* 3.5.1 (ed. Rousseau and Doutreleau, 54.23–56,1).
31   Iren., *Haer.* 3.5.2 (ed. Rousseau and Doutreleau, 60.62–64).

ity church-aligned Alexandrians really is not so far from what the Gnostics, marginalized within the majority church, believed and, from a historical perspective, were the first among Christian theologians to do so. The polemics of Irenaeus, who in contrast to Clement was not seeking to rehabilitate a majority church Christian Gnosis, can only be understood as follows: (Valentinian or Ptolemaean) Gnostics as regarded by Irenaeus distinguished between exoteric teachings for the interested public and the newly converted on the one hand, and teachings for the initiated elite on the other—exactly as the often-cited duality ἐξωτερικός—ἐσωτερικός originally meant. There is no doubt that, at least among individual Gnostic groups, this distinction between more public and more private teachings was associated with the obligation to maintain secrecy arising from the Pythagorean tradition—the various titles of Gnostic writings are sufficient proof of this, encompassed by the Greek term or loanword ἀπό-κρυφος, even those which originate not from urban Roman Valentinianism, but from a different Gnostic tradition, that is, a tradition which current research often refers to as "Sethianism."

At this point, I am unable to assess whether the writings of individual Gnostic groups in their literary forms are more exoteric or more esoteric in nature. This is because there is a preliminary question which must be addressed, that is, the question of whether, in interpreting this familiar duality, the ancient sense is not in fact eluding us somewhat, or is impossible to accurately account for. We have already seen that the question of whether the term "esoteric" was associated with purely oral, unwritten teachings in the Roman Empire (as Konrad Gaiser evidently believed towards the end of his life), is not easy to answer. Nor is it easy to detail how widespread the idea that the truly secret core elements of philosophical or philosophizing teachings could only be transmitted orally, or at least not in simple earthly language, was in the second and third century CE. If Gaiser's interpretation also applied to the Roman Empire and if the Gnostics adhered to such an understanding of exoteric and esoteric teachings, then one would have to conclude that no esoteric teachings have been passed down to us in written form at all, because they were largely or exclusively subject to oral transmission. This is indicated, for example, by the renowned "Great Notice," the first chapters in the anti-Gnostic work of Irenaeus, which report on the teachings of the pupils of Ptolemy (they referred to themselves as "Valentinians" after the urban Roman teacher Valentinus, who had long since emigrated to Cyprus),[32] and which are used as a philosophizing artistic myth and

---

32   Iren., *Haer.* 1.1.1–1.8.4. Regarding this text see also Markschies 1997a and 1997b.

thus—either way—correspond to the *exoteric* form in which Platonic philosophy was presented in the artistic myths of the Dialogues: the artistic myth of Ptolemy (or his pupils), as I have shown elsewhere,[33] can only be understood if its mythic elements are interpreted in the same manner as, for example, Plato's *Republic* is usually interpreted through the Allegory of the Cave. Such an interpretive methodology against the backdrop of unwritten, oral and secret teachings would have wide-reaching consequences for the reconstruction of not just Valentinian (or Ptolemaean) Gnosis. We would need to carry out the interpretation of their extant, exoteric texts on the basis of a reconstruction of their "actual" esoteric teachings, for which we have no written sources—and that is precisely because there never were any written sources for purely oral, esoteric teachings.

Of course, that is by no means the only possible interpretation of the findings: one could continue to claim—and not solely motivated by a critical opinion of Gaiser's theories on the significance of orality in Plato's unwritten teachings—that both exoteric and esoteric teachings were transcribed in Valentinian Gnosis, as they were transcribed in the Sethianist Gnosis (for example, in the form of the "Apocryphon of John"). Evidence for this classic view of the problem comes from the overwhelmingly exoteric form of Gnostic teachings in the letter from the urban Roman Gnostic Ptolemy to the matron Flora, as handed down to us by the Late Antique Bishop Epiphanius of Salamis.[34] If this epistle represents the exoteric form of Gnostic teachings, then Irenaeus' address to his pupils, the source referred to by Sagnard as the "Great Notice,"[35] would be the esoteric form of the teachings. I have ventured to provide a dual outline of these very complex facts in simplified form showing, *on the one hand,* the classic model of allocating the terms "esoteric" and "exoteric" to Valentinian Gnostic texts, and *on the other hand,* a proposed new allocation:

Classic model:

esoteric	exoteric
Great Notice (via Irenaeus)	Ptolemy's *Epistle to Flora*

---

33   Markschies 2009b.
34   Markschies 2000 and 2011; the Greek text, for example, in Quispel 1966.
35   Sagnard 1947; most recently, the comprehensive commentary by Chiapparini, 2012. I will return to this stimulating work elsewhere.

New model:

esoteric	exoteric
secret	not secret
internal	public
oral	written
ἄγραφα δόγματα	Myths of the Platonic Dialogues (e.g. Cave
Dogmatics to be reconstructed	Allegory)
	Ptolemy's *Epistle to Flora*
	Great Notice (via Irenaeus)

Were the schema here defined as the "new model" to form the basis for interpreting Gnostic texts, that would—as already indicated—have wide-reaching consequences for the interpretation of Valentinian (and presumably also Sethian) texts. It would require investigating which oral, secret, esoteric teachings stood behind that which is passed down to us in texts. This could lead, for example, to a discussion of whether the somewhat polytheistic interpretation of—as the North African Christian theologian Tertullian stated polemically—a huge band of divine figures has been adequately interpreted, as it were, in an oral dogmatic adherence to principles by a strictly Judeo-Christian monotheism. And we might also ask whether the notion of teaching three different classes of people, which is supposedly characteristic for Gnosticism, was not perhaps developed further at the level of a dogmatic adherence to principles as three dimensions within every one of us.

I can only sketch in the consequences here and put them aside for later, more thorough investigation. The philological basis for justifying this model, which supports the merely provisional evaluation of the terminology of "esoteric/exoteric" and its Christian reception[36] in this article, must first be expanded.

Whether this new model will actually form the basis for interpretation of Gnostic, particularly Valentinian texts in the future is a matter for further discussion. No matter what one thinks at this point: it seems to me that a comparison of ancient pagan—and particularly Platonic traditions—regarding esoteric knowledge will produce some enlightening results for the understanding of Gnostic texts, and indeed the whole phenomenon of Gnosis—and here I have merely made a cautious start for such comparative investigations.

---

36   I give a more thorough representation of this point of view in the articles compiled in
      Markschies 2009a.

Acknowledgements

I would like to thank my assistant, Dr. Renate Burri, for her careful editing of the manuscript. My own contribution to this topic is a rather brief abstract of a detailed exposition that I am intending to write: Markschies 2010.

Bibliography

Bardy, Gustave. 1950. "Apokryphen." Pages 516–517 in *Reallexikon für Antike und Christentum*. Stuttgart: Hiersemann.

Brakke, David. 2010. *The Gnostics: Myth, Ritual, and Diversity in Early Christianity*. Cambridge, Mass.: Harvard University Press.

Chiapparini, Giuliano. 2012. *Valentino Gnostico e Platonico. Il valentinianesimo della 'grande notizia' di Ireneo di Lione: fra esegesi gnostica e filosofia medioplatonica*. Milan: Vita e pensiero.

Clement of Alexandria. *Clemens Alexandrinus: Stromata Buch I–VI*. Edited by O. Stählin, new edition by L. Früchtel, 4th edition with supplements by U. Treu. Die griechischen christlichen Schriftsteller 52. Berlin: Akademie Verlag.

DiTommaso, Lorenzo. 2001. *A Bibliography of Pseudepigrapha Research 1850–1999*. Journal of the Study of Pseudepigrapha, Supplement Series 39. Sheffield: Sheffield Academic Press.

Dörrie, Heinrich. 1990. *Der Platonismus in der Antike: Der hellenistische Rahmen des kaiserzeitlichen Platonismus*, Vol. 2. Revised by Matthias Baltes. Stuttgart: Frommann-Holzboog.

Gaiser, Konrad. 1972. "Exoterisch/esoterisch." Pages 865–867 in *Historisches Wörterbuch der Philosophie 2*. Darmstadt: Wissenschaftliche Buchgesellschaft.

Gaiser, Konrad. 1984. *Platone come scrittore filosofico: saggi sull'ermeneutica dei dialoghi platonici*. Naples: Bibliopolis.

Gaiser, Konrad. 1988. "Platons esoterische Lehre." Pages 13–40 in *Gnosis und Mystik in der Geschichte der Philosophie*. Edited by Peter Koslowski. Zurich: Artemis.

Hilgenfeld, Adolf. 1963. *Die Ketzergeschichte des Urchristentums, urkundlich dargestellt*. Darmstadt: Wissenschaftliche Buchgesellschaft.

Irenaeus of Lyon. *Irénée de Lyon: Contre les Hérésies, Livre III*. Edited by A. Rousseau and L. Doutreleau. Sources Chretiennes 211. Paris: Cerf.

Jenott, Lance. 2011. *The Gospel of Judas: Coptic Text, Translation, and Historical Interpretation of the "Betrayer's Gospel."* Studien und Texte zu Antike und Christentum 64. Tübingen: Mohr Siebeck.

Kasser, Rodolphe and Gregor Wurst. 2007. *The Gospel of Judas, together with the Letter of Peter to Philip, James and a Book of Allogenes from Codex Tchacos: Critical Edition*. Washington, DC: National Geographic.

Lucian of Samosata. 1992. *Luciani vitarum auctio. Piscator.* Edited by Joel Itzkowitz. Bibliotheca Teubneriana 23.

Markschies, Christoph. 1994. "Die Krise einer philosophischen Bibel-Theologie in der Alten Kirche, oder: Valentin und die valentinianische Gnosis zwischen philosophischer Bibelinterpretation und mythologischer Häresie." Pages 227–269 in *Gnosis und Philosophie. Miscellanea.* Edited by R. Berlinger and W. Schrader. Foreword by A. Böhlig, Elementa 59. Amsterdam: Rodopi.

Markschies, Christoph. 1997a. "Nochmals: Valentinus und die Gnostikoi. Beobachtungen zu Irenaeus, haer. I 30,15 und Tertullian, Val. 4,2." *Vigiliae Christianae.* 51:179–187.

Markschies, Christoph. 1997b. "Valentinian Gnosticism: Toward the Anatomy of a School." Pages 401–438 in *The Nag Hammadi Library after Fifty Years. Proceedings of the 1995 Society of Biblical Literature Commemoration.* Edited by J.D. Turner and A.M. McGuire. Nag Hammadi and Manichaean Studies 44. Leiden: Brill.

Markschies, Christoph. 2000. "New Research on Ptolemaeus Gnosticus." *Zeitschrift für Antikes Christentum* 4:225–254.

Markschies, Christoph. 2002. "Valentin/Valentinianer." Pages 495–500 in *Theologische Realenzyklopädie* 34. Berlin: De Gruyter.

Markschies, Christoph. 2009a. *Gnosis und Christentum.* Berlin: Berlin University Press.

Markschies, Christoph. 2009b. "Welche Funktion hat der Mythos in gnostischen Systemen? Oder: ein gescheiterter Denkversuch zum Thema 'Heil und Geschichte'." Pages 513–534 in *Heil und Geschichte. Die Geschichtsbezogenheit des Heils und das Problem der Heilsgeschichte in der biblischen Tradition und in der theologischen Deutung.* Edited by J. Frey, S. Krauter, and H. Lichtenberger. Wissenschaftliche Untersuchungen zum Neuen Testament 248. Tübingen: Mohr Siebeck.

Markschies, Christoph. 2010. *Die Gnosis.* 3rd ed. Munich: Beck.

Markschies, Christoph. 2011. "Individuality in Some Gnostic Authors. With a Few Remarks on the Interpretation of Ptolemaeus, Epistula ad Floram." *Zeitschrift für Antikes Christentum* 15:411–430.

Markschies, Christoph and Jens Schröter, 2012. *Antike christliche Apokryphen in deutscher Übersetzung,* 7th ed. Tübingen: Mohr Siebeck.

Oepke, Albrecht. 1938. "κρύπτω κτλ." Pages 959–979 in *Theologisches Wörterbuch zum Neuen Testament* 3. Stuttgart: Kohlhammer.

Peek, Werner. 1930. *Der Isishymnus von Andros und verwandte Texte.* Berlin: Weidmann.

Quispel, Gilles. 1966. *Ptolémée, Lettre à Flora. Analyse, texte critique, traduction, commentaire et index grec.* Paris: Éditions du Cerf.

Rudolph, Kurt. 1994. *Die Gnosis: Wesen und Geschichte einer spätantiken Religion,* unamended reprint of the 3rd revised and supplemented edition. Uni-taschenbücher 1577. Göttingen: Vandenhoeck & Ruprecht.

Sagnard, François Louis Marie Matthew. 1947. *La Gnose Valentinienne et le témoignage de Saint Irénée.* Études de philosophie médiévale 36. Paris: Vrin.

Totti, Maria. 1985. *Ausgewählte Texte der Isis- und Sarapis-Religion.* Subsidia Epigraphica 12. Hildesheim: Olms.

Van den Broek, R. 2005. "Prodicus." Pages 974–975 in *Dictionary of Gnosis and Western Esotericism* 2. Leiden: Brill.

Waldstein, Michael and Frederik Wisse, eds. 1995. *The Apocryphon of John. Synopsis of the Nag Hammadi Codices II,1; III,1; and IV,1 with BG 8502,* Nag Hammadi and Manichaean Studies 33. Leiden: Brill.

Whittaker, John. 1980. "Self-generating principles in Second-century Gnostic Systems." Pages 176–193 in *The Rediscovery of Gnosticism. Proceedings of the International Conference on Gnosticism at Yale, New Haven, Connecticut, March 28–31, 1978: The School of Valentinus.* Vol. 1. Studies in the History of Religions 41.1. Edited by Bentley Layton. Leiden: Brill.

Wyrwa, Dietmar. 1983. *Die christliche Platonaneignung in den Stromateis des Clemens von Alexandrien.* Arbeiten zur Kirchengeschichte 53. Berlin: De Gruyter.

CHAPTER 4

Visual Representations of Early Christian Teachers and of Christ as the True Philosopher

Robin M. Jensen

Elite or educated members of the Roman aristocracy in the early Imperial era frequently incorporated portraits of philosophers into their domestic décor along with depictions of ancestors, household gods, and even the more official divinities like Apollo, Zeus, Hercules or Asclepius. In the period known as the Second Sophistic, images of famous teachers even came to be subjects of a certain degree of veneration and usually bore recognizable physical characteristics, including a full beard, balding pate, and the recognizable philosopher's cloak, in Latin called a *pallium*, usually worn over the bare chest. The desire to be associated with these esteemed thinkers or to be represented as learned citizens, prompted Roman men of the third century to have themselves similarly portrayed, especially on their funerary monuments. This practice of depicting the intellectual in visual art continued within Christianity, as Jesus came to be included in the pantheon of revered teachers and, along with other Christian figures like John the Baptist and the Apostle Paul, was depicted in much the same guise, and sometimes in the same setting, as those antecedent philosophers.

For example, in his treatise, *Against Heresies*, Irenaeus of Lyons mentions a certain female student of Carpocrates named Marcellina who, he says, came to Rome and led many astray. Apparently, among her various transgressions, she possessed a portrait of Jesus made from life, which according to Irenaeus' informant, was copied (or perhaps commissioned) by Pontius Pilate. Supposedly, Marcellina displayed this object in a portrait gallery along with images of Pythagoras, Plato, and Aristotle where it—like them—received a variety of votive offerings, including the bestowal of a crown (*Haer.* 1.25.6).[1]

Although the story of Marcellina's image has no precise parallel elsewhere in early Christian literature, it was reprised in a comment attributed to the late second-or early third-century Roman teacher, Hippolytus who, without mentioning Marcellina, repeats that followers of Carpocrates possessed images of

---

[1] On Marcellina and with discussion of the Carpocratian's alleged images, see Snyder 2017.

Christ fashioned by Pilate (*Ref.* 7.32.8 ed. Marcovich). The story also found its way into the work of the fourth-century heresy-fighter, Epiphanius of Salamis who repeated the assertion that Carpocratians had images of Jesus made by Pilate out of precious materials and that they venerated them, after the manner of the "heathens" alongside of images of Pythagoras, Plato, and Aristotle (*Pan.* 27.6.9–10). The sixth-century Piacenza pilgrim to Jerusalem actually reports seeing a portrait of Christ, said to be made from life, set up in a basilica identified as built on the site of Pilate's praetorium (*Itin.* 23).

While Hippolytus' and Epiphanius' references clearly draw upon Irenaeus' text, some of the details of the Carpocratian's alleged images resonate with another second-century account of an early Christian portrait, mentioned in the *Acts of John*. In this instance, the apostle encounters his own portrait, set up to be venerated by the grateful husband of a woman whom John had miraculously healed and whose own life, lost through grief, had been restored (*Acts of John* 26–30). According to the story, John scolded the husband, Lycomedes of Ephesus, both for having acquired the portrait and for treating it like the image of a god, crowning it with garlands and placing lamps and altars before it. John pointed out that a portrait is merely an external appearance, seen by the eye, and not a true likeness of a person's soul.

Intriguingly, Irenaeus' reference to Marcellina's portrait resonates with a later (fourth- or fifth-century) detail included in the probably specious *Historia Augusta's* entry on Severus Alexander.[2] Although dubious in any factual sense, this curious document asserts that Alexander (208–235) maintained an art collection that not only included traditional portraits of his ancestors and deified emperors but more unexpected representations of Christ, Apollonius of Tyana, Abraham, and Orpheus (*Vit. Alex. Sev.* 29.2). While one can only speculate how the *Historia's* anonymous author got—or why he would have invented—this information, its very existence demonstrates that at least he and perhaps many of his ancient readers were willing to believe that an imperial collection of gods' and heroes' portraits could have included images of Jesus and Abraham.[3]

Little other textual evidence and—perhaps more significantly—almost no surviving material artifacts attest to the existence of images showing Jesus as a

---

2   The secondary literature is extensive. For a recent summary of the most well-known theories about date and authorship, as well as a rebuttal of several, see Cameron 2010, 743–746.

3   The *Historia Augusta Vit. Hel.* 3.5 also reports that Alexander's predecessor, Elagabalus incorporated the religions of Christians, Jews and Samaritans in his temple to the god Elagabalus in Rome and, presumably, this would include an image of Jesus. In addition, according to Eusebius, *Hist. eccl.* 6.21.3–4, Alexander's mother, Julia Mamaea, had requested Origen of Alexandria to come to Antioch to give her instruction in the Christian religion, which could have prompted Alexander to include Jesus in his pantheon.

teacher or philosopher prior to the fourth century. The earliest extant depictions of Jesus show him primarily as a miracle worker or healer (for example, see Fig. 4.4). Apart from one rare example illustrated below, Jesus is not depicted as a teacher among his disciples before the fourth century.

1 Philosopher Portraits in Roman Visual Art

Whether or not ancient Carpocratians or Severus Alexander actually possessed, displayed, and even venerated portraits of Jesus among the likenesses of other heroes, gods, and philosophers, galleries like his are described elsewhere.[4] The *Historia Augusta* also reports that Marcus Aurelius (121–180) kept golden statues of his revered teachers in his lararium, regularly making them offerings of flowers and sacrifices (*Vit. Marc. Anton.* 3). Juvenal mocked the ignorant who filled their houses with plaster busts of Chrysippus, Aristotle, or Pittacus, and purchased antique statues of Cleanthes to watch over their bookcases (*Sat.* 2.1–7). Evidently, both the Roman nobility and affluent private citizens eagerly procured portraits of famous intellectuals to adorn their palaces and villas, most of them likely copies of Greek originals.

Although collectors had created a demand for illustrious poets' and philosophers' portraits for part of their domestic décor from the late Republican period onwards, the popularity of these portraits increased in the second through fourth centuries, when members of the elite classes sought busts of famous teachers in order to enhance their own social presentation as learned or cultured intellectuals. The remarkable group of shield and bust portraits of philosophers found at Aphrodisias is a particularly good example.[5] Similar to accumulating scrolls for their personal libraries, possessing and displaying images of famous thinkers suggested that their owners were well acquainted with their works. While many collectors of such images could have been genuine students of philosophy, it was not actually necessary, for the display of their portraits alone could suggest a level of respect for the life of the mind.

Pretense to culture was probably as likely as real intellectual engagement was. In addition, almost all of these popular images portrayed illustrious men who had lived in the distant past, rather than contemporary personages whose reputations might have been more ambiguous. In fact, most philosopher portraits probably were purchased almost randomly and primarily for purely decorative purposes. Such affectation even became the subject of satire. Clearly,

---

4   On this see Dillon 2006, esp. chap. 2, "Displaying Portraits of the Greeks."
5   See Smith 1990, 127–155, 177.

many of these objects were intended primarily for show, and said little about the actual intelligence or achievements of their owners. This fascination with ancient philosophers explains the multitude of surviving Roman copies of much earlier Greek portraits of illustrious poets and sages in the world's great museums.

Yet, while these copies were more or less faithful reproductions of their models, their purpose was different. As art historian Paul Zanker has argued, whereas the Greek originals were meant as honorific portraits and destined for the agora or temples, the Roman copies primarily functioned as "icons in a peculiar cult of Greek culture and learning."[6] They were not, therefore, commemorative works so much as decorative art pieces, designed to give visitors the impression that a householder was a person of intellectual refinement. Instead of galleries filled with images of famous statesmen, war heroes, or even their distinguished ancestors, the owners of these objects favored portraits of renowned intellectuals—figures less caught up in the mundane demands of civic or public duties.

Such monuments demonstrate the extent of a burgeoning Roman preoccupation with Hellenic culture and learning, particularly in the second and third centuries CE, a preoccupation that many of an older generation viewed with some distaste.[7] Roman values and virtues were juxtaposed with Greek ideals; a life traditionally defined by piety and prudence leavened by the pursuit of philosophy, art, and poetry. Yet, such captivation by a cultured past was, to a large degree, limited to the private sphere, where otherwise proudly conventional Romans could imitate the manners and tastes of cultivated Greeks. This movement inspired the recovery of Greek styles of the plastic arts and a renewed interest in the gods and their myths along with the acquisition of the works (and portrait likenesses) of great philosophers. These citizens may also have amassed impressive libraries to go with the statues of sages for their gardens, dining rooms, and atria.

The inscription of a name occasionally appeared on the bases of certain busts, but if that was lacking, portraits might possess some identifying physical features that were usually recognizable. Romans believed that physiognomy revealed certain qualities of character, thus making it an essential aspect of portraiture. Nobility or wisdom was clearly evident in one's face, or at least in the way a sculptor might render it.[8] While emperors like Augustus were rendered as idealized youths well into old age, philosophers and other respected statesmen

---

6 Zanker 1995, 10.

7 The study of this subject is vast, but recommended background on the influence of Greek learning and culture on society in this period includes Bowersock 1996.

8 On this subject see Fejfer 2008, 98–99.

FIGURE 4.1 Conversation among philosophers, mosaic from Pompeii, 1st cen. CE

were more likely to be portrayed as venerable than beautiful, confirmation that their personal appearance was insignificant in comparison to their intellectual acumen.

Rare wall paintings and mosaics depicting philosophers have been found in addition to portrait statues and busts, and like these, reflect the ways that these individuals were characterized. For example, a group of philosophers are gathered into a group portrait for a first-century mosaic pavement, usually titled "Plato's Academy," found in the Pompeian villa of Titus Siminius Stephanus and now in the Naples Archaeological Museum (Fig. 4.1).

Depicted as a symposium of seven philosophers (possibly the seven sages of Greek tradition) they sit together under the shade of an olive tree. Their pen-

FIGURE 4.2 Mosaic of Socrates and the sages, Apamea, 3rd cen. CE

sive expressions are intended to signal to the viewer that the men are either deep in thought or in the midst of a learned discussion. The walled citadel at the upper right might be Athens' acropolis; the large epistyle at the left could be that city's sacred Dipylon gate—situated close to Plato's Academy. The central figure under the tree may be Plato himself. He appears to be pointing a staff either at the globe sitting in a wooden chest at the bottom center or to the shadow cast by his left foot (perhaps a reference to the myth of the cave). The sundial at the center might be a reference to the transience of life; the globe perhaps an allusion to the celestial sphere or a lesson on astronomy.[9]

A much later mosaic, dating from the mid-360s, and from Apamea, Syria, also depicts seven sages, six on each side of their teacher Socrates who is identified by name (Fig. 4.2). The group is more simply arranged as if around a semicircular table in the midst of a symposium. The late fourth-century date of this mosaic along with the bust of a philosopher in the Getty Museum (Fig. 4.3) shows that depictions of philosophers with or without their disciples surrounding them remained fashionable well into the Christian imperial era.

---

9   Elderkin 1935.

FIGURE 4.3 Portrait of a philosopher, about 400 CE

Yet, despite this continuing popularity of philosopher portraits, comparable depictions of Jesus as a teacher surrounded by his followers or apostles only just began to emerge around this same time.

2   Philosophers' Physical Appearance

As is evident in these images, certain attributes were associated with philosophers: distinctive items of dress, particular physical characteristics, and specific objects. Among these were the customary philosopher's cloak (*pallium*), the beard, and the book roll (*volumen*). Other common features include going bare-footed or wearing sandals rather than boots, having dirty fingernails, and allow-ing the hair to be tangled and shaggy. Facial expressions, such as knitted brows suggested deep thought. In portrait production, such items were intended to show a disdain for conformity with conventional standards of grooming or self-presentation. They demonstrated the sage's repudiation of personal van-ity, symbolized his lack of concern for worldly matters, showed his practice of ponderous cogitation, and signaled his retreat from the civic sphere for the sake of pursuing the intellectual life.[10]

According to these images, philosophers draped a rectangular mantle or *pallium* over a tunic or simply over their bare chest. The *pallium* (or Greek *hima-tion*), the basic uniform of the philosopher, was basically a large rectangular mantle, draped over one shoulder and wrapped around the waist. Although it was originally a regular and practical item of clothing for Greek men, in the Roman context it reflected the fashionable interest in all things Greek, and in particular bespoke the garb of a teacher, poet, philosopher, or rhetorician—i.e., the "learned man."

The bare-chested version typically signified a Cynic, by reputation someone who cared little for personal grooming or appearance and who affected other anti-social behaviors. The sophist philosopher, Dio Chrysostom, remarked that when people see someone in a cloak but no tunic, with flowing hair and full beard, they know him to be a philosopher, wearing the garb prescribed for his profession (*Dis.* 72.2). Some ancient writers wrote derisively about the impli-cations of these habits. Seneca, for example, referred to them as repellent, and linked with slovenly self-display and showy contempt for luxuries like sleeping couches and silver dishes. Seneca, rather, believed that philosophers could lead simple lives without being unkempt or dirty (*Ep.* 5).

The *pallium* made a conscious contrast with the traditional Roman toga, the formal costume of a respectable and politically engaged citizen. The *pallium* was an unacceptable garment in certain social contexts, particularly if it was worn without an undertunic and was tattered or soiled. An especially ragged *pallium* was distinguished with its own name: *tribōn*.[11] However, whether pris-tine and worn over a tunic or shabby and wrapped around a bare chest, it

---

10   Hoff 1994, 27–33 and 43–47 enumerates these elements of the philosopher portraits. Dillon, however, points out that many of these characteristics are also found on stat-ues of Roman statesmen and civically involved intellectuals of other classes, so cau-tions against overly generalizing these features to philosophers alone. See Dillon 2006, 125.

11   See Urbano 2014.

signaled its owner's desire to be regarded as an individual who had both the leisure and allowance to pursue intellectual activities.

Typically, philosophers also wore beards, which was an anomaly in the late Republic and through the first century but became more common during the second and third centuries. Wearing of beards, for long regarded as un-Roman, is often associated with the reign of the Emperor Hadrian, the first Roman emperor who was known to wear a full beard and moustache. Historians have usually judged this to be a sign of his particular devotion to philosophy or perhaps simply his desire to be regarded as an intellectual, although the dubious *Historia Augusta* claims he did this primarily to hide facial warts (*Hist. Aug.* 26.1–2). Whatever the reason for his forging this fashion, Hadrian is credited with a cultural renaissance and a love of all things Greek.[12] This new trend in personal grooming continued under Hadrian's successors, Antoninus Pius and Marcus Aurelius, the latter of course, philosophically inclined and author of the *Meditations*, influenced by the works of Epictetus.

Baldness was also a common trait of philosophers, as a high forehead was believed to denote wisdom, but hair on the head also might be rather long and unkempt. Facial expressions also were meant to express intense contemplation (e.g., the hand on the chin, a furrowed brow, a penetrating gaze). When not merely busts, they usually were depicted as either reading an unfurled book roll or merely grasping a scroll, like three of the seven philosophers in this mosaic. Although this mosaic does not show it, a leather case (*capsa*) filled with scrolls is often a featured prop.

3   Christians Writers on Philosophers' Physical Appearance

According to both Justin Martyr and Tertullian, second- and third-century Christian teachers properly wore the philosopher's mantle because they considered themselves to be teachers of true wisdom. Justin Martyr introduces the summary of his dialogue with the Jew Trypho by reporting that Trypho immediately recognized him as a philosopher because of his manner of dress. He also notes that Trypho cordially greeted him on that basis, explaining that his friendly approach was prompted by advice from his teacher in Argos, Corinthus the Socratic. According to Trypho, Corinthus had taught him not to despise those who dressed in the *pallium* but rather to be open to learning some-

---

12   Zanker 1995, 217–220. Another possibility is that Hadrian initially adopted a beard as a sign of mourning for his adoptive father (and predecessor), Trajan.

thing profitable from an amiable conversation with them (*Dial.* 1). Justin did, in fact, regard himself as a philosopher insofar as he had studied with Stoics, Pythagoreans, and Platonists, before becoming a disciple of the Syrian Christian who expounded true (Christian) philosophy (*Dial.* 2).

Trypho's recognizing Justin as a *pallium*-wearing philosopher does not mean that he thought Justin was something other than a member of the Christian sect. To the contrary, according to Justin, as soon as he realized his identity, Trypho eagerly engaged Justin in debate about the nature of the deity and the validity of Christian versus Jewish interpretations of scripture and expectations for the Messiah. Nevertheless, Justin's account of their interaction implies that Trypho encountered something he may have found surprising: a convert to Christianity who unapologetically regarded his new religion as a form of philosophical teaching.

Meanwhile, many early Christian writers ridiculed contemporary (vs. ancient) self-styled philosophers as interested only in futile arguments and pretentious debates rather than seeking genuine truth. They regarded them as conceited and ignorant.[13] Even so, the early third-century teacher, Tertullian of Carthage, who famously asked what Athens has in common with Jerusalem (*Praescr.* 7), wore the *pallium* and urged other Christian teachers to do likewise. In a treatise devoted to the garment, *On the Pallium*, he, like Justin, recognized that *pallium*-wearers had a bad reputation in certain quarters. Tertullian insisted, however, that the *pallium* was the most appropriate attire for those who taught "better philosophy," e.g., Christianity. In contrast with the toga, Tertullian regarded the philosopher's mantle as both sensible and unpretentious. It did not require fancy folding and draping by a trained servant, but was easy to throw over one's head and simply let fall to cover the body (*Pall.* 5.1.3). But more than merely donning a more practical garment, Tertullian deemed wearing the *pallium* as signaling a renunciation of secular concerns and public duties— a renunciation not only appropriate for all philosophers, but especially fitting for Christian catechists who eschewed the ambitions, civic responsibilities, and worldly distractions that wearing the toga symbolized. In his treatise, he lets the mantle make its own case (*Pall.* 5.4.2):

> "I owe nothing to the forum," it says, "nothing to the Campus Martius, nothing to the Senate House. I do not watch for a magistrate's function, do not occupy any platform for speakers, do not attend to the governor's office; I do not smell the gutters, nor adore the bar in court, nor wear

---

13 For examples see Clement of Alexandria, *Protr.* 5; *Strom.* 8.1.2.

out the benches, nor disturb proceedings nor bark pleas; I do not act as a judge, a soldier, or a king; I have withdrawn from public life. My only activity concerns myself; I do not have any care, except for this: to have no care. A better life can be enjoyed in seclusion than out in the open."[14]

Thus, according to Tertullian, adopting the *pallium* was an obvious exhibition of a Christian teacher's disdain for secular affairs. Furthermore, it suited their role as teachers of a "true" philosophy.

Such teachers, including Clement of Alexandria, similarly characterized Christianity in the second and third century. Theirs was not an anti-intellectual religion or one that eschewed the teachings of pre-Christian thinkers. Rather they carried on in the ancient and venerable tradition of their predecessors, presenting and debating ideas about the deity and the nature of the virtuous life and incorporated the writings of their pagan predecessors by arguing that these had even laid the groundwork for the true teachings that would supersede them. Clement even urged Christian men to grow their beards, claiming that the beard was a sign of maturity, virility, and authority (*Paed.* 3, 3 and 11). Tertullian concludes his treatise with these words, "Rejoice, *pallium*, and exult! A better philosophy has deigned you worthy, from the moment that it is the Christian whom you started to dress (*Pall.* 6.4)."[15]

Not everyone agreed with Tertullian's preference for wearing the *pallium*, however. His African contemporary, Minucius Felix, for example, argues that Christians need not display their philosophical wisdom through their mode of attire (*Oct.* 38.6). More pointedly Cyprian of Carthage directly rebuked *pallium* wearers, contending that true philosophers show their wisdom simply by their actions, which speak more loudly than words (or clothes). Cyprian's censure of the *pallium* supplements his general suspicion of philosophers, whom he judges to be filled with pride, self-deceiving, and unaware of how affected they looked with their naked chests (*Bon. pat.* 2–3).[16]

---

14   Tertullian, *Pall.* 5.4.2, trans. Hunink 2005, 59; also cited by Urbano 2014, 185. Further see Brennan 2008. Tertullian adds a comment in this chapter also on the wearing of boots, saying that going barefooted or wearing only sandals was much preferable and better for the feet.

15   Tertullian, *Pall.* 6.4 (tr. Hunink 2005, 63).

16   See also Cyprian, *Ep.* 55.16.1 respecting his view of philosophers.

FIGURE 4.4
Jesus healing the blind man, detail
from an early Christian sarcophagus, Rome, 4th cen. CE

4   The Intellectual on Early Christian Funerary Monuments

As noted above, despite these textual references to Christians wearing the *pallium* and full beards, the earliest surviving images of Jesus do not depict him
as a teacher among his disciples, nor with any of the characteristic features of
the philosopher's appearance. Prior to the late fourth century, Jesus is almost
always represented as a miracle worker or healer and as beardless and wearing
a tunic under his *pallium* (Fig. 4.4).

He often also holds a bookroll. While the other men that appear with him
(presumably his apostles or other followers) normally wear closely cropped
beards, rather than long or shaggy ones, they similarly wear tunics beneath
their *pallia*. A single surviving exception, discussed below, is an image of Jesus
wearing only the *pallium* (over a bare chest) along with a full, bushy beard,
appearing on a third-century marble plaque, now housed in Rome's Museo
Nazionale (see below, Fig. 4.9).

By contrast, the image of a pallium-draped, bearded, and bare-chested male
is more common for Christian sarcophagus reliefs, in which the figure is prob-

FIGURE 4.5 Sarcophagus with seated reader, good shepherd, and orant, Rome, ca. 260 CE

ably meant to represent the deceased. On these examples, found on Rome's Via Salaria and commonly known as the Ram's Head sarcophagus (Fig. 4.5), the individual in question is shown as seated, often in profile, and with a scroll unfurled on his lap. This convention was already common on the sarcophagi of non-Christians and seems to have been intended to represent the departed as a man of learning and culture.

Depicting the deceased as a learned reader was already a popular motif for the funerary monuments of the middle and upper classes.[17] Instead of exhibiting statues of revered statesmen or philosophers whose reputation would rub off upon their owner, these funerary portraits perpetually portrayed the deceased themselves as well-educated and culturally refined individuals (Fig. 4.6).

Almost always male, this figure of the learned reader typically sits on a folding stool and appears to be studying the text of an unfurled scroll. A bundle of scrolls sits on the ground, near his feet. Frequently a female muse joins him. The bookroll is a particularly effective signifier of the man's erudition and cultural refinement.[18] Instead of the image of the unkempt philosopher, however, the seated reader usually is depicted as clean-shaven and neatly barbered. Admirers (friends and family members) often stand nearby, and in certain instances these supporters are—by contrast—bare-chested, bearded, and shaggy-haired as if they might be his intellectual mentors.

17   On the philosopher sarcophagi see Ewald 1999, 30–53; id. 2010, 285–288; and Birk 2013.
18   On the bookroll as an iconographic symbol in both Christian and Graco-Roman art, see Birt 1907, esp. pp. 77–80 ("Christus mit der Rolle") and 173–175 (unrolled scrolls on sarcophagi).

FIGURE 4.6 Sarcophagus with philosopher (Plotinus?) and family, Rome, late 3rd cen. CE

The endurance of this motif into Christian iconography suggests the desire for self-presentation across religious allegiances, if not necessarily social class distinctions. The seated male reader is often joined by a praying figure (*orant*) who is almost always a veiled female who stands with her hands outstretched in the customary posture of supplication. The female praying figure (*orant*) might be meant to be a personification of the virtue of *pietas*, just as the reader could perhaps personify Christian *paideia*. On the Ram's Head Sarcophagus (Fig. 4.5) a seated woman—perhaps the deceased's wife—holds a rolled up scroll that similarly signals her as a person of learning. On many of these sarcophagi, women also appear holding rolled scrolls, signaling that they too were educated intellectuals.[19]

The central image of (what appears to be) the Good Shepherd has prompted viewers to identify this object as having been commissioned by a Christian, although almost every other detail could as readily appear on a pagan monu-

---

19   On the learned woman, see Birk 2013, 77–91.

FIGURE 4.7   Christian sarcophagus from the church of Sta. Maria Antiqua, Rome, late 3rd cen.
CE

ment. The veiled *orant* turns toward the shepherd at the center of the composition, who appears to return her gaze. He carries a ram over his shoulders; two
other rams graze nearby.

The prominence of a seated reader, shown with the characteristic garb of a
philosopher was a convention found on many Roman funerary monuments. In
this case, it seems to have been preferred also by late third-century Christians,
who apparently had the same desire to represent themselves as practitioners
of *paideia*, *pietas*, and marital *concordia*. Here, husband and wife are depicted
as seated with scrolls (although usually only the man's is unrolled). Friends or
family members attend each of the spouses.

Because its iconography is religiously ambiguous, the Rams' Head sarcophagus could be regarded as an instance of a sarcophagus commissioned by or
fabricated for a couple with mixed commitments. By contrast, the well-known
sarcophagus in the church of Sta. Maria Antiqua, incorporates explicitly Christian motifs: both a Jonah scene and a depiction of John baptizing Christ are
joined with the seated reader, praying figure, and shepherd (Fig. 4.7).

Here, again the seated reader figure is bare chested and bearded. As on the
Via Salaria sarcophagus (Fig. 4.5), he is joined by a standing female *orant* and
a Good Shepherd. However, in this instance the faces of both reader and *orant*
are incomplete, a puzzling detail that is common also on parallel pagan sarcophagi, and might be the result of haste, but could be an intentional omission
in order to suggest that either the dissolution of the self in death, or perhaps
that the buyer regarded the figures as generic types rather than representations
of the deceased.[20]

---

20   On the lack of finished faces on both pagan and Christian sarcophagi of this type see Birk
      2013, 126.

On the Sta. Maria Antiqua sarcophagus, the *orant*, rather than a matronly, seated woman, appears to be the male reader's female counterpart. One may suppose that she was intended to be a personification of piety rather than the portrait of a specific woman and that, similarly, the male reader was to personify *paideia*. Thus, the composition was possibly designed to represent the virtues of the deceased individual (or couple) buried in the tomb, rather than their actual likenesses. Given the composition's other, clear Christian imagery, these figures then could be adapted to suggest that the interred was a man devoted to the pursuit of Christian learning, while his wife was assiduous in her practice of Christian prayer. Thus, iconographic conventions that expressed traditional Roman virtues (*paideia* and *pietas*) were rendered more explicitly Christian.

As noted above, an image of John the Baptist baptizing a child-sized Jesus joins the seated reader and praying woman on the Santa Maria Antiqua sarcophagus. Here, John has a thick, curly beard and wears the philosopher's *pallium* draped over his bare chest. This depiction of the Baptist adds a special dimension to his character, perhaps as the philosophical forerunner to Jesus as the teacher of true wisdom.

In Christian art of the fourth century, the Apostle Paul is the only other figure who most seems to possess some of the features of a typical philosopher. Although identifiable portraits of Paul cannot be dated much before the mid-fourth century, his likeness is easily recognizable and consistent in its features. In contrast to his closely-cropped colleague Peter, with whom he is often paired, Paul is portrayed with a long, pointed beard, receding hairline, and relatively narrow face. Yet, like the other apostles and Jesus himself, Paul normally wears the *pallium*, draped over an undertunic rather than a bare chest. Nevertheless, Paul could be identified with the philosopher type not only by his facial features or garb but also by the fact that he usually holds a scroll or stands next to a basket (*capsa*) or case of scrolls (Fig. 4.8).

In a letter purported to be from Eusebius of Caesarea to the Emperor Constantine's sister, Constantia, a certain woman is reported to have owned a portrait of both Apostles Peter and Paul portrayed in the guise of philosophers (Eusebius, *Ep. Constantia*). According to one historian, Paul's portrait may have been modeled after depictions of the Neoplatonist teacher Plotinus in order to emphasize his role as the earliest Christian philosopher/theologian.[21]

---

21 See L'Orange 1973. On portraits of Paul, see Jensen 2011.

FIGURE 4.8
Paul with basket of scrolls, from
the catacomb of Domitilla, Rome,
4th cen. CE

5 Christ as Teacher in Early Christian Art

Although it does not emerge before the early fourth century, a depiction of Christ as a teacher soon became a popular Christian iconographic motif.[22] Prior to that, Christ appears either at his baptism, upon his mother's lap and visited by the magi, or as a miraculous healer or wonderworker, curing the infirm, raising the dead, multiplying loaves and fishes, and changing water to wine. In many of these, Christ holds a bookroll, as do many of the male witnesses that surround him. However, in the emerging depictions of Christ as teacher, he usually shows wears a tunic and *pallium* and is beardless and youthful in appearance.

As noted above, a unique and notable exception is a polychrome fragment of a plaque or sarcophagus, now in Rome's Museo Nazionale (Palazzo

---

22   See Kollwitz 1936.

FIGURE 4.9 Scenes of Christ teaching and working miracles, Rome, ca. 290–310 CE

Massimo) and which art historians usually date to the late third or turn of the fourth century (Fig. 4.9).

Here Christ appears several times within a single panel, in each instance holding a book roll. On the left and right sides, he heals a supplicant; in the center he is depicted as seated and teaching. He wears the *pallium* in all three scenes but over a tunic only in the image to the left. In the other two images he is bare chested (as well as barefooted). In a different section of the same fragment, Christ appears to have just healed the paralytic (carrying away his bed) and multiplying loaves of bread. In the paralytic scene, he wears a tunic under his *pallium*, while in the multiplication image he is, again, bare chested.

The center image of Christ teaching differs somewhat from the other scenes as his beard and hair are made to look especially full and longer. He is posed frontally rather than in profile, raises his right hand in a conventional gesture of speech, and holds up a partially rolled scroll with his left. At his feet six small figures in short tunics pay him rapt attention. Historians have sometimes identified this composition as portraying the Sermon on the Mount.[23]

These early depictions of Christ with a beard and bare chest are exceptional, however. Depictions of Jesus sitting among his apostles that resonate more with the depiction of Socrates and his circle on the Apamea mosaic (Fig. 4.1) begin to appear in the first half of the fourth century. Examples of this type include paintings from the Christian catacombs of Domitilla (Fig. 4.10 and 4.11), Ermete, the Via Anapo and the Coemeterium Maius.

---

23 Hellemo 1989, 19; Mathews 1993, 70.

FIGURE 4.10   Christ enthroned among the apostles, from the catacomb of Domitilla, Rome, 4th cen. CE

FIGURE 4.11   Christ among the apostles; from the catacomb of Domitilla, Rome, 4th cen. CE

A representation of Christ as a teacher surrounded by his disciples also appears in a later fourth-century mosaic found in the apse of the chapel of Sant'Aquilino, annexed to the Basilica of San Lorenzo in Milan (Fig. 4.12).

In these examples, Jesus sits, facing forward, in a high-backed chair that elevates him above his disciples. He holds a partially unfurled scroll and raises his right hand in the speaking gesture. In the Milan mosaic, a leather *capsa* filled with scrolls sits below Jesus' feet. The disciples are gathered into two groups of six on either side of Christ and either gaze toward him or look out of the frame directly at the viewer. Some hold bookrolls or make animated gestures, allowing the scene to evoke a lively discussion. Unlike the Socrates mosaic or

FIGURE 4.12   Christ Teaching the apostles, mosaic apse from the chapel of Sant'Aquilino,
                Milan, late 4th cen. CE

the sarcophagus fragment from Rome, the catacomb paintings and the Milan mosaic show Jesus as beardless, and, like his apostles, he always wears a tunic under his *pallium*.

A depiction of Christ teaching also occurs on numerous later fourth-century sarcophagi, including one in Arles, named for its occupant, the Bishop Concordius (Fig. 4.13), and another in the Louvre (Fig. 4.14).

In these sculptural examples, Jesus sits slightly above his apostles and his feet rest on a distinctive footstool that indicates his superior status. Significantly, on the Arles sarcophagus Christ is bearded, while on the Milan sarcophagus he is clean-shaven. In both he wears the *pallium*, and seems to be in mid-lecture, pointing to a page in the codex (rather than a scroll) that he holds. His flanking disciples appear to be actively responding to his instruction, some of them looking straight at him, others turning back to their companions as if in conversation; on the Arles sarcophagus one of them even seems to be reading along in his own scroll. The composition again evokes the scene of an animated teaching session.

The fact that Christ has a beard in some of these new images is significant. In fact, it is in these representations of Christ as a teacher among his apostles that Christ first appears as bearded. Although his appearance varies for a while— sometimes bearded, sometimes clean-shaven—this shift seems to emphasize his role as transmitter of truth over against his almost exclusive earlier presentation as a youthful (and beardless) wonderworker. Rather than demonstrating his divine power through prodigies and miraculous healings, these new com-

FIGURE 4.13   Christ teaching among the apostles, 4th cen. CE

FIGURE 4.14   Christ teaching among the apostles, 4th cen. CE

positions show Jesus as expounding his teaching and forming a following of those who would become its adherents.

Thus, the iconic figure of the intellectual evolved in Christian art from the late third through the late fourth century. Initially it was a straightforward borrowing of a Roman type that could be adapted to represent any educated individual, or perhaps more generically to the virtue of *paideia*. In certain instances, the *pallium*-wearing and bearded philosopher characterization applied to portrayals of John the Baptist or the apostle Paul. However, by the middle of the fourth century, one of the most common ways of representing Christ was as the teacher or transmitter of a new philosophy. He sits among his disciples like Socrates, holding a book in his hands and evidently instructing them in the tenets of wisdom that was transcendently superior to earlier and imperfect manifestations. Christian iconography, like Christian catechesis, extolled the value of *paideia*, while proclaiming that the true knowledge was found exclusively in this new teaching.

This adoption of the iconography of Christ as a teacher during the middle of the fourth century points to a change in the way that Christians regarded Jesus. Earlier visual depictions emphasized his role as a wonderworker by showing him as healing the sick, raising the dead, multiplying bread, and changing water to wine. In these images he appeared as a beardless youth. During the fourth century he was more frequently represented as a teacher and he gradually began to be depicted as a mature male figure with a full beard. In the depictions of him as a teacher he holds a book or a scroll and is surrounded by his disciples. It appears that Christian iconography finally and fully absorbed the second sophistic cult of learning by showing Jesus himself in the guise of the philosopher.

This transition has struck at least one commentator as arising from an elitist context and reflecting Jesus' visual evolution from an egalitarian savior whose message was directed at slaves, the poor, and the uneducated into a teacher of wisdom who satisfied the social aspirations of the sophisticated upper classes or those Christians who had felt demeaned by critics of their religion as a superstition.[24] However, one of the early apologists' primary aims was to show exactly this: that Jesus was the teacher of true philosophy and not only a miracle worker, and that Christianity was not a religion solely aimed at simple belief in a new savior god but a whole system of thought. Thus, the arrival of this iconography seems a little late, given the early emphasis on Christian teaching as the true *paideia*. At last, one might say, Christian iconography caught up to the culture: showing Christ as a teacher and the faith as a superior form of wisdom.

---

24   This is the argument of Zanker 1995, 296–297.

Bibliography

Birk, Stine. 2013. *Depicting the Dead: Self-Representation and Commemoration on Roman Sarcophagi with Portraits*. Aarhus: Universitetsforlag.

Birt, Theodor. 1907. *Die Buchrolle in der Kunst: archäologische-antiquarische Untersuchungen zum antiken Buchweisen*. Leipzig: Strauss & Cramer.

Bowersock, G.W. 1996. *Hellenism in Late Antiquity*. Ann Arbor, Mich.: University of Michigan Press.

Brennan, T. Corey. 2008. "Tertullian's *De Pallio* and Roman Dress in North Africa." Pages 257–270 in *Roman Dress and the Fabrics of Roman Culture*. Edited by J. Edmondson and A. Keith. Toronto: University of Toronto Press.

Cameron, Alan. 2010. *The Last Pagans of Rome*. Oxford: Oxford University Press.

Deichmann, Friedrich Wilhelm. 1967. *Repertorium der christlich-antiken Sarkophage*. Wiesbaden: Franz Steiner Verlag.

Dillon, Sheila. 2006. *Ancient Greek Portrait Sculpture: Context, Subjects, and Styles*. Cambridge: Cambridge University Press.

Elderkin, G.W. 1935. "Two Mosaics Representing the Seven Wise Men." *American Journal of Archaeology* 39:92–111.

Ewald, Björn C. 1999. *Der Philosoph als Leitbild. Ikonographische Untersuchungen an Römischen Sarkophagreliefs*, Roemische Abteilung, Ergänzungsheft 34. Mainz: Von Zabern.

Ewald, Björn C. 2010. "Myth and Visual Narrative in the Second Sophistic: A Comparative Approach: Notes on an Attic Hippolytos Sarcophagus in Agrigento." Pages 261–308 in *Life, Death and Representation: Some New Work on Roman Sarcophagi*. Edited by J. Elsner and J. Huskinson. Berlin: De Gruyter.

Fejfer, Jane. 2008. *Roman Portraits in Context*. Berlin: De Gruyter.

Hellemo, Geir. 1989. *Adventus Domini: Eschatological Thought in 4th-Century Apses and Catecheses*. Leiden: Brill.

Hoff, Ralf von den. 1994. *Philosophenporträts des Früh- und Hochhellenismus*. Munich: Biering and Brinkmann.

Hunink, Vincent. 2005. *Tertullian, De Pallio: A Commentary*. Leiden: Brill.

Jensen, Robin. 2011. "Paul in Art." Pages 507–530 in *The Blackwell Companion to Paul*. Edited by Stephen Westerholm. Malden, Mass.: Wiley-Blackwell.

Kollwitz, Johannes. 1936. "Christus als Lehrer und die Gesetzesübergabe an Petrus in der konstantinische Kunst Roms." *Römische Quartalschrift für christliche Altertumskunde und Kirchengeschichte* 44:45–66.

L' Orange, H.P. 1973. "Plotinus-Paul." Pages 32–42 in *Likeness and Icon: Selected Studies in Classical and Early Mediaeval Art*. Odense: Odense University Press.

Marcovich, Miroslav, ed. 1986. *Hippolytus: Refutatio Omnium Haeresium*. Berlin: Walter De Gruyter.

Mathews, Thomas. 1993. *Clash of Gods: A Reinterpretation of Early Christian Art*. Princeton: Princeton University Press.

Smith, R.R.R. 1990. "Late Roman Philosopher Portraits from Aphrodisias." *Journal of Roman Studies* 80:127–155, 177.

Snyder, H. Gregory. 2017. "'She Destroyed Multitudes': Marcellina's Group in Rome." Pages 39–61 in *Women and Knowledge in Early Christianity*. Edited by U. Tervahauta et al. Leiden: Brill.

Urbano, Arthur. 2014. "Sizing Up the Philosopher's Cloak: Christian Verbal and Visual Representations of the *Tribōn*." Pages 175–194 in *Dressing Judeans and Christians in Antiquity*. Edited by K. Upson-Saia, et al. Surrey: Ashgate.

Zanker, Paul. 1995. *The Mask of Socrates. The Image of the Intellectual in Antiquity*. Translated by A. Shapiro. Berkeley: University of California Press.

CHAPTER 5

Christians as and among Writer-Intellectuals in Second-Century Rome

Heidi Wendt

1 Introduction

In his classic micro-history of a Catholic inquiry into the sixteenth-century Italian miller Domenico Scandella, called Menocchio, Carlo Ginzburg reconstructs a climate of unbridled religious innovation that is, in certain respects, apropos of second-century Rome.[1] Accused of having uttered heretical and impious words about Christ and, what is more, of proselytizing others with his dogma, Menocchio's trials disclose an idiosyncratic cosmogony informed by literary materials ranging from a vernacular Bible to Christian devotional texts to the Qur'an. Numerous details that emerge from these accounts invite comparison with the second-century Christians at the center of this volume: the relationship between Menocchio's literacy and his propensity for theological speculation; the motley writings whence he adduced profound "scriptural" mysteries; his unexpected occupation for undertaking these activities, and how artisan networks not only facilitated the exchange of writings that enabled them, but also supplied an audience for his insights; and, in this vein, the audacity of one with no obvious avenue for claiming religious expertise being emboldened to do so at all.[2] The yield of Ginzburg's study is a detailed snapshot of the

---

1　Ginzburg 1992. Jason BeDuhn (2015, 31) makes a similar connection between Ginzburg's study and third-century Christian diversity with a focus on the Manichaeans. I do not wish to overstate my own comparison, particularly with respect to the role of representatives of the Catholic Church in stemming or attempting to constrain possibilities for religious innovation. Whereas similar interests have been posited of Roman religious actors and institutions—that is, of attempting to limit religious pluralism or even engage in religious persecution—many have called into question the Romans' desire and basic ability to legislate religious norms. The bibliography is vast, but see, e.g., Orlin 2010, esp. 162–190, 191–214; North 2011; Fuhrmann 2012. For an overview of these complexities with a focus on the problematic model of civic or *polis* decline, see Harland 2006.

2　Although Menocchio wore the traditional miller's costume, he identified also as a "carpenter, sawyer, mason, and other things" (Ginzburg 1992, 1). This sort of professional "eclecticism" both encompassed and characterized his religious practices.

religious creativity that can ferment in unexpected places, cultivated by unlikely agents, and nourished by texts.

Not unlike post-Reformation Europe, the Roman imperial period was a time of fertile cultural and intellectual experimentation, wherein novel religious phenomena abounded and would-be religious experts jockeyed for occasional audiences or regular followers. Whereas these dynamics have long been theorized at the level of corporate entities—rival cults, religious communities, religions, or religious systems—scholarship of the past decade has foregrounded the behavior of individual agents in assessing broader patterns of religious diversity and change under the empire.[3] This shift in focus permits greater nuance: it is easier to imagine the ingenuity and latitude of particular actors, both religious experts and also those who sought them out, than to map the tremendous diversity or complex histories of putative traditions and institutions. All the more so when the *apparent* cogency of such traditions and institutions was deeply indebted to the efforts of such individuals, often writers, who were not merely defending the integrity of entities already in existence, but actively laboring to bring them into being.[4]

With respect to the study of early "Christianity" the turn to individuals allows for a methodological alternative to introducing the problematic language of orthodoxy (or proto-orthodoxy), heresy, and Gnosticism into this early period.[5] The stubborn persistence of these categories in the face of multiple avenues of sustained critique signals the need for a more thoroughgoing reconceptualization of the actors and phenomena they comprise and are employed to explain.[6] To begin instead from would-be experts whose claims somehow involved Jesus Christ—or cognate figures such as Savior—offers an approach to the first and second centuries that is not beholden to *a priori* schemes of orthodoxy and its discontents. If Menocchio serves as a reminder of the vibrant theological worlds that can coexist alongside the Church, how much more so at a time when such an institution had yet to emerge and when what it meant to be a Christian expert depended largely, if not entirely, on being able to persuade others of this claim?[7]

---

3 See Rüpke and Spickermann 2013; Rüpke 2016.

4 See esp., Eshleman 2012.

5 So I argue in Wendt 2016. "Christianity" and "Christian" will appear without further qualification henceforth. When I use the former, it is either with respect to the intellectual history of this category or else to capture how particular authors—Justin, for instance—presented their own constellations of thought and practice as bounded, normative entities. "Christian" is not always accurate, particularly with respect to Paul and his associates, but I employ the term more loosely on occasion for the sake of simplicity.

6 See Dunderberg 2008, 19; Brakke 2010, 1–28; King 2011.

7 I remain skeptical of the presumption that there was "a Church" at Rome, despite the

The present volume's focus on Christians as and among other kinds of Roman intellectuals is especially germane to such an approach: on the one hand, literary artifacts, and ones that attest a multiplicity of intellectual discourses and practices, are the *only* evidence for Christ-phenomena in the first three centuries. On the other, it is on the basis of this evidence that scholars have extrapolated fully formed religious communities and traditions whose hypothetical status, once posited, not only obscures other social settings from which the texts might plausibly have arisen, but also renders Christians incomparable to non-Christian (and non-Jewish) religious actors and groups of the Greco-Roman world.[8]

Nowhere are these observations more apparent than in scholarship on the fourfold gospel of the New Testament. Recent publications have adduced multiple points of contact between the gospel authors and their approximate literary contemporaries. However, these studies tend to stop short of considering the (later) canonical texts as products of the same social processes and interests that gave rise to non-canonical Christian writings, to say nothing of the copious non-Christian compositions that circulated within this timeframe: the books of Hystaspes, Orphica, Hermetic literature, Pythagorean pseudepigrapha, various textual oracles, and so-called magical papyri, among other examples.[9]

My objectives in this chapter are twofold: First, I situate Christian writers of the second century within a wider matrix of intellectuals, and then a specific subset of intellectualizing religious experts who not only shared numerous skills but also drew on these to common ends. Literacy and other intellectual abilities were not only diffuse in the Roman period, but also crossed many social registers. I am interested in figures who engaged in these practices in the context of religious activity, a domain that overlapped with philosophy, medicine, education, and law, to the extent any specialty were distinct.[10] More-

---

recurrence of this assertion in early Christian sources and scholarly literature (Wendt 2016, 212–215).

8   See Stowers 2011.

9   Of course, the literary record of the second century is far more plentiful than this list indicates. I am particularly interested in writings that seem to have participated in dynamics of self-authorization and competition among would-be religious experts. For elaboration of this literary category, see Wendt 2016, 129–141.

10   That is, an exorcist might have much in common with a doctor, practically speaking, and even employ the language of *pneuma* and other philosophical or medical terminology to explain a patient's affliction. Yet his epistemological premise of his diagnosis and remedy would still be rather different. In the case of Josephus' Judean exorcist Eleazar (*Ant.* 8.46–48), for instance, these would be possession by a malevolent spirit and the performance of

over, my focus falls on religious experts who were largely self-authorized, by which I mean that their authority and legitimacy accrued not from existing institutions but from their own displays of expertise, typically of an intellectual variety.

The first and second centuries teemed with assorted specialists, including many who alleged expertise in religious matters: diviners, initiators, magi, astrologers, exorcists and other healers, inspired prophets, and exegetes of literary prophecy, among others. I have argued elsewhere that the affinities between these actors are more significant than the exact content of their teachings, which ethnic idiom they invoked, or which texts they interpreted. Not only did they navigate common challenges and possibilities, but they also suffered the same legislative actions, sometimes even co-implication in an expulsion, proscription, or confiscation of literary materials.[11] Their rivalries also spanned different specialist guises. Many experts were jacks-of-all trade, purveying skills and benefits that not only defied neat categorization but also amplified the number of figures with whom one was plausibly in competition. Notwithstanding, competition was rifest within the same "areas" of expertise: between figures attributing their wisdom or teachings to the same sage, initiators into the mysteries of the same god, or exegetes of the same text.[12]

The expectation that Christians of the second century either adhered to or departed from an earlier Jesus tradition has precluded viewing them as full-fledged participants in this sort of religious activity, alongside a variegated cast of freelance actors with similar interests. In what follows I situate them within it and offer examples of how the behaviors of these other experts might illuminate the motivations of Justin, Marcion, Valentinus, and their ilk, particularly with respect to the production or interpretation of writings in the service of one's expertise. From here I offer a preliminary theorization of early Christian literary activity, and the composition of gospel literature in particular, within this framework: as a tactic of legitimation among figures claiming the same or closely related specialty, in this case, experts whose programs were rooted in the exegesis of Judean religious texts and involved the figure of Christ. And while it is less controversial to view the writings of "heretics" as the products of such dynamics, I propose that the canonical gospels, too, might be investi-

---

a rite rooted in the wisdom of an inspired ancient sage as opposed to a diagnosis of illness to be treated pharmacologically. One sees how this distinction operated, for example, in Justin's boast that Christians have successfully exorcised many whom others were unable to heal, including exorcists, enchanters, and doctors (2 *Apol.* 5–6).

11   Wendt 2015a and 2015b.
12   See Edmonds 2008; Wendt 2017, 149, 156–157.

gated as texts written to privilege aspiring authorities on Christ, possibly even Christian intellectuals of the second century, at the expense of their immediate rivals.[13]

2   Christians as Freelance Experts

There is a long tradition in the study of the New Testament and early Christianity of beginning from the premise that Christianity was an unprecedented and radical development in Roman society.[14] While one can think of many notable exceptions, even scholarship that has sought to restore early Christians to their Greco-Roman cultural milieu tends to default to a premise of essential difference between them and their religious contemporaries. Christians might be *like* other writers, or voluntary associations, or schools in any number of interesting ways, but they were ultimately different, even unique, owing to some quality: their beliefs, their theology, their ethics, their adherence to scripture, their charitability, and so forth.

This impression of essential social or religious difference stems in part from the nature and quality of the evidence that survives for early Christians. In the first two centuries, the record is dominated by writings in which Christian authors explain and justify their beliefs and rites; profess utter disinterest in worldly pursuits, over and against profit-mongering charlatans or unenlightened philosophers; compare themselves favorably to rivals, to Judeans, to sinful gentiles, or to irrational pagans; and insist time and again upon their own uniqueness. And yet, if these discourses—along with the proprietary terminology of "faith," "baptism," "apostle," etc.—are redescribed, the practices of Christian writers are strictly comparable to those of numerous other religious figures and phenomena of the empire.[15]

The disproportionate survival of Pauline letters and other early "Christian" literature partially conceals the participation of their authors in a broader religious phenomenon that also included some Judeans, but was not specific to these domains of expertise.[16] Over the first two centuries of the empire, there

---

13   For the sake of simplicity, I refer henceforth to the four gospels that would eventually become canonical without additional qualification, even though neither their canonicity nor their "scriptural" status is a foregone conclusion in the first and second centuries.

14   For extensive critique of approaches that cast the rise of Christianity in unique and teleological terms, see the essays in Vaage 2006; Ando 2008, ix–xvii, 149–157.

15   For illustrations, see Cameron and Miller 2004 and 2011; Crawford and Miller 2017.

16   The phenomenon is not specific, that is, to "Jews" and "Christians," even though "Judaism"

seems to have been an expansion in the visibility and influence, and likely also number, of self-authorized or "freelance" experts in many specialties, including religion. The language of freelance reflects my attempt to categorize a diverse set of actors whose recognition, authority, and legitimacy depended on demonstrations of skill and learning rather than relationships to established institutions or well-defined traditions.[17] Freelance *religious* experts, according to my category, were a particular population within a wider field that included many philosophers, teachers of *paideia*, and doctors, but whose specialized teachings and other practices—divination, prognostication, initiation, purification, healing, and so forth—were understood to involve the participation of divine beings.[18] The edges between these putative areas of expertise were hazy: many experts balanced religious skills or practices with other dimensions of their programs, and to greater and lesser degrees.[19]

Although they predate the Roman period, with the empire's expansion freelance religious actors became more prominent, more ambitious in the skills and benefits they alleged to offer, and more global in the ethnic coding of their wisdom and practices. One would expect this trend to persist at least until its apogee under Trajan; if the second-century preoccupation with "charlatans" and "false prophets" is any indication, would-be experts of many varieties continued to thrive in this period.[20] Given the dramatically changing

---

and "Christianity" are typically the primary scholarly categories for treating this literary evidence. See Wendt 2016, 146–189, 190–216. That being said, these texts contain any number of straightforward indications that their authors participated in this sort of religious activity. Perhaps it is more accurate to say that their later exegetical and intellectual histories do this work of concealment more so than the authors themselves.

17   While the category of freelance expertise could be applied profitably to certain philosophers, teachers, doctors, and astrologers, many of the best examples enlisted directly in their practices gods and similar beings (*daimones*, divine *pneuma*, or the dead). That being said, the boundaries between these putative areas were both porous and also secondary to challenges that all freelance experts negotiated by virtue of engaging in a similar form of social activity.

18   Unlike, say, a philosopher, who might write a theological treatise or explain the properties of *pneuma*, an expert such as Paul, whose indebtedness to Greco-Roman philosophy is well documented, performed pneumatic demonstrations (e.g., 1 Thess 1:5; Rom 15:19; 1 Cor 2:4), taught that those "in Christ" were in the process of undergoing an ontological transformation after receiving a first installment of God's or Christ's own material pneuma (e.g., Rom 5:5, 8:9), and regularly refers to this *pneuma* as an agent that precipitates revelations, searches people's minds or hearts, and otherwise acts upon them.

19   The intermingling of religious and intellectual practices became especially pronounced over the course of the second and third centuries. See Marx-Wolf 2016.

20   Fraudulent religious experts are a particular preoccupation of second-century satirists,

territory and population demographics of the imperial period, many were perceived as foreigners who took advantage of widespread interest in exotic *paideia*, wisdom, deities, rites, or divinatory techniques.[21] And while the empire owed its general climate of religious innovation to any number of factors, the phenomenon of freelance expertise seems to have contributed substantially to larger transformations.

These developments coincided with an effervescent literary culture at Rome, fueled by an abundance of public and private libraries as well as a thriving commercial book industry.[22] In keeping with the heightened profile of writing under the empire, aspiring experts of all stripes wielded sundry intellectual tools—e.g., philosophical discourses, textual exegesis, and the composition of new writings—to impress audiences who valued these offerings.[23] From the writings of Petronius, Juvenal, Lucian, and Apuleius one can infer a considerable demand for the religious expert whose initiations were gleaned from ancient wisdom or prophecies, or whose healing methods aligned with contemporary currents in medicine and philosophy. While few inhabitants of the Roman world possessed the abilities required to occupy such a specialized niche, those who did wasted no opportunity to display them. Even experts who were illiterate, or largely so, could appeal to the distant literary foundations of their wisdom or incorporate textual artifacts into their practices. The latter might amount to nothing more than a piece of metal inscribed with crude, nonsensical characters, but the plentiful attestation of such objects underscores the cachet of writing among those claiming some form of religious expertise.[24]

For their intellectual leanings, many specialists exemplified a relationship between textuality and religious authority that predates the imperial period. In a recent study of late-republican theological writings, Duncan MacRae argues that this literature offered an ideal venue for displaying specialized knowledge and facilitating the pursuit of alternative modes of distinction, above all for men without illustrious pedigrees who nevertheless sought a place in Rome's

---

whose catalogues of specialists, their pretensions to expertise, chicaneries, and even costumes seem intended for an audience familiar enough with these religious actors that they will get the joke.

21   For the appeal of exotic *paideia* in this period, see Stowers 2011, 104–109, 113–117.

22   For libraries, reading, the book industry, and other mechanisms of literary distribution at Rome, see Houston 2008; Johnson and Parker 2009; Johnson 2010; König, Oikonomopoulou, and Woolf 2013. For Christian authors as participants in these wider literary networks, see Gamble 1995 and 2012; Kruger 2013; Stroumsa 2016; Larsen 2018.

23   For the relationship between allegorical exegesis and authority, see Struck 2004; Konstan 2005; Niehoff 2011.

24   See, e.g., Gordan 2015; Bremmer 2015.

sociopolitical elite.[25] Although composing a learned text on such weighty matters as theology or philosophy was, in itself, insufficient to insinuate oneself into the Roman aristocracy, the skills required to do so might, MacRae argues, underwrite one's credentials in other social arenas. There are, of course, significant differences between theological writers such as Cicero or Varro and freelance religious experts, especially with respect to ambition and potentiality. But they were not so dissimilar in skills or strategy, even if the latter's literary activities were put to the task of impressing potential clients or establishing groups of followers, rather than gaining entry into the senate or one of Rome's priestly colleges.

Intellectualizing religious experts are prominent in earlier periods but seem to have flourished especially under the empire.[26] So too did writings that either enabled or plausibly arose from this sort of religious activity: Hermetica; Orphica; Sibylline, Chaldean, and Judean oracles; Pythagorean pseudepigrapha; the books of Hystaspes; the letters of Paul, of Apollonius of Tyana; almanacs attributed to Petosiris and Thrasyllus; manuals for calculating horoscopes, casting lots, and interpreting dreams; copious so-called magical or ritual spells. This list could be expanded considerably. Although they represent a range of aptitude, such writings appear to have bolstered the authority of religious experts acting in a freelance capacity and were indispensable to their practices. As with Menocchio's cosmology, most were indebted to other literature and betray mutual intellectual preoccupations, foremost with the works of Plato.[27]

A shift in focus away from the specific content of such literature, including early Christian writings, toward the skills, ambitions, and possible social settings of their authors allows for a more thoroughgoing redescription of religious actors who not only had many affinities, but also, in many cases, viewed one another as direct competitors. I echo the sentiments of scholars who have emphasized the intimate contact Christian intellectuals had with one another, irrespective of whether they would be coopted into later orthodox tradition or classified as heretics, as well as with non-Christian intellectuals.[28] But it is also

---

25 MacRae 2016.
26 Radcliffe G. Edmonds III notes a similar increase in intellectualizing religious experts in late classical Athens, when books became an indispensable marker of expertise for intellectuals of any type (2013, 112–116).
27 Although wisdom traditions or literary corpora were often ethnically coded, recent scholarship has emphasized that many books and teachings that were presented as Persian, Egyptian, Judean, and Chaldean reflected a common intellectual milieu. See, e.g., Stowers 2017, 249–250.
28 See, e.g., Snyder 2000; Dunderberg 2008; Eshleman 2012; Secord 2012.

clear from second-century sources that self-identifying Christians had in their sights not only other Christians and Judeans, but also *magi*, astrologers, myriad diviners, exorcists, healers, prophets, exegetes of prophecy, and so on.[29] Sorting these figures into distinct categories—Judaism, Christianity, Gnosticism, magic, mystery cults, or philosophy—on the basis of their textual proclivities or select features of their practices masks any number of resemblances that stemmed from a common sphere of activity and the competitive dynamics that encompassed them.

The intellectual dimension of freelance expertise lays the foundation for situating second-century Christian writers within a landscape of diverse religious specialists, many for whom texts and intellectual activities were inseparable from their authority and legitimacy. It is noteworthy that competition among writer-intellectuals was acute in this period, particularly under Hadrian, whose emphases on philosophy and the classical past incentivized religious offerings framed in compatible terms.[30] Hence, it is to be expected that expertise was cut increasingly along the lines of literacy, textuality, and facility with marked intellectual currencies. These incentives join other hallmarks of the era that were not exclusive to but especially pronounced in Rome: the widespread availability of texts; numerous mechanisms and venues that promoted literary exchange; and a general enthusiasm for forms of religion with a textual or intellectual bent.

From this starting point arise a number of questions about the social climate of Christian writers of second-century Rome and, by extension, of comparable urban centers such as Alexandria, Athens, Corinth, and Ephesus. To appreciate their place among other intellectuals inhabiting these cities requires a more nuanced appreciation of the literate networks that spanned them, as well as the assorted figures with whom Christian writers were (or wanted to be) in dialogue. The sort of questions I have in mind range from the social relations between specific intellectuals to the work accomplished by particular genres of literature and individual writings. With respect to the former, we might ask what features differentiated a historiographer such as Josephus from the author of Luke-Acts, or "Luke" from other historiographers. Or, about how to theorize interlocution between writers who were not only exact contemporaries but, in

---

29   Wendt 2016, 198–202.

30   As Marco Rizzi (2010) argues, it was in this climate that apologists such as Justin began to present Christians as a kind of philosophical school, distinct from and superior to not only the so-called Judean philosophies, but also to any other philosophical group or school of thought. These claims were, in turn, predicated on the superior exegesis of oracles gleaned from the famed holy writings or oracles of the Judeans.

some cases, even cohabited the same urban spaces: Galen and Justin or, later, Plotinus, Porphyry, and Origen.[31] Merely cataloguing the similarities that Paul or Justin bore to their respective philosophical contemporaries might reveal each to be conversant in the intellectual jargon of his day, yet without necessarily dislodging either from a distinctly Christian sphere of activity. The paradigm changes considerably when both are presented as variations on a wider phenomenon of freelance expertise wherein creative intellectual sampling was the norm.

I am especially interested in how Christian writings of the second century square with contemporaneous non-Christian literature that was implicated in the activities of would-be religious experts. What is to be learned from Justin's inclusion of "the prophets," by which he surely means Israelite or Judean writings, among the books of Hystaspes, the Sibylline Oracles, and other oracular corpora whose private possession, he alleges, is punishable by death in second-century Rome?[32] What of his claim that authorities on Mithras and his mysteries mine Isaiah for prophecies that reinforce their teachings about this god?[33] What of his denunciations of Greek poets, another allusion to writings that might have sustained freelance expertise, as did poetry attributed to Orpheus in earlier times?[34] While Justin's contestations with Marcion or Trypho suffer no lack of scholarly attention, far less has been devoted to teasing apart these other rivalries or the implication of widespread exegetical interest in Judean literature.[35]

The fleeting glimpses of Christians jostling with other teachers, philosophers, instructors in religious wisdom, exegetes of literary prophecy, initiators, diviners, and exorcists are invaluable for the task of reconstructing their activities in a manner that does not presume the uniqueness of Christianity. To imagine them as better attested, but fully integrated participants in a phenomenon not limited to Judeans or Christians invites fresh and more thoroughgoing comparisons with similarly self-authorized figures of their day. The subset of intellectualizing experts is especially ripe for this work, since many relied upon textuality to demonstrate or defend the expertise they claimed. And while it might suffice to situate known Christian writers within this milieu, I also wish

---

31   I will return to the implications of these particular examples momentarily.

32   Justin, *1Apol.* 44.12; Wendt 2016, 51, 199.

33   Justin, *Dial.* 78.6; Wendt 2016, 198–199.

34   This is most apparent in the Derveni papyrus, the scholarship on which is rich and increasingly plentiful. For an overview with gestures toward the text's relevance for early Christianity, see Fitzgerald 2014 and 2015.

35   There are notable exceptions, many of which are cited in the present essay. See, e.g., Snyder 2007 and 2013; Secord 2012 and 2013.

to raise the possibility that the canonical gospels arose from the same social processes that scholars are more comfortable positing for non-canonical and non-scriptural texts.

3 Second-Century Christian Literature as Artifacts of Competition

What is to be gained from theorizing the location of early Christian writers among other kinds of intellectuals in Rome, and other intellectualizing religious experts more specifically? On the one hand, there is nothing wholly new about the map I have sketched above: the points of overlap and apparent exchange between Christians and other intellectuals, and even between particular figures such as Justin and Galen, have been noted by many.[36] Nor are scholars of early Christianity ignorant of the literary culture in which all of these figures partook; far from it. On the other hand, such promising contributions have yet to be synthesized into a more comprehensive picture of how the second century might stand to transform more traditional narratives about earliest Christianity.

Hence in what remains I outline a few problematic assumptions that color some of the (ostensibly) earliest literature to inform this history, the canonical gospels, in order to gesture in a preliminary fashion toward how the approach I am suggesting might be brought to bear on these texts. As the starting point for what is, at present, still a thought experiment, I heed the reminders of scholars who have drawn attention to the flimsy basis for dating the canonical gospels prior to the mid-second century, when there is suddenly a good deal of evidence for their circulation, namely in the writings of authors such as Justin, Clement, Irenaeus, and other intellectuals active in Rome or Alexandria.[37] The tendency has been to characterize these authors as curatorial bystanders of first-century sources, even if ones more fluid than fixed and which the authors would not recognize as gospels per se until the latter part of the second century.[38]

An absence of evidence is not, of course, evidence of absence. Moreover, the suggestion that gospel literature originated as such in the service of would-

---

36 E.g., Snyder 2013.

37 See, e.g., Detering 2000; Vinzent 2012 and 2014, esp. viii–ix. The first half of Vinzent's 2014 book, in particular, offers a detailed overview of sources that underscore the absence of secure evidence for the traditional dating schemes of the gospels.

38 As opposed to as Greek *hypomnēmata* or Latin *commentarii*, both of which terms have a broad range of applications to different kinds of writings.

be experts for whom textuality was inextricable from pretensions to religious authority works just as well for a first-century climate; Paul's letters and the prophetic exegesis that informs them are apt examples.[39] However, taken with other developments that I have sketched above, the combination of a first-century lacuna followed by a significant increase in attestations of the canonical texts in sources that can be dated confidently to the middle part of the second century permits cautious consideration of factors that favor this context for their composition. At a minimum, entertaining the possibility of a later timeframe places the canonical texts on an equal footing with non-canonical writings, including other gospels, that are dated without scruple to this period.

Beyond the nature of the evidence, there are several methodological justifications for the approach I am suggesting. First and foremost, scholarly accounts of the origins of gospel literature have long posited that these texts arose from and reflected the sentiments of pious communities of early Christ believers, if not also the actual teachings of the historical Jesus.[40] While such accounts grant that authors or redactors helped to shape this literature, individual inflections or variations on the basic gospel narrative have been seen to be largely in keeping with the needs of the communities on whose behalf the evangelists wrote. There is far less consideration of how individual interests or power relations informed their compositions; rather, the writer is assumed to have acted as the voice of the group, the scribe of a theology derived from his community's particular situation and needs.

As a handful of scholars have noted, there is little precedent for this textual paradigm in the ancient world. That is, one does not typically presume that communal interests motivated or informed the composition and circulation of, say, Juvenal's satires or the writings of Josephus.[41] Rather, these authors are understood to have participated in webs of literary patronage, performance, and exchange, and also to have accrued a number of material and symbolic benefits from their activities. Nor are they thought to be entirely reliant on earlier sources in crafting their own compositions; to the contrary, they are granted as a necessary precondition for their literary activities authorial interests and self-expression that are rarely entertained for the gospel authors. Alternatively,

---

39   See Wendt 2016, 146–189.

40   For example, Stanley Stowers 2011, 239–245 calls attention to the Romantic underpinnings of much scholarship on the origins of the canonical gospels, namely, the notion that they arose from and mirrored the values of pious communities of believers in the decades following Jesus' death.

41   To the contrary, recent scholarship on these figures stresses their embeddedness in wider networks of literate exchange at Rome. See Uden 2014, 1–19; Mason 2005 and 2011. For a more sociologically nuanced discussion of elite reading cultures, see Johnson 2010.

when a literary composition is known to have arisen from a group setting—for instance, the *Discourses* of Epictetus, diligently recorded by his student, Arrian—the text in question is understood to privilege the wisdom of a single teacher, to codify and reinforce that figure's proprietary teachings, and, in some cases, to establish the boundaries of group membership.[42] Many writings of the first and second centuries arose from networks of literate specialists who not only wrote prolifically, but also did so to defend either their own authority or else that of a teacher or expert with whom they were closely aligned.

To explore the possibility that the canonical gospels served a similar purpose restores plausible authorial interests to them while also suggesting different types of social formations—networks of writers, teacher–student relationships, schools, circles of initiation, voluntary associations, etc.—that their composition and interpretation may have supported. Discarding or even deferring the expectation that these texts took shape within early "churches" or pious communities of believers, a model that begs important questions about why they were written and how they were utilized, sets them alongside other early Christian literature (gospels, revelatory or cosmogonic writings, apologies, heresiologies), and the gospel authors among their literate contemporaries.

Indeed, whereas the characterization of Rome as a hostile environment for early Christians and one that was therefore inhospitable to their literary activities has naturalized the impression that Christian authors formed exclusive networks comprised only of fellow believers, recent scholarship would suggest otherwise.[43] As Richard Last notes, "writers generally enjoyed social relationships on the basis of common occupation, levels of literacy, and pursuits for *paideia* rather than exclusively on the basis of common cultic affiliation." There are no *prima facie* grounds for portraying Christian writers otherwise and, to the contrary, compelling evidence that they were thoroughly embedded in the same literary matrices as non-Christian writers. Comparing the gospel authors to Greek historiographers, Last concludes that the gospels are more likely to have arisen from urban literate networks than from insular pietistic settings.[44]

---

42   Eshleman 2012, 15 and *passim*.

43   See Last 2012 and 2015, esp. 224–225.

44   Examining the social relationships and intellectual practices of local *ephēboi*, teachers of grammar and rhetoric, artists, *collegia* of writers, the social elites who attended historical lectures, and other contributors to the cultural life of Greco-Roman cities, Last concludes that "the range of social activities performed by the gospel authors was likely broader, and less fully situated in 'Christianity,' than is often assumed" (2015, 227).

Likewise, Steve Mason's meticulously documented argument that the author of Luke–Acts made ample use of the writings of Josephus, or else very similar literature, offers further evidence that these writers were indebted to a wider literary culture.[45] Although influential among certain circles, the significance of this hypothesis has not received the attention it deserves in mainstream New Testament scholarship. That at least one gospel author was likely informed by the work of a prominent Judean writer resident at Rome in the Flavian period undermines the myth of Christian literary isolation (to say nothing of the historicity of his works). Nor is Luke the only gospel with indications of an outward-looking intellectual orientation. Stowers has demonstrated Matthew's intentional refashioning of a Jesus inherited from Mark to accord with the Stoic sage, and his teachings with Stoic ethics.[46] Such efforts reveal more than this author's mere *familiarity* with Stoicism. Rather, they are suggestive of the kinds of figures with whom he viewed himself to be in competition, the sort of audiences to whom his writing was intended to appeal, and the types of skills and knowledge for which he sought recognition. Although Mason and Stowers proceed along different lines, the implication of both studies is that "Matthew" and "Luke" were not only aware of other writer-intellectuals, but also sought to distinguish their own abilities through the composition of gospels.[47]

While these and similar lines of inquiry have raised important questions about the educational backgrounds of the gospel authors and their use of sources, to my mind they invite a more ambitious reimagining of the social settings in which these writers operated. In particular, aligning them with other figures whose literary activities offered venues for displays of expertise and legitimacy has the advantage of coordinating the gospels' literary features with the social practices of their authors. Insofar as many religious experts of the period boasted a "multidisciplinary" vocabulary and wielded assorted intellectual tools, what can these elements *within* the texts tell us about the aspirations and social entanglements of those who wrote them? Instead of the disinterested reflections of pious communities, might the gospels have been written instead to lend credence to the proprietary religious program of one figure or group at the expense of others? The apparent literary relationship between the Synoptic Gospels, in particular, makes a good deal of sense within this framework, namely, as a relic of three authors with distinct interests, if not mutually

---

45   Mason 2003, 251–295.
46   Stowers 2010.
47   The same point could, of course, also extend to these authors' reliance on common source material or even Luke's use of Matthew, depending on one's solution to the Synoptic Problem.

aware rivals, seeking to differentiate themselves within the same field of expertise, in part, by improving upon existing compositions.[48]

In this vein, another area where the phenomenon of freelance religious expertise might be brought to bear on canonical gospel scholarship involves consideration of *how* these texts might have operated in such a context. For the Sibylline or Chaldean Oracles, it is clear that, questions of authorship aside, the texts were designed to be cryptic, to require the aid of a specialized interpreter, and to convey prophecy in ambiguous terms. Likewise, it has been suggested that the Greek so-called magical papyri granted and affirmed the reader's own expertise, essentially creating feedback loops of skill among networks of would-be specialists.[49]

There is far less consideration of how the gospels *worked*, so to speak, possibly owing to anachronistic ideas about them being read aloud during a church service or serving as the basis for a Christian sermon.[50] And yet, recent scholarship on other early Christian literature suggests intriguing possibilities in this direction. In a series of articles on the *Gospel of Thomas*, for example, William Arnal abandons the quest for the text's underlying community in favor of the intellectual dynamics it fostered.[51] *Thomas*, he suggests, imposes obscurity on its *logia* through a series of literary techniques that cultivate and reinforce expertise.[52] To be a competent reader of this text, "one must in the first place (obviously) be literate; they must additionally have interpretive or exegetical skills well beyond mere reading; they must exercise memory in unusual ways; and they must have the background knowledge of (some of) the philosophical tropes of Middle Platonism as exegetical traditions around specific texts (especially Genesis) that will enable them to make sense of *Thomas'* cryptic references."[53] Importantly, the text's value may lie more in the act of deploying such skills than in anything about its content. What the reader gains is affir-

---

48   This is stated clearly in Luke's preface (1:1–4), and, if one accepts arguments for Markan priority, at the expense of another canonical gospel author. So too has much recent scholarship argued for Luke's reactionary use of Marcion's gospel, rather than the other way around. See, e.g., Joseph B. Tyson 2006; Klinghardt 2008; BeDuhn 2012 and 2013. For an overview of this position in the history of the scholarship on Marcion, see Roth 2015, 10–45.

49   So argues Edmonds 2017.

50   A notable exception is Henderson 2009, who has a similar piece forthcoming about Mark's historically designed audience(s) and how the text functions at one level as a sort of apostolic training manual for would-be specialists.

51   Arnal 2005, 2014, and 2016.

52   Arnal 2016, 271–272. The same behavior, Arnal notes, is exhibited also in the Gospel of Mark, especially chapter four. For a more exegetical treatment of the text, see Arnal 2005.

53   Arnal 2016, 274.

mation of his or her cultural refinement and distinction, all the more so since literacy, reading, possessing books, and philosophical competency were elite habits that carried great prestige in this period.[54]

Imagining early Christian literature, both canonical and non-canonical, doing work in the service of interested authors and audiences encourages us to move beyond the mere cataloguing of resemblances toward a theorization of Christians among other experts for whom literary composition and interpretation furthered various ambitions: to display and safeguard religious authority; to elevate one's expertise above that of assorted rivals; to cater to a demand for religious offerings that required and rewarded the skills of potential audiences; and to form various types of groups dedicated to one's particular teachings and practices. These considerations move toward a more plausible account of why and to what ends *some* early Christians took up literary activities, one that also explains similarities between their texts and other writings implicated in such processes.

Again, a second-century context is less important than and also separable from my argument that the canonical gospels make the most sense as products of the particular social setting I have delimited: rivalries among would-be authorities on Christ who shared a number of skills, interests, and intellectual resources, including access to various Judean writings and familiarity with contemporary philosophical discourses. That being said, there are compelling reasons to take seriously the dearth of evidence for these texts prior to the second century, not the least of which is that their traditional dating scheme is rooted in a binary methodological framework that privileges them as necessarily earlier, more integral, and, therefore, more authoritative than gospel literature that did not achieve canonical status. Even if the former did, indeed, predate and/or originate in contexts different from the latter, there would still be value in normalizing further explanatory accounts of their genesis by interrogating the *a priori* premises on which the received wisdom rests.

While an argument that the gospels were written by Christian rivals of the second century would require a more sustained treatment than the present space permits, the recent arguments of Markus Vinzent provide a rich starting point for this reorientation. Vinzent marshals a trove of patristic sources to support his provocative thesis that the concept of a written gospel originated with Marcion and was then taken up by his rivals at Rome.[55] "As one would expect in competing classrooms in a city," he explains, "Marcion's venture was soon

---

54 Arnal 2016, 274, 276.
55 This hypothesis first appears in Vinzent 2011 and is subsequently elaborated with more support in Vinzent 2014.

replicated by other teachers who contributed, altered, broadened, or nuanced both the [Pauline] letters and [Marcion's] Gospel according to their respective needs and interests."[56] Vinzent presumes a high degree of mutual awareness and exchange among would-be Christian authorities of the mid-second century and posits Rome as the setting for much early Christian literary composition.

Regardless of whether one is persuaded by the particularities of Vinzent's model and its implications for the dating and authorship of the canonical gospels, the ancient witnesses he amasses underscore how thoroughly enmeshed second-century Christian writers were in Rome's diffuse intellectual armature: the book market, public lectures and debates, the composition or acquisition of pseudepigrapha, and the exegesis of ancient, oracular texts, to name a few prominent examples. Several sources also align Christians incidentally with non-Christian authors navigating the same literary challenges and possibilities. Allegedly, Marcion contended that a copy of his *Evangelion* was circulated before publication, at which point it was embellished, most likely with material drawn from biblical prophecy which he purportedly rejected.[57] His complaint about the breach of a text not, or not yet, intended for publication echoes the frustrations of Cicero, Quintillian, and Galen, among other known authors with the same axe to grind.[58] Similarly, Valentinus differentiated "publicly available books" from "writings in the church," lamenting that many of the things written in the former, "evidently available on the market, borrowable from houses or at hand in classrooms," made their way into the latter.[59] Apparently Irenaeus had a habit of collecting the works of his perceived opponents in order to refute their teachings. He also appealed to future scribes to avoid distortion by reviewing with care their copies of his own text

---

56   Vinzent 2011, 88.

57   See Tertullian, *Marc.* 4.5.4. As Vinzent notes, "Tertullian's report makes it plain that in response to Marcion's Gospel others had forged a Judaized version of it. Tertullian, following Irenaeus, however, turned Marcion's argument upside down and claimed not that Marcion's opponents had 'judaized', but that Marcion had 'circumcised' Scripture" (2011, 88). See also Vinzent 2016 for a fuller treatment of this passage.

58   See, e.g., Secord 2019, 17–18: "Other signs of hostility and competitiveness in Roman intellectual life come from the concerns of Christian and non-Christian scholars about the dissemination of literature. These concerns are abundantly on display throughout Galen's *oeuvre*, which demonstrates how difficult it was for a scholar to maintain control over the transmission of work bearing his name. ... Irenaeus, in comparison, wrote much less, but he still shared Galen's desire to keep control over his works." For a useful overview of the evidence for leaked texts with a view to similar accusations that appear in the highly controversial "secret" Gospel of Mark, see Jay 2008.

59   Clement of Alexandria, *Strom.* 6.52.3–4; Vinzent 2011, 100.

and admits to doing his part to remove from circulation works that he believed to be heretical, namely by destroying them. All of these tactics had corollaries among non-Christian intellectuals, as did the regular ruptures and factions that fueled second-century Christian diversity.[60]

The apparent social spaces of early Christian activity are also consistent with the places where other specialists and their followings are known to have gathered: private homes or rental apartments, as well as public venues such as baths and marketplaces.[61] As Jared Secord remarks of the contemporaries Irenaeus and Galen, "Though their paths almost certainly never crossed, Irenaeus and Galen both operated in similar scholarly environments. Their examples help to show that the lives and experiences of Christian and non-Christian scholars had much in common in the second century, even if they were still operating for the most part in separate worlds."[62] H. Gregory Snyder takes this general observation a step farther in a pair of articles that emplace the school of Justin Martyr, of which Irenaeus was likely once a part, in a social arena known to be highly conducive to specialist activity, while also making the case that Justin's fulfillment citations, which Justin introduces as "proof" in favor of his Christian beliefs, answered directly Galen's charge that Christians lacked any such support for their claims.[63] In these and numerous other instances, we glimpse Christian writers of the second century not merely reacting or responding to a *general* intellectual climate, but to particular intellectual rivals there within. And while it may prove impossible to gauge how much influence they wielded, whether their rivalries were reciprocated, or what qualities, if any, were particular to how they participated in the wider phenomenon of intellectualizing religious expertise, the onus ought to fall on demonstrating, not assuming, that Christians and their literature, including that of the New Testament, were somehow singular in this context.

---

60 Secord offers Irenaeus' story of Cerdo (*Haer.* 3.4.3) as an example of how "a cumulative buildup of interactions between Cerdo and other Christians in more or less public settings" resulted in his withdrawal from "fellowship with the brothers." Secord concludes, "The break ... was thus an informal arrangement between rival scholars, much like the many conflicts described by Galen a few decades later, which might feature one party choosing to make a dramatic exit. It was also a mutual decision: Cerdo was reproved for the content of his teaching before he withdrew from fellowship. ... Cerdo and his rivals were simply behaving in the way that scholars did, as is abundantly clear from Galen's works. The example of Cerdo helps to establish that Christian scholars were operating in a world similar to the one described by Galen" (2019, 14).

61 See Eshleman 2012, 25–26.

62 Secord 2019, 20.

63 Snyder 2007 and 2013.

4   Conclusions

Although there were differences in the wealth, prestige, and social standing of Christian writers and other intellectuals at Rome, these should not fore-close important affinities in their practices. While some of these similarities stemmed from common educational backgrounds and methods of argumentation, they go beyond such considerations and for reasons, I have argued, having to do with the sort of religious activity in which "Christian" writers of the first and second centuries engaged, alongside other would-be specialists with a common intellectual orientation. Given Rome's thriving culture of literacy and the premium placed on literate offerings and forms of religion in this period, it stands to reason—and indeed there are many indications—that Christian writers were part of a broader literary network that supported these interests.

To situate the composition of gospels, both canonical and non-canonical, in the midst of this world improves upon traditional accounts of their literary development in at least two immediate ways.

First, jettisoning the communities model of gospel literature invites new conceptualizations of the relationship between literary composition and religious expertise, not only among rival Christian writers, but also among a more variegated field of intellectualizing religious experts who enlisted texts and exegetical practices to common ends. Whereas it has been a foregone conclusion that the first Christians were intensely interested in traditions about the historical Jesus, this reorientation puts pressure on the narratological or scriptural character of earliest Christianity. If the gospels are a secondary development, then the image of Christians gathering to recite, listen to, meditate on, and receive sermons rooted in their narrative(s) gives way to the sort of religiosity captured in the Pauline Epistles: initiation based, bound up in pneumatic demonstrations, speaking in and interpreting tongues, healing, celebrating special ritual meals, and so forth, and more invested in literary divination than literary composition or sermonizing. Notably, the portrait of Christian activity that Pliny pieces together through interrogation is more consistent with this picture. Nowhere in his epistle to Trajan does he mention literary activities, either the reading of gospels or the delivery of sermons based on their contents; rather, he reports gatherings at dawn during which participants sang hymns to Christ, swore oaths to behave ethically, and consumed a special, if rather ordinary, meal.[64] The absence of writings from this account may serve as a reminder that the mere survival of literary evidence for early Christians

---

64   Pliny, *Ep.* 10.96, 97.

has given undue weight to the significance of texts and intellectual practices in this period. This picture has changed by the time that Lucian depicts Christians reading aloud from their sacred books as he mocks them for accepting Peregrinus' commentaries on these texts as well as his own scriptural compositions.[65]

This is not to say that literary activities are absent from our early evidence for "Christians." To the contrary, Paul's own expertise depended in large part on his claim to have special insight into the "oracles of God," whence, in conjunction with revelations, he derived many of his teachings about Christ. The significance of Paul's ability to write down and transmit his religious program across vast distances cannot be overstated. Without letter-writing to reinforce them, his claims would likely be less ambitious or intricate, with fewer moving parts; his epistles were necessary for the clarification, defense, and elaboration of a complex eschatology that required specific preparations for escaping an ominous outcome. So too would his authority be less durable in absentia, as is evident in how many Pauline verses are concerned with the apostle's sincerity, credibility, and disinterest, to say nothing of his many rivals.

For Paul and others like him, intellectual demonstrations, particularly ones involving texts, were indispensable tools for conveying one's expertise and persuading audiences of the legitimacy of (and urgent need for) one's offerings. After all, it is by pointing to prophecies in the holy writings of the Judeans—and by characterizing these texts as oracular in the first place—that Paul furnishes proof for his boldest claims. What he does not do is impress his audiences by appealing to stories about Jesus performing miracles, healing the sick, or resurrecting the dead, abilities that would have been highly germane to Paul's own teachings. Nor, for that matter, does he ever depict Jesus as a teacher, his followers as disciples—roles and settings that accord nicely with the ambitions of many second-century Christian writers. But granting the importance of texts and intellectual practices for those who would position themselves as *authorities* on Christ is different from presuming that all Christian phenomena of the first and second centuries had a pronounced and pervasive emphasis on literary traditions.

On this point, the other gain of the approach I have advocated is that it highlights the role of Christian intellectuals, foremost those who cohabited Rome in the middle part of the second century, in projecting coherence and unity onto the preceding period of "Christian" history. As Arnal aptly advises, "Christian origins are really to be sought in the ways in which a rapidly self-defining

---

65   Lucian, *Peregr.* 11.

movement of the *second* century invented a tradition for itself. It did so by laying claim to, and thus retrojecting its own sense of identity onto, scattered and variegated past artifacts: stories, sayings collections, letters, and individual characters such as Peter and Paul."[66]

Whether these artifacts included robust traditions about Jesus or were dominated by the writings of Paul, which are notoriously silent about him, there is a compelling case for commencing the quest for Christian origins in the second century and moving earlier as the evidence demands. Either way, all of this literature and the authors who produced it gain new explanatory possibilities when restored to a world in which texts and intellectual practices were inseparable from pretensions to religious expertise.

Bibliography

Ando, Clifford. 2008. *A Matter of the Gods: Religion and the Roman Empire.* Berkeley: University of California Press.

Arnal, William. 2005. "The Rhetoric of Social Construction: Language and Society in the Gospel of Thomas." Pages 27–47 in *Rhetoric and Reality in Early Christianities.* Edited by Willi Braun. Waterloo, Canada: Wilfred Laurier University Press.

Arnal, William. 2011. "The Collection and Synthesis of 'Tradition' and the Second-Century Invention of Christianity." *Method and Theory in the Study of Religion* 23:193–215.

Arnal, William. 2014. "Blessed Are the Solitary: Textual Practices and the Mirage of a Thomas 'Community.'" Pages 271–281 in *The One Who Sows Bountifully: Essays in Honor of Stanley K. Stowers.* Brown Judaic Studies 356. Edited by Caroline Johnson Hodge, Saul M. Olyan, Daniel Ullucci, and Emma Wasserman. Atlanta: SBL Press.

Arnal, William. 2016. "How the Gospel of Thomas Works." Pages 261–280 in *Scribal Practices and Social Structures among Jesus Adherents: Essays in Honour of John S. Kloppenborg.* Edited by William Arnal, Richard Ascough, Robert Derrenbacker, and Philip Harland. Leuven: Peeters.

BeDuhn, Jason David. 2012. "The Myth of Marcion as Redactor: The Evidence of 'Marcion's' Gospel Against an Assumed Marcionite Redaction." *Annali di Storia dell'Esegesi* 29:21–48.

BeDuhn, Jason David. 2013. *The First New Testament: Marcion's Scriptural Canon.* Salem, Ore.: Polebridge.

BeDuhn, Jason David. 2015. "Am I a Christian? The Individual at the Manichaean-

---

66   Arnal 2011, 201–202 (emphasis original).

Christian Interface." Pages 31–53 in *Group Identity and Religious Individuality in Late Antiquity*. Edited by Éric Rebillard and Jörg Rüpke. Washington, D.C.: The Catholic University of America Press.

Brakke, David. 2010. *The Gnostics: Myth, Ritual, and Diversity in Early Christianity*. Cambridge, Mass.: Harvard University Press.

Bremmer, Jan N. 2015. "From Books with Magic to Magical Books in Ancient Greece and Rome?" Pages 241–270 in *The Materiality of Magic*. Edited by Dietrich Boschung and Jan N. Bremmer. Paderborn: Wilhelm Fink.

Cameron, Ron and Merrill P. Miller, eds. 2004. *Redescribing Christian Origins*. SBL Symposium Series. Atlanta: SBL Press.

Cameron, Ron and Merrill P. Miller, eds. 2011. *Redescribing Paul and the Corinthians*. Early Christianity and Its Literature 5. Atlanta: SBL Press.

Crawford, Barry S. and Merrill P. Miller, eds. 2017. *Redescribing the Gospel of Mark*. Early Christianity and Its Literature 22. Atlanta: SBL Press.

Dunderberg, Ismo. 2008. *Beyond Gnosticism: Myth, Lifestyle, and Society in the School of Valentinus*. New York: Columbia University Press.

Edmonds, Radcliffe G. III. 2008. "Extra-Ordinary People: *Mystai* and *Magoi*, Magicians and Orphics in the Derveni Papyrus." *Classical Philology* 103:16–39.

Edmonds, Radcliffe G. 2013. *Redefining Ancient Orphism: A Study in Greek Religion*. Cambridge: Cambridge University Press.

Edmonds, Radcliffe G. 2017. And You Will be Amazed: The Rhetoric of Authority in the Greek Magical Papyri. Paper presented at "Colloquium in Response to *At the Temple Gates: The Religion of Freelance Experts in the Roman Empire* by Heidi Wendt (Oxford 2016)." Ohio State University, Columbus, Ohio. September 30.

Eshleman, Kendra. 2012. *The Social World of Intellectuals in the Roman Empire: Sophists, Philosophers, and Christians*. Cambridge: Cambridge University Press.

Fitzgerald, John T. 2014. "Myth, Allegory, and the Derveni Papyrus." Pages 229–244 in *Myth and Scripture: Contemporary Perspectives on Religion, Language, and Imagination*. Edited by Dexter E. Callender, Jr. Atlanta: SBL Press.

Fitzgerald, John T. 2015. "The Derveni Papyrus and Its Relevance for Biblical and Patristic Studies." *Early Christianity* 6:1–22.

Fuhrmann, Christopher J. 2012. *Policing the Roman Empire: Soldiers, Administration, and Public Order*. Oxford/New York: Oxford University Press.

Gamble, Harry Y. 1995. *Books and Readers in the Early Church: A History of Early Christian Texts*. New Haven: Yale University Press.

Gamble, Harry Y. 2012. "The Book Trade in the Roman Empire." Pages 23–36 in *The Early Text of the New Testament*. Edited by Charles E. Hill and Michael J. Kruger. New York: Oxford University Press.

Ginzburg, Carlo. 1992. *The Cheese and the Worms: The Cosmos of a Sixteenth-Century Miller*. Translated by John and Anne Tedeschi. Baltimore: The Johns Hopkins University Press.

Gordon, Richard L. 2015. "From Substances to Texts: Three Materialities of Magic in the Roman Imperial Period." Pages 133–176 in *The Materiality of Magic*. Edited by Dietrich Boschung and Jan N. Bremmer. Paderborn: Wilhelm Fink.

Harland, Philip A. 2006. "The Declining *Polis*? Religious Rivalries in Ancient Civic Context." Pages 21–49 in *Religious Rivalries in the Early Roman Empire and the Rise of Christianity*. Edited by Leif E. Vaage. Waterloo, Canada: Wilfred Laurier Press.

Henderson, Ian H. 2009. "Reconstructing Mark's Double Audience." Pages 6–28 in *Between Author and Audience in Mark: Narration, Characterization, Interpretation*. Edited by Elizabeth Struthers Malbon. Sheffield: Sheffield Phoenix.

Houston, George W. 2008. "Tiberius and the Libraries: Public Book Collections and Buildings in the Early Roman Empire." *Libraries & the Cultural Record* 43:247–269.

Jay, Jeff. 2008. "A New Look at the Epistolary Framework of the Secret Gospel of Mark." *Journal of Early Christian Studies* 16:573–597.

Johnson, William A. 2010. *Readers and Reading Culture in the High Roman Empire: A Study of Elite Communities*. New York: Oxford University Press.

Johnson, William A. and Holt N. Parker. 2009. *Ancient Literacies: The Culture of Reading in Greece and Rome*. New York: Oxford University Press.

King, Karen L. 2011. "Factions, Variety, Diversity, Multiplicity: Representing Early Christian Differences for the 21st Century." *Method and Theory in the Study of Religion* 23:216–237.

Klinghardt, Matthias. 2008. "The Marcionite Gospel and the Synoptic Problem." *Novum Testamentum* 50:1–27.

König, Jason, Katerina Oikonomopoulou, and Greg Woolf, eds. 2013. *Ancient Libraries*. Cambridge: Cambridge University Press.

Konstan, David. 2005. "Introduction." Pages xi–xxx in *Heraclitus: Homeric Problems*. Religions in the Graeco-Roman World 14. Edited and translated by Donald A. Russell and David Konstan. Leiden: Brill.

Kruger, Michael J. 2013. "Manuscripts, Scribes, and Book Production within Early Christianity." Pages 15–40 in *Social and Literary Contexts for the New Testament*. Edited by Stanley E. Porter and Andrew W. Pitts. Leiden: Brill.

Larsen, Matthew D.C. 2018. *Gospels before the Book*. New York: Oxford University Press.

Last, Richard. 2012. "Communities that Write: Christ-Groups, Associations, and Gospel Communities." *New Testament Studies* 58:173–198.

Last, Richard. 2015. "The Social Relationship of Gospel Writers: New Insights from Inscriptions Commending Greek Historiographers." *Journal for the Study of the New Testament* 37:223–252.

MacRae, Duncan. 2016. *Legible Religion: Books, Gods, and Rituals in Roman Culture*. Cambridge, Mass.: Harvard University Press.

Marx-Wolf, Heidi. 2016. *Spiritual Taxonomies and Ritual Authority: Platonists, Priests, and Gnostics in the Third Century* C.E. Divinations: Rereading Late Ancient Religion. Philadelphia: University of Pennsylvania Press.

Mason, Steve. 2003. *Josephus and the New Testament*. Peabody, Mass.: Hendrickson Publishers.

Mason, Steve. 2005. "Of Audience and Meaning: Reading Josephus' *Bellum Iudaicum* in the Context of a Flavian Audience." Pages 70–100 in *Josephus and Jewish History in Flavian Rome and Beyond*. Edited by Joseph Sievers and Gaia Lembi. Leiden: Brill.

Mason, Steve. 2011. "Josephus, Publications, and Audience: A Response." *Zutot* 8:81–94.

Niehoff, Maren R. 2011. *Jewish Exegesis and Homeric Scholarship in Alexandria*. Cambridge: Cambridge University Press.

North, John A. 2011. "Pagans, Polytheists, and the Pendulum." Pages 479–504 in *The Religious History of the Roman Empire: Pagans, Jews, and Christians*. Edited by John A. North and Simon R.F. Price. Oxford/New York: Oxford University Press. Originally printed as 124–143 in *The Spread of Christianity in the First Four Centuries: Studies in Explanation*. Edited by William V. Harris. Leiden: Brill.

Orlin, Eric M. 2010. *Foreign Cults in Rome: Creating a Roman Empire*. New York: Oxford University Press.

Rizzi, Marco. 2010. "Hadrian and the Christians." Pages 7–20 in *Hadrian and the Christians*. Millennium-Studien 30. Edited by Marco Rizzi. Berlin: De Gruyter.

Roth, Dieter T. 2015. *The Text of Marcion's Gospel*. New Testament Tools, Studies, and Documents 49. Leiden: Brill.

Rüpke, Jörg. 2013. *The Individual in the Religions of the Ancient Mediterranean*. Corby: Oxford University Press.

Rüpke, Jörg. 2016. *On Roman Religion: Lived Religion and the Individual in Ancient Rome*. Townsend Lectures. Cornell Studies in Classical Philology. Ithaca: Cornell University Press.

Rüpke, Jörg and Wolfgang Spickermann, eds. 2012. *Reflections on Religious Individuality: Graeco-Roman and Judaeo-Christian Texts and Practices*. Religionsgeschichtliche Versuche und Vorarbeiten 62. Berlin: De Gruyter.

Secord, Jared. 2012. "The Cultural Geography of a Greek Christian: Irenaeus from Smyrna to Lyons." Pages 25–34 in *Irenaeus: Life, Scripture, Legacy*. Edited by Sara Parvis and Paul Foster. Minneapolis: Fortress.

Secord, Jared. 2013. "Medicine and Sophistry in Hippolytus' *Refutatio*." Studia Patristica 65:217–224.

Secord, Jared. 2019. "Irenaeus at Rome: The Greek Context of Christian Intellectual Life in the Second Century." Pages 1–20 in *Irénée entre Asie et Occident*. Collection des Études Augustiniennes. Edited by Agnès Bastit-Kalinowska. Turnhout: Brepols.

Snyder, H. Gregory. 2000. *Teachers and Texts in the Ancient World: Philosophers, Jews, and Christians*. Religion in the First Christian Centuries. London: Routledge.

Snyder, H. Gregory. 2007. "'Above the Bath of Myrtinus': Justin Martyr's 'School' in the City of Rome." *Harvard Theological Review* 100:335–362.

Snyder, H. Gregory. 2013. "The Classroom in the Text: Exegetical Practices in Justin and

Galen." Pages 663–685 in *Christian Origins and Greco-Roman Culture: Social and Literary Contexts for the New Testament*. Edited by Stanley E. Porter and Andrew W. Pitts. Leiden: Brill.

Stowers, Stanley. 2010. "Jesus the Teacher and Stoic Ethics in the Gospel of Matthew." Pages 59–76 in *Stoicism in Early Christianity*. Edited by Tuomas Rasimus, Troels Engberg-Pederson, and Ismo Dunderberg. Grand Rapids, Mich.: Baker Academic.

Stowers, Stanley. 2011a. "Kinds of Myth, Meals, and Power." Pages 105–150 in *Redescribing Paul and the Corinthians*. Edited by Ron Cameron and Merrill P. Miller. Atlanta: SBL Press.

Stowers, Stanley. 2011b. "The Concept of 'Community' and the History of Early Christianity." *Method and Theory in the Study of Religion* 23:238–256.

Stowers, Stanley. 2017. "The Dilemma of Paul's Physics: Features Stoic-Platonist or Platonist-Stoic." Pages 231–253 in *From Stoicism to Platonism: The Development of Philosophy, 100 BCE–100 CE*. Edited by Troels Engberg-Pedersen. Cambridge: Cambridge University Press.

Stroumsa, Guy G. 2016. *The Scriptural Universe of Ancient Christianity*. Cambridge, Mass.: Harvard University Press.

Struck, Peter T. 2004. *Birth of the Symbol: Ancient Readers at the Limits of their Texts*. Princeton: Princeton University Press.

Tyson, Joseph B. 2006. *Marcion and Luke-Acts: A Defining Struggle*. Columbia, S.C.: University of South Carolina Press.

Vaage, Leif E., ed. 2006. *Religious Rivalries in the Early Roman Empire and the Rise of Christianity*. Waterloo, Canada: Wilfred Laurier Press.

Vinzent, Markus. 2014. *Marcion and the Synoptic Gospels*. Studia Patristica Supplements 2. Leuven: Peeters.

Vinzent, Markus. 2016. *Tertullian's Preface to Marcion's Gospel*. Studia Patristica Supplements 5. Leuven: Peeters.

Vinzent, Markus. 2011. *Christ's Resurrection in Early Christianity and the Making of the New Testament*. Surrey: Ashgate.

Uden, James. 2014. *The Invisible Satirist: Juvenal and Second-Century Rome*. Oxford/New York: Oxford University Press.

Wendt, Heidi. 2015a. "*Ea Supestitione*: Christian Martyrdom and the Religion of Freelance Experts." *Journal of Roman Studies* 105:183–202.

Wendt, Heidi. 2015b. "*Iudaica Romana*: A Rereading of Judean Expulsions from Rome." *Journal of Ancient Judaism* 6:97–126.

Wendt, Heidi. 2016. *At the Temple Gates: The Religion of Freelance Experts in the Roman Empire*. New York: Oxford University Press.

Wendt, Heidi. 2017. "From the Herodians to Hadrian: The Shifting Status of Judean Religion in Post-Flavian Rome." *Forum* 6:145–170.

CHAPTER 6

Problems of Profiling Marcion

Winrich Löhr

Marcion was one of the more important and interesting Christian teachers of the second century. Although we know more about him, his works, and his teachings, than about several other of his Christian contemporaries, the evidence presents a number of problems which have been discussed with varying attention in modern scholarship. Virtually all the early sources are biased against him: the bias, however, is not uniform, but is modulated according to the particular perspective of each source, its polemical strategies and its engagement with Marcion and his doctrine. In the following, I will focus on some (but certainly not all) key problems (most of them well known) of the evidence about Marcion, discuss possible solutions and try to indicate how they affect in one way or another the reconstruction of the profile of the historical Marcion.[1]

1 Biography

According to Justin Martyr, Irenaeus, Rhodon and Tertullian, Marcion's origins were in Pontus, a name designating in Antiquity either the whole region of the Black Sea or only the Black Sea coast of Asia Minor.[2] Only Epiphanius of Salamis, writing in the 4th century, mentions more precisely the commercial port of Sinope as Marcion's place of origin. But this is only a learned guess—Justin Martyr, Marcion's contemporary in Rome, knows nothing about it, although he is careful to specify the place of origin of both Simon Magus and Menander.[3] Harnack's speculation about a possible Jewish origin of Marcion is

---

1 In this paper I wish to question certain assumptions I still took for granted in Löhr 2010.

2 Justin, *1Apol.* 26.5; 58,1; Irenaeus, 1.27.2; Eusebius of Caesarea, *Hist. eccl.* 5.13.3; Tertullian, *Marc.* 1.1.3 etc.

3 Epiphanius, *Pan.* 42.1.3; Justin Martyr, *1Apol.* 26. If Epiphanius' specification of Sinope as place of Marcion's origin is not to be trusted, this applies *a fortiori* to his further narrative about Marcion's youth which presupposes that Marcion's father had been the bishop of Sinope—if any more arguments to dismiss this fiction are really needed.

© KONINKLIJKE BRILL NV, LEIDEN, 2020 | DOI:10.1163/9789004428010_008

without foundation: the fact that Tertullian's heresiology tries to portray Marcion's exegesis of Old Testament as "Jewish" is no sufficient reason for accepting it.[4]

Rhodon, a Roman pupil of Tatian, is the first source to call Marcion a "sailor" or a "ship captain" (Greek: *nautês*).[5] Tertullian calls Marcion five times a *nauclerus*: the Oxford Latin Dictionary translates this term simply as "a ship's captain," whereas Lewis-Short offers "a ship-owner, a ship-master, skipper."[6] The *opinio communis* has settled on Marcion the "ship-owner" rather than Marcion the "captain" or, *horribile dictu*, Marcion the "sailor." It certainly seems difficult to imagine that a simple sailor should have been able to donate a substantial sum of money to the Roman church (see below).[7] However, as far as I can see, the designation of Marcion as "sailor," "ship man," "ship captain" or "ship owner" is ignored by our two earliest sources, Justin and Irenaeus, and appears only after Marcion's death in the writings of Rhodon and Tertullian, as invective, invariably in a polemical context and often connected with the appellation of "Ponticus."[8] A contemporary source, Julius Pollux, reminds us in his *Onomasticon* (which was addressed to the emperor Commodus) that "*nautês*" belongs to those professional designations that admit of polemical applications.[9] Tertullian himself can also use *nauclerus, nautici* and *nautae* in order to ridicule the Valentinian pleroma.[10] It would therefore be hazardous to build too much

---

4   Harnack 1985, 22, 31, 67 f., 96. But see Dungan 1974, 186 f. Vinzent 2013 (see also 2014, 137) tries to develop Harnack's view.

5   Eusebius of Caesarea, *Hist eccl.* 5.13.3. Besides the translations mentioned Liddell-Scott-Jones, s.v. also offers "passenger by the sea" or "mates in a drinking bout": The second meaning may be close to the use of the word as a sobriquet, see below.

6   *Oxford Latin Dictionary*, 1160; Lewis and Short, *A Latin Dictionary*, 1190.

7   Moll 2010, 29 f. (note 22).

8   Eusebius (*Hist. eccl.* 5.13.3) writes: "But others, such as the *nautês* [Marcion] himself, introduced two principles. To them belong Potitus and Basiliscus. These followed the Pontic wolf, not perceiving the division of things ..." (transl. K. Lake, modified). According to the apparatus of Schwartz 1908, 195, the three Greek manuscripts ATE omit "*nautês*." Schwartz brackets "Markion": in good polemical fashion Rhodon may have replaced the name of Marcion by sobriquets. The expression "Pontic wolf" may derive from Justin, *1Apol.* 58.2. For Marcion as "*nauclerus*," see Tertullian, *Praescr.* 30.1; *Marc.* 1.18.4; 3.6.3 (polemical allusion to the maritime law of Rhodos); 4.9.2 (reference to Luke 5:1–11); 5.1.2: Here the *nauclerus* is clearly a ship owner whose ships may transport illicit cargo; Braun 2004, 72 takes the—possibly playful—polemic of Tertullian at face value and suspects an "insinuation perfide sur les malhonnêtetés possibles de Marcion dans sa vie professionnelle." Marcion becomes a potential pirate or smuggler—Braun's suggestion adds yet another tantalizing trait to his profile.

9   Julius Pollux, *Onom.* 6.128 (ed. Bethe, 2.35).

10   Tertullian, *Val.* 12.2–3. See the commentary *ad locum* of Fredouille 1981, 264 who—listing

on Marcion as *nauclerus*, and—as has often been done—to infer from it too readily a social context for one of the more important Christian theologians of the 2nd century.[11]

With regard to the chronological framework of Marcion's life and activities, the indications of the ancient sources largely agree. Justin Martyr, writing about 155 CE, mentions him as still active.[12] Tertullian, wishing to demonstrate the recent origin of heresies, argues that Valentinus and Marcion lived under the emperor Antoninus Pius (138–161 CE) and still clung to the Catholic faith under bishop Eleutherus.[13] If we assume for the tenure of Eleutherus the dates offered by Eusebius of Caesarea, Valentinus and Marcion were still alive in 177–189 CE, that is, late in the reign of the emperor Marcus Aurelius—which seems unlikely.[14] Clement of Alexandria places the three heretics Marcion, Basilides and Valentinus, within a period stretching from the emperor Hadrian to the emperor Antoninus Pius, that is from 117 CE to 161 CE.[15]

Tertullian's remarks in *Marc.* 1.19.2 are often assumed to allow us to date Marcion's Roman activities more precisely. In the following, the passage is translated in its context (*Marc.* 1.19.1–3):

1. "Yes, but our god," the Marcionites rejoin, "though not revealed from the beginning, or by virtue of any creation, yet has by his own self been revealed in Christ Jesus." One of my books will have reference to Christ

---

those passages where Tertullian calls Marcion a *nauclerus*—curiously insists that here, too, it does not designate so much the captain's ship as rather that person that "has the commercial responsibility for the transport of passengers and goods."

11 For a plausible and valuable portrait of Marcion as a *nauclerus*, see May 2005, 51–62. May is, of course right, to point out that the testimonies of Rhodon and Tertullian are independent of each other: if Tertullian knew the (probably earlier) treatise of Rhodon, which was possibly addressed to a certain Kallistio (Eusebius, *Hist. eccl.* 5.13.8), there is no proof that he did. It is, however, entirely possible that Rhodon and Tertullian reflect a (possibly Roman) polemical tradition about Marcion, and in any case, the fact that Marcion was a *Ponticus* by birth, may have suggested a maritime sobriquet to more than one polemicist. One could also entertain the possibility that Rhodon or—more likely—Tertullian took what was initially meant as a sobriquet at face value and yet developed it in playful polemic. Vinzent 2016, 150–157 portrays Marcion as a successful businessman and a theological teacher. In this context one could of course also mention the Roman theologian Theodotus the banker (Eusebius, *Hist. eccl.* 5.28.9) and the Roman bishop (?) Kallistus (Hippolytus, *Ref.* 9.12) both of whom managed to combine business acumen with an interest in theology.

12 Justin, *1Apol.* 26.5.

13 Tertullian, *Praescr.* 30.2.

14 Eusebius, *Hist. eccl.* 5.1.1; 5.22.1.

15 Clement of Alexandria, *Strom.* 7.107.1.

and all that he stands for: for the divisions of our subject have to be kept distinct, so as to receive more complete and orderly treatment. For the time it must suffice to follow up our present argument so far as to prove, and that in few words, that Christ Jesus is the representative of no other god than the Creator. 2. "In the fifteenth year of Tiberius Caesar Christ Jesus deigned to glide down from heaven, a salutary spirit." In what year of the elder Antoninus the pestilential breeze of Marcion's salvation, whose opinion this was, breathed out from his own Pontus, I did not undertake to inquire. But of this I am sure, that he is an Antoninian heretic, impious under Pius. Now from Tiberius to Antoninus there are about a hundred and fifteen and a half years and half a month. The same length of time do they posit between Christ and Marcion. 3. Since therefore it was under Antoninus that, as I have proved, Marcion first brought this god on the scene, at once, if you are in your senses, the fact is clear. The dates themselves put it beyond argument that that which first came to light under Antoninus did not come to light under Tiberius: that is, that the god of Antoninus' reign was not the God of the reign of Tiberius, and therefore he who it is admitted was first reported to exist by Marcion, had not been revealed by Christ.[16]

It was Richard Adalbert Lipsius who—reacting to an article of Gustav Volkmar—proposed an interpretation of the crucial sentence in 1.19.2 (*A Tiberio autem usque ad Antoninum anni fere centum quindecim et dimidium anni cum dimidio mensis*) that—with some modification—was then adopted by Adolf von Harnack and has since then been left more or less unchallenged.[17] Recently Judith Lieu, one of the very few scholars wholly unfascinated by Harnack's Marcion, has questioned in passing the Lipsius-Harnack theory.[18]

According to Lipsius-Harnack, the statement relates a chronology proposed by the Marcionites themselves: in the sentence immediately following (*Tantumdem temporis ponunt inter Christum et Marcionem*) the third person plural, Lipsius believes, refers to the Marcionites. The 115 years and 6 ½ months are then the period from the appearance of Christ in the 15th year of Tiberius[19] to the appearance of Marcion: if one places the first event in the spring of 29 CE, the latter event would have to be dated to the autumn of 144 CE. This date would

16   Transl. Evans, altered.
17   Lipsius 1875, 241–244; Harnack 1897, 306 f.; Harnack 1985, 20*f. Compare Hoffmann 1984, 68–70.
18   Lieu 2015, 296.
19   The Marcionites adopt the chronology of Luke 3:1.

designate either the start of Marcion's activity in Rome or—but Lipsius considers this conjecture less probable—his first public appearance in his home region of Pontus.

But does the Lipsius-Harnack interpretation hold? Let us look more closely at the passage and its context.

Before entering into any detailed discussion with the Marcionites, Tertullian wants to point out that Marcion, who proclaims a new, hitherto unknown God, has lived much later than Jesus Christ. If Marcion contends that an unknown God revealed himself in Jesus Christ, Tertullian maintains that the unknown God of Marcion was not revealed through Jesus Christ under the emperor Tiberius, but much later by Marcion himself under the emperor Antoninus Pius. Tertullian calls his preliminary argument a "very quick proof" (*expeditissma probatio*). Already in *De praescriptione* 30 he had used the late appearance of the heretics—their lateness being here contrasted with the ancientness of the tradition of the Church—as an argument against them.

Tertullian starts by pointing out that Marcion himself assumes that Jesus Christ, the salvific spirit, has revealed himself by "deigning to flow from heavens."[20] However, Tertullian continues by emphasizing that he does not bother to fix precisely the date of Marcion's first appearance on the scene.[21] For Tertullian's argument, it is sufficient to state that Marcion is clearly a contemporary of the reign of Antoninus Pius (138–161 CE), or as Tertullian's wordplay puts it: *Antoninanus hereticus est, sub Pio impius*. The following statement (*A Tiberio autem usque ad Antoninum anni fere centum quindecim et dimidium anni cum dimidio mensis*) is clearly meant to determine the length of time that has elapsed between the reign of Tiberius and the reign of Antoninus Pius.

But if that is correct, the calculation is wrong or at least very imprecise. If we consider the year of the accession of each emperor, the period would run from 14 CE to 138 CE and the length of time would have to be calculated as (roughly) 125 instead of 115 years.[22] If the number of years was not written out in some ancestor manuscript (such as the archetype), an accidental mis-

---

20   "Iesus de caelo manare dignatus est": Braun 1990, 186, note 1 rightly notices the satirical intent of the phrasing.

21   "quoto quidem anno Antonini maioris de Ponto suo exhalaverit aura canicularis non curavi investigare ..."

22   According to the critical apparatus of the Oehler's edition, one manuscript, the Codex Leidensis latinus 2 (15th century) does in fact read "centum viginti quinque." However, the Codex Leidensis is a late manuscript, a copy of the Codex Florentinus Magliabechianus I, VI.10 (15th century), see Mahé 1980,51; Braun 1990, 81. I have not seen either manuscript; it is possible that the reading of the Codex Leidensis is a learned (or not so learned) conjecture by a humanist scribe.

take such as deforming "CXXV" into "CXV" could have easily occurred.[23] It is also possible that Tertullian may here simply rely on an incorrect chronology proposed by someone else or, alternatively, may have himself miscalculated the exact number of years and months. One needs only to consult the chronological calculations of Tatian or Clement of Alexandria to become aware how easily mistakes occurred—either because the original author of the chronology had miscalculated or—more likely—because of negligent copying.[24]

But this is admittedly mere speculation. It is, however, beyond possible contestation that Tertullian's calculation is meant to determine the length of time between the reigns of the two emperors, not between Christ and Marcion. It is only the following sentence that possibly (re)introduces the Marcionites.[25] Here, Tertullian does not simply say that they propose the length of time mentioned in the previous sentence as the period between Christ and Marcion, but he rather points out that they assume (*ponunt*) the *same length of time* (*tantumdem temporis*) as that between Christ and Marcion. With this phrasing, he indicates that the calculation refers to the interval of time between the reigns of the two emperors and is only secondarily invoked in order to estimate the interval of time that has elapsed between Christ and Marcion. Tertullian's wording need imply no more than that Marcion/the Marcionites dated Christ to the reign of Tiberius (more precisely to the 15th year of Tiberius) and acknowledged the well-known fact (*constat*) that Marcion appeared in the reign of Antoninus Pius.[26] That the periods of time between Tiberius and Antoninus Pius on the one hand, and Christ and Marcion on the other hand, are not precisely identical is indicated by the (anticipatory) *fere* inserted by Tertullian into the chronolog-

---

23   Shortly before the "15th year of Tiberius" is mentioned, which the manuscript could have transcribed as "anno xv Tiberii."

24   See, for example, the text critical apparatus to Tatian, *Or.* 31 (Goodspeed 1914/1984, 296) or Clement of Alexandria, *Strom.* 1.144–145 (ed. Stählin/Früchtel/Treu 1985, 89–90).

25   One could also translate the sentence as "the same length of time is posited between Christ and Marcion." I have, however, found no convincing parallel to this impersonal use of *ponunt* in Tertullian.

26   Lieu 2015, 296 writes: "Indeed it may be entirely mistaken to read 'that much time they put (ponunt) between Christ and Marcion' as evidence that the precise figure was one celebrated by Marcion's followers rather than the result of Tertullian's opaque computation of the gap between Tiberius and Antoninus, which is what he states." But she continues: "Even so, this is not so different from *The Chronicle of Edessa* for when Marcion left 'the catholic church,' even if this is equally anachronistic." *The Chronicle of Edessa* dates Marcion's separation from the church to 138 CE, i.e. to the first year of the reign of Antoninus Pius; see *Chronica Minora I* (ed. Guidi, CSCO I, 1, p. 3 [Syriac text]; transl. Guidi, CSCO I, 2, p. 4 [Latin translation]). Harnack's tortuous attempt to square this date with his own theory fails to convince (1985, 29*f).

ical calculation. It signals that the calculation based on the dates of the reigns of the two emperors is a kind of rough-and-ready device for approximately determining also the interval of time between Christ and Marcion, employed by someone who explicitly protests not wishing to calculate it more precisely (*quoto quidem anno Antonini maioris ... non curavi investigare*).[27]

In order to corroborate this interpretation of *Marc.* 1.19.2, two more passages from the same work have to be considered.

The first passage is *Marc.* 1.15.1:

> Meanwhile, whatever this material reality (*substantia*) is [Tertullian refers to the transcendent creation of the unknown god], it ought to have appeared at the same time as the god whose it is. Yet how is it that their

---

27   Moll 2010, 33 seems to get it interestingly wrong when he argues: "Reading Tertullian's first sentence [Moll here refers to the chronological statement] one could easily get the impression that his calculation is simply referring to the time difference between the Emperors. But (...) it is the use of the word *fere* which excludes this possibility: no one would make such an exact calculation down to the very day and say: it is *more or less* 115 years and 6 ½ months. Therefore, it is obvious that Tertullian is referring to a calculation made by the Marcionites themselves, which he then approximately (*fere*) equates with the time between Tiberius and Antoninus." Against this argument it must be said that 1) it is flatly contradicted by the chronological statement which explicitly calculates the interval of time between the emperors, and 2) it is also at odds with Tertullian's unambiguous statement that he has not undertaken to find out in which year of the reign of Antoninus Pius Marcion appeared. If Tertullian's chronological statement presented a Marcionite chronology determining the appearance of Marcion, I see no reason why Tertullian should have obscured this fact by resorting to so much confusing circumlocution—he would have had no reason not to use it as a straightforward argument against his opponents. It is also no good arguing that Tertullian based his claim that Marcion was a *haereticus Antoninianus* on a Marcionite chronology dating the first appearance of Marcion to about 144 CE. This inference is clearly precluded by the drift of the argument as presented by Tertullian which starts from the assumption that he does not know in precisely which year of Antoninus' reign Marcion had his outing. Lipsius (1875, 243) misleadingly talks of a "affectirte Unwissenheit Tertullians über das Jahr von Markions Übersiedlung vom Pontos nach Rom." Again, the nuance of Tertullian's remarks is missed: Tertullian states 1) that he did not bother to find out about the exact year of the reign in which Marcion burst on the scene, but that 2) it happened in any case (*de quo tamen constat*) in the reign of Antoninus—which is the (minimum) information Tertullian needs for his approximate estimate as set out in the immediately following chronological statement. Vinzent 2016, 273 now tries to argue that Tertullian here alludes to two different versions of Marcion's gospel (this is a hypothesis of Vinzent, with—as far as I can see—little confirmation in any of the hereseological sources; see below). Tertullian did not investigate when the first draft was written, but indicates very precisely the date of the second draft: 144 CE.

lord has been revealed since the fifteenth year of Tiberius Caesar, but of that there is absolutely no indication of this material reality right down to this fifteenth year of the emperor Severus?[28]

As in *Marc.* 1.19.2, Tertullian here tries to show that Marcion's unknown god is but a recent invention. The argument evokes the transcendent creation of the unknown god: although, Tertullian argues, the lord—the unknown god who is identical with his Christ—has already been revealed in the 15th year of the emperor Tiberius, at the time of Tertullian's writing (in the 15th year of the emperor Septimius Severus [i.e. 207/208 CE]), this new creation, which should have appeared together with its creator, is still quite unknown. In this case, the interval of time Tertullian chooses fixes his own present as the *terminus ad quem*. This is plausible because the creation (*substantia*) of the unknown God should not be a revelation at a particular point in time, but rather something that—as with creation!—can be seen and experienced by all. It is therefore Tertullian himself who can reliably testify to its non-existence.

In *Marc.* 4.4.5 Tertullian remarks with heavy irony:

> As corrector apparently of a gospel which from the times of Tiberius to those of Antoninus had suffered subversion, Marcion comes to light, first and alone, after Christ had waited for him all that time, repenting of having been in a hurry to send forth apostles without Marcion to protect them.[29]

As in *Marc.* 1.19.2, here again the interval of time between the reign of Tiberius and the reign of Antonius (*Antoniana tempora*) is evoked without being calculated: it is the period of time in which, according to Marcion (says Tertullian), the gospel had lain ruined before its corrector (*emendator*), that is Marcion, appeared. In this passage, no length of time is calculated.

Even if one were to accept the assumption of Lipsius and Harnack that Tertullian presents in *Marc.* 1.19.2 (a Marcionite chronology), one would have still to ask about its Marcionite rationale: why calculate the length of time that has elapsed between Christ and Marcion? One reason may be indicated by the passage just quoted (*Marc.* 4.4.5): the Marcionites wished to highlight the period of time during which the gospel had been obscured and falsified, and they celebrated the restitution of the pure gospel message by the work of Marcion. But if

---

28   Braun 1990, 168–169; tr. Evans, much altered in light of Braun's translation.
29   Braun 2001, 80 (tr. Evans).

that were correct, it would presuppose that the Marcionites did indeed accept the priority of the (corrupted) gospel tradition of their opponents and saw the work of their master as recovering the original gospel message from distortions and falsifications that had occurred early on. This view has been (again) challenged in recent scholarship (see below). Moreover, this view of Marcion's role, which casts him as a prophet or reformer,[30] seems to draw on Neander's and Harnack's Neo-protestant interpretation of Marcion, according to which the *nauclerus* from Pontus was no less than the "first Protestant."[31]

One may further ask which event in 144/145 CE is precisely targeted by Marcionite chronology: it has been suggested that it is Marcion's arrival in Rome. But it seems that Marcion initially belonged to the Roman church and consequently must have been "orthodox" and therefore would not have "revealed" his unknown god right from the beginning of his Roman period (see below). Similar reasoning should also prevent us from assigning Marcion's first public appearance in Pontus to the year 144/145 CE Again, those who simply claim that in 144/145 CE. Marcion separated from the Roman church seem to neglect the notice on Marcion and Valentinus in Tertullian, *Praescr.* 30.2–3 which suggests that there was no neat and simple separation of Marcion from the church of Rome (but see below).[32] A fourth solution, namely, to refer the year 144/145 CE to the death of Marcion seems to be precluded by Justin Martyr, *1Apol.* 26, where it is implied that Marcion is still alive at the time of Justin's writing, which is ca. 155 CE. All of these attempts to identify a significant event in the life of Marcion or his church that can be placed in the year 144/145 CE are equally problematic and without any basis in the text of *Marc.* 1.19.2.

As regards Marcion's activity in Rome, most scholars agree that in the first time after his arrival in Rome he still belonged to the Roman church (in what-

---

30   Harnack 1985, 20* writes: "Die römischen Marcioniten haben ihn [the period between Christ and Marcion] berechnet und auch in dieser Berechnung ihre hohe Meinung von der Bedeutung ihres Stifters zum Ausdruck gebracht; erst in der Gemeinde Muhameds stößt man wieder auf Ähnliches." To support his case, Harnack could also have cited the possible parallel of the prophet Mani. He believed that the Marcionite chronology calculates the interval between the "Christ day" (i.e. the epiphany of Christ: Harnack proposes either January 6th or January 1st 29 CE) and the Marcion day on which the Marcionites celebrated the founding of their church, see Harnack 1985, 20*f, note 3. All this is, however, no more than a learned flight of fancy without sufficient evidence to support it: No ancient source mentions a "Marcion day" celebrated by Marcionite communities.

31   Harnack 1985, 198. It was August Neander who was apparently the first to see Marcion as a true Protestant, see May 2005, 111–117.

32   Lieu 2015, 296 who remarks on the anachronism of assuming "a decisive act of 'excommunication.'" See also her remark concerning the *Chronicle of Edessa*, quoted above.

ever institutional form that entity existed).[33] Harnack suggested that Marcion
had published his new doctrine already in his hometown of Sinope and had
therefore been excommunicated by his father who was the local bishop.[34] Carrying with him letters of recommendation from his adherents in Sinope,[35] Marcion had then moved to Asia and had met Polycarp in either Smyrna, Ephesus
or, possibly Hierapolis, where Polycarp rejected him as the firstborn of Satan.[36]
All this suggests to Harnack that Marcion had developed his teaching some
time before his arrival at Rome, where his excommunication in Sinope was
either unknown or irrelevant.[37] If Harnack's way of piecing together the patchy
evidence for a pre-Roman career of Marcion may be somewhat less than convincing,[38] it is certainly a useful reminder that the assumption that Marcion in
the first time after his arrival in Rome still belonged to the Roman church does
not necessarily prejudice the question whether or not he published his teaching before or after his arrival at Rome. That he was initially a member of the
Roman church is for most scholars sufficiently demonstrated by his donation of
the considerable sum of 200,000 sesterces to his church.[39] The separation from
the Roman church was probably not as neat and clear-cut as the restitution
of the donation which happened on this occasion seems to suggest. Tertullian,
Praescr. 30.2 f. talks of a repeated expulsion of Marcion from the Roman church.
Shortly before his death, Tertullian alleges, Marcion repented and was read-
mitted into the church on the condition of bringing back into the fold those
who had followed him into separation. Death, however, prevented the reconciliation from being carried out. If this story of a last-minute repentance of

---

33   This view is confirmed by Marcion's donation to the Roman church and by the assump-
        tion that the letter of Marcion tries to justify his separation from the Roman church (see
        below).

34   Harnack 1985, 23, citing Hippolytus of Rome (i.e. Epiphanius, *Pan.* 42.1.3 f.; Ps.-Tertullian,
        Haer. 6.2) in support of his claim.

35   Harnack 1985, 11* cites the "anti-marcionite" prologue to the Gospel of John (that refers to
        Papias of Hierapolis as a source), conveniently printed with parallel material, translations
        and a rich commentary in Norelli 2005, 448–471. However, Zwierlein 2015 (who prefers
        the longer version; see his reconstruction [24]) shows that the notice about Marcion is
        not taken from Papias but draws on later legendary tradition (70–77).

36   Harnack 1985, 24; see Irenaeus, *Haer.* 3.3.4.

37   Harnack 1985, 24–25.

38   See Norelli 2005, 469 f who largely follows Regul 1969 in his critical assessment of all infor-
        mation regarding the pre-Roman activity of Marcion. See also Zwierlein 2015, 74–77.

39   Tertullian, *Praescr.* 30.2; *Marc.* 4.4.3. See Lampe 1989, 207–209 for an attempt at evalu-
        ating this sum of money. It is unclear if "cum ducentis sestertiis ..." in *Praescr.* 30.2 the
        figure 200,000 is to be taken literally or if it simply indicates a large sum of money; see
        Lampe 1989, 207 f., note 295.

Marcion looks very suspicious indeed,[40] the fact of the circulation of the story may still suggest that for a considerable period of time, there was no neat separation of Marcion and his followers from the Roman church, but rather protracted divorce proceedings (including the return of the dowry!), with continuing engagement and negotiations on both sides. This picture seems all the more plausible as it seems rather unlikely that at that early date, the Roman church would have had the institutional structures required to effect a clear break with a rich sponsor and his possibly considerable following among its members.[41]

Marcion left disciples who were engaged in discussions among themselves and with rival Christian schools. Rhodon (who probably in lived in Rome during the time of Marcus Aurelius) mentions Potitus, Basiliscus and Syneros as disciples who were engaged in debates about the number of principles.[42] Other disciples are Lucanus and Apelles.[43] The very existence of these disciples and their continuing activity in Rome and elsewhere suggests that Marcion had set up a school in Rome and was engaged in some (regular or irregular) teaching activity. In this respect, Marcion is then comparable to Justin Martyr or Valentinus or the Carpocratians, teachers of Christian philosophy who had moved to Rome in order to spread their doctrines in the capital of a prospering global empire.

It would fit Marcion's portrait as a Roman teacher if he himself had been the disciple of another Roman teacher, Cerdo. But even if Cerdo is an historical person and possibly even one of Marcion's teachers, nevertheless, the hereseological doxography about his doctrines is rightly suspected of constructing him in the image of his more famous disciple.[44]

As was usual with teachers of philosophy, their teaching was discussed and contested by opponents and pupils alike. Justin Martyr started the attacks, viewing Marcionite theology as akin to Platonic theories of principles.[45] In the next generation, Rhodon, a pupil of Justin Martyr's disciple Tatian, and

---

40 See, e.g. Moll 2010, 45, note 100. As regards the double excommunication of Marcion, the parallel with Cerdo as reported by Irenaeus, *Haer.* 3.4.2 looks also a bit suspicious—in one way or another, see Refoulé 1957, 127, note 3.

41 This is generally acknowledged in modern research, see, e.g., Vinzent 2014, 134. The Roman church of the second century seems to have generated several stories of the spectacular separation and dramatic reconciliation of heretics; see also Eusebius, *Hist. eccl.* 5.28.7–12. The mode of self-definition and exclusion adopted here is by dramatic performance rather than institutional fiat.

42 Eusebius of Caesarea, *Hist. eccl.* 5.13.3 f.

43 Löhr 2010, 166–173.

44 Irenaeus, *Adv. Haer.* 1.27.1. See Deakle 2002; May 2005, 63–73.

45 Justin, *1 Apol.* 26.5. See Lieu 2015, 332 f.

thus, a member of a rival school, highlighted divisions among Marcion's disciples about the number of principles.[46] The criticism of Marcion's teaching that had started during Marcion's lifetime continued for some time after his death. The following authors wrote treatises exclusively directed against Marcion: Justin Martyr, Irenaeus (?), Theophilus of Antioch, Philip of Gortyna, Modestus, Bardesanes, Tertullian, and Hippolytus.[47] This list seems to suggest that the teaching of Marcion was a live issue during the last third of the second century and that the controversy surrounding it somewhat abated after the first quarter of the third century: Tertullian (together with Bardesanes) was already a latecomer. The heyday of anti-Marcionite polemics coincides with the time of the first spread of "Marcionitism" beyond Rome; it was also the time when his intellectual disciples—who were far from unanimous amongst each other—discussed and propagated his work. Tertullian's work against Marcion refers several times to his disciples rather than to Marcion himself and it is against them—who are apparently still very much around in Africa—that he directs his polemics.[48]

2   The Works of Marcion

Regarding the works of Marcion, no consensus has so far been achieved as to their contents, scope or date.

We know of three works: 1) the Letter, 2) the Antitheses, 3) the "bible" of Marcion, apparently consisting of a gospel and ten letters of Paul.

As to the Letter, it is mentioned in three passages of Tertullian:

1)   His [i.e. Marcion's] disciples will not deny that at the beginning he shared our faith (*primam illi fidem nobiscum fuisse*)—as his Letter testifies (*ipsius litteris testibus*)—so that for this reason alone he could be defined as a heretic ... (*Marc.* 1.1.6).

---

46   Eusebius, *Hist. eccl.* 5.13. 3 f. See also Hippolytus, *Haer.* 7.31; 10.19.

47   Justin (Irenaeus, *Haer.* 4.6.2—is this identical with the treatise mentioned by Justin himself in *1 Apol.* 26.8, the *Syntagma*?); Irenaeus, *Haer.* 1.27.4, announces a separate treatise against Marcion (Eusebius, *Hist. eccl* 4.25 implies that he actually published it, although he may be simply relying on the said announcement; see *Hist. eccl.* 5.8.9); Theophilus of Antioch (Eusebius, *Hist. eccl.* 4.24); Philip of Gortyna (Eusebius, *Hist. eccl.* 4.21, 25; he lived under Marcus Aurelius and was mentioned by Dionysius of Corinth); Modestus (Eusebius, *Hist. eccl.* 4.25), active during the time of Marcus Aurelius. His refutation of Marcion was still available for Jerome, *Vir. ill.* 32; Bardesanes (Eusebius, *Hist. eccl.* 4.30), dialogues against the Marcionites and others; Tertullian, *Marc.* I.–V.; Hippolytus (Eusebius, *Hist. eccl.* 6.22). For a full list, see Vinzent 2013, 177–179.

48   Tertullian, *Marc.* 1.19.2; 4.15.3 f.; 4.29.16.

2) What if the Marcionites will deny that his first faith was on our side (*primam apud nos fidem*), against also his own Letter? What if they do not even acknowledge the Letter? (*Marc.* 4.4.3).

3) This is because you, being not a Christian, are dead, since you do not believe what to believe makes a Christian. And you are all the more dead, the more you are not a Christian, you, who when you were a Christian, dropped out by annulling what you had earlier believed, as you yourself admit in a certain Letter and your supporters do not deny ... (*Carn. Chr.* 2.4).

Neither the date nor the addressee of the Letter are specified. All three passages indicate that, in his Letter, Marcion mentions a profound change of mind, but we are not told whether the Letter announces, explains or defends this change of mind. For Tertullian, the Letter seems to refer to the separation of Marcion from the church. Harnack suggested that the Letter may have been preserved in the archives of the Roman church and that Marcion possibly wrote it to explain his change of mind to the Roman church.[49] Since the addressee of the Letter is unknown, Harnack's suggestion is not confirmed by any source.

Jean-Pierre Mahé has argued that it is in his Letter that Marcion had explained the reasoning behind his dualist doctrine with reference to Luke 6:43 and Isaiah 45:7.[50] For Mahé then, Marcion wrote his Letter not so much as a justification of his separation addressed to the Roman church, but rather as an introduction to his dualist message whose purpose was missionary and whose addressee was the wider public.[51] Mahé may be right, but the evidence is insufficient to fully support his thesis.

Sebastian Moll endorses the gist of Mahé's theory and elaborates it further. As an additional element, he refers to the letter a remark made by Tertullian in *Marc.* 4.9.3. According to Tertullian, Marcion developed his argument in the presence (*apud*) of someone he called his companion in misery and hatred (*quem syntalaipôron, commiseronem, et symmisoumenon, coodibilem*). For Moll, then, Marcion addressed the Letter to a member of his own community, during his stay in Rome.[52] However, the context of Tertullian's remark in *Adv. Marc.* 4.9.3 makes it very clear that the traditional view that ascribes this dedication to Marcion's *Antitheses* rather than to the Letter is correct.

---

49 Harnack 1985, 22*.
50 Tertullian, *Adv. Marc.* 1.2.1–2; cf. 2.24.3–4.
51 Mahé 1971, 358–371.
52 Moll 2010, 115–118. Moll acknowledges Hilgenfeld 1884/1966, 525, as the source of this suggestion.

Most important for determining the intellectual profile of Marcion are, of course, his major works, the *Antitheses* and his "bible." Within the limited compass of this paper it is, however, impossible to reconstruct either of them. However, it is possible to formulate some preliminary observations and conclusions which may help to evaluate those reconstructions that have been proposed:[53]

- Tertullian is the only ancient source that gives us the full title of the *Antitheses*: *Antitheseis Markiônos* (if Tertullian read the work in Greek) or *Antithesis Marcionis* (if he read it in Latin).[54]

- The work not only had a title, but also a dedication.

- It can be excluded that it served as the introduction to, or preface of, Marcion's bible.[55]

- For his disciples, it was the *Antitheses*, rather than his bible, that was the most important work of Marcion.

- The contents and scope of the *Antitheses* are difficult to determine: for his refutation of Marcion, Tertullian preferred to focus on his bible rather than the *Antitheses*.[56] There is no agreement between scholars whether the *Antitheses* were just a collection of contradictory propositions, drawn from the bible of Marcion and the Old Testament, or whether they also contained exegetical remarks of some kind.[57] In one passage, Tertullian may have revealed the contents and/or the structure of the *Antitheses*: they compared the Christ and the creator God as to their moral natures, their legislation and their miracles.[58] This summary (?) seems to suggest that the *Antitheses* drew on a larger moralizing discourse about the character of a (divine or human) person as expressed in, or contradicted by, his or her sayings and actions rather than on any Pauline dialectics of the gospel and the law.[59]

- David L. Dungan had already suggested that the *Antitheses* were not only "a list of contrasts between Law and Gospel, Good God and Just God, Old and New Testament" but also "contained attacks pure and simple upon the God of the Old Testament, ridiculing His record of inconsistencies, weaknesses, immoral and unjust actions." And Dungan concludes: "... the 'contradictions'

---

53   Also treated in Löhr 2016, 73–80.
54   For a collection of passages, see Löhr 2016, 74, note 34.
55   Lieu 2015, 283 f. (but see 275 f.!); Löhr 2016, 77–80.
56   For a maximalist view, Harnack 1985, 74–92; for a possibly minimalist view, May 2005, 47–48. See also Moll 2010, 107–114; Löhr 2010, 153–155; Löhr 2016, 73–80. See also the discussion in Lieu 2015, 272–289.
57   Löhr 2016, 77 f.
58   Tertullian, *Marc.* 2.29.1.
59   See Löhr 2002, 145; Lieu 2015, 275, 278 f.

Marcion lists are just as much between what Marcion considered *fitting for the Deity* and the anthropomorphisms and inconsistencies recorded in the Old Testament accounts, as they are lists of contradictions between the Old and New Covenants and two Gods, Creator versus Savior."[60]

- Dungan's view of Marcion's *Antitheses* has certainly this to recommend itself, that it tries to situate them in the larger context of contemporary discourses conducted by philosophically minded Jews, pagans and Christians: How does one talk about God in a manner that is fitting for God or the gods (in Greek: *theoprepês*)? And how does one deal hermeneutically with those texts (be they revealed scripture or—as in the case of Homer— inspired poetry) whose anthropomorphisms seem to violate that canon of sound philosophical religion and good taste?[61] Moreover, Dungan argues, Marcion only adapted an argumentative technique used by contemporary Jews, pagans and Christians alike when he insisted on a literal interpretation of the Old Testament, only to highlight the contradictions between passages from the Gospel and from the Law.[62] If Dungan is right, his view of the *Antitheses* would fit a profile of Marcion as a teacher of Christian philosophy that is engaged in an intellectual critique of the Old Testament.[63]
- Regarding Marcion's bible, it seems certain that it consisted of a gospel closely related to the Gospel of Luke and ten letters of Paul, in the order, Gal, 1 and 2 Cor, Rom, 1 and 2 Thess, Eph, Col, Phil, Phm.[64]

Epiphanius reports in his *Panarion omnium haeresium* (published in 375 CE) that Marcion's bible consisted of two codices, one presumably containing the gospel, the other one, the ten letters of Paul (the "*Apostolos*").[65] Tertullian is the only ancient author to comment on the scandalous fact that Marcion's gospel did not indicate its author.[66] Marcion's gospel is here explicitly and unfavorably compared to the canonical gospels of Tertullian's bible, whose titles by

---

60 Dungan 1974, 188–189.

61 See also Aland 1992,94; Löhr 2002, 146.

62 Dungan 1974, 188–198 cites many examples. Marcion was not the only author who wrote *Antitheses*; see Löhr 2010. For Marcion's disciple Apelles whose thirty-eight books of syllogisms tried to refute the Law of Moses and in this way probably continued the work of the *Antitheses*, see *ibidem*, 170.

63 Löhr 2016, 80, note 63.

64 Tertullian, *Marc.* 5; Epiphanius of Salamis, *Pan.* 42.9.3 f.—Lieu 2015, 186 cautions against attributing to Marcion the idea of a New Testament: His opponents do not "credit Marcion with holding his "Gospel" and "Apostolikon" together in the way that they themselves were doing ..."

65 Epiphanius, *Pan.* 42.10.2; Adamantius, *Dial.* 2.5; 2.10; 2.12 (ed. van de Sande Bakhuyzen 66, 76, 80).

66 Tertullian, *Marc.* 4.2.3.

that time securely attributed them to Mark, Matthew, Luke and John. However, the fact that the title of Marcion's Gospel probably omitted any mention of its author (and therefore did not have a full title, as emphasized by Tertullian) was probably less unusual than Tertullian's critique suggests. As has already been pointed out,[67] a contemporary of Marcion, the Alexandrian teacher Basilides, also wrote a commentary "*eis to euangelion.*" Again, no author is mentioned.[68]

It is certainly beyond the scope of this article to evaluate and critique the numerous recent and not-so-recent attempts to reconstruct the text of either Marcion's Gospel or Marcion's *Apostolos*.[69] If Marcion was a Christian teacher who also edited the gospel and the ten letters of Paul, one would like to know about 1) the scope and profile of his editorial work, and 2) possible connections between his editorial work and his other works, particularly the *Antitheses*.

The traditional view of the intention of Marcion's bible-edition follows Irenaeus, *Haer.* 1.27.2, who claims that:

1) Marcion—convincing his disciples that he was more truthful than those who had transmitted the Gospel—made cuts in the Gospel of Luke, eliminating everything relating to the birth of the Lord and also suppressing much of the teaching of the Lord, in which the Lord confesses openly that the creator of this universe is his father.

2) Marcion mutilated also the Letters of Paul, cutting out all passages where the apostle openly talks about the creator and where he mentions prophecies that announce the coming of the Lord.

According to Irenaeus, the textual criticism of Marcion was fully coherent with his doctrine, according to which Jesus Christ is not the son of the creator of this world, but rather of the god who is above the creator god. Irenaeus announces that he will refute Marcion in a separate writing, demonstrating his errors on the basis of Marcion's mutilated bible.[70] This announcement shows that Irenaeus was probably aware that the textual criticism of Marcion had not eliminated all passages that referred to the creator god.

Tertullian endorses and develops Irenaeus' critique of Marcion's bible. Regarding the gospel, he claims that Marcion corrected (*corrigere*) or adulterated the Gospel of Luke, a gospel which he considered falsified (*Marc.* 4.4.4; 4.4.5;

---

67 E.g. Löhr 2016, 69.
68 Eusebius *Hist. eccl.* 4.7.7. See Löhr 1996, 12; Löhr 2016, 69–73.
69 Tsutsui 1992 (Gospel), Schmid 1995 (*Apostolos*); BeDuhn 2011 (Gospel); Roth 2015 (Gospel); Klinghardt 2015 (Gospel). More attention should probably be paid to the possibility that our witnesses to Marcion's bible may have recorded (and criticized) a text that had already been worked on by Marcion's disciples and therefore did not represent in every detail Marcion's own editorial work.
70 Irenaeus, *Haer.* 1.27.4.

4.6.1).[71] Moreover, erasing from his Gospel all those texts that contradict his view and that according to him have been inserted by the protagonists of the creator god, Marcion has retained those that are in accordance with his doctrine.[72] Adopting the method already announced by Irenaeus, Tertullian proceeds to refute Marcion on the basis of those passages he has retained in his gospel. The same method is applied to the ten letters of Paul.[73]

Other than Irenaeus, Tertullian mentions Marcion's *Antitheses* and sees a strong connection between them and Marcion's bible: he claims that for Marcionites, the *Antitheses* are his most important work.[74] Moreover, Tertullian calls the *Antitheses* a dowry (*dos*) for Marcion's gospel.[75] And in *Marc.* 4.4.4 he remarks, arguing for the priority of the Gospel of Luke:

> If the gospel that is attributed to Luke by us—it does not matter if it is also attributed to Luke by Marcion[76]—is identical with the gospel that Marcion in his Antitheses has accused of having been interpolated by the guardians of Judaism in order to incorporate into it the law and the prophets and on this basis to fabricate a Christ, then it is any rate clear that he [i.e. Marcion] could not have accused it if he had not already found it in place.[77]

How is this passage to be understood? What is the precise relation between the argument of the *Antitheses* and Marcion's edition of the gospel? Perhaps

---

71 See also Tertullian, *Marc.* 1.20.1: The Marcionites themselves seem to have claimed that by separating the law and the gospel their master had recovered the original doctrine.

72 Tertullian, *Marc.* 4.6.2. See also Tertullian, *Praescr.* 38.9.

73 Tertullian, *Marc.* 5.1.8. I disagree with Vinzent 2014, 90–93 who claims that Tertullian's critique distinguishes between Marcion the "author" of the gospel and the "redactor" of the *Apostolos*.

74 Tertullian, *Marc.* 1.19.4: "*Separatio legis et euangelii proprium et principale opus est Marcionis, nec poterunt negare discipuli eius quod in summo instrumento habent …*" See also *Marc.* 4.4.3–4 and Löhr 2016, 76, note 45.

75 Tertullian, *Marc.* 4.1.1; Löhr 2016, 75, note 41.

76 "*Si enim id euangelium quod Lucae refertur penes nos—uiderimus an et penes Marcionem*" … Vinzent 2014, 94 translates: "If that Gospel which among us is ascribed to Luke—may it also be ascribed to Marcion" and on the basis of this incorrect translation claims: "On the contrary, Marcion must have made it quite clear that it was 'his own' Gospel, as Tertullian reports." But Tertullian criticizes Marcion for omitting the name of the author from the title of his gospel. For the translation of "*uiderimus an*," see Braun 2001, 78 f., note 4; Zwierlein 2015, 79, 82. Vinzent 2016, 329, seems to correct his translation.

77 "*arguit ut interpolatum a protectoribus Iudaismi ad concorporationem* [*scil. ei*] *legis et prophetarum, quo etiam Christum inde confingerent …*" Here I now follow (compare Löhr 2016, 76) the translation and interpretation of Zwierlein 2015, 79 f.

the *Antitheses* were meant to justify the textual criticism of Marcion: since—as the *Antitheses* demonstrated—selected passages from the gospel and selected passages from the law are antithetical to each other, Marcion felt justified in eliminating these verses (probably not all of them) from the gospel in which Jesus is designated (or designates himself) as the son of the creator god. By showing the contradictions between the gospel and the law, the *Antitheses* would lay bare the contradictions within the text of the interpolated gospel (of Luke).

Tertullian's critique of Marcion offers no more than one possible reconstruction of the relation between the *Antitheses* and the gospel edition of Marcion.

However, almost since the very beginning of modern critical research on the text of Marcion's Gospel and *Apostolos*, some scholars have remained robustly skeptical regarding the claim that discrepancies between its text and the text of the canonical gospels and the canonical letters of Paul (insofar as they can be ascertained) can all be explained by reference to Marcion's theological dualism as presumably set out in one form or other by the *Antitheses*. The portrait of Marcion the editor-cum-censor who arrives at his version of the text by rigorously applying doctrinal criteria has more or less continuously been questioned.[78] At the present state of research, the possibility that Marcion may have used an existing gospel text (of whatever date, authorship or provenance, somehow related to the Gospel of Luke) has to be seriously considered.[79] The emancipation from the patristic view of Marcion's activity as an editor-cum-censor coined by Irenaeus and developed by Tertullian can be called the more or less undisputed premise of the most recent attempts to reconstruct Marcion's profile as an editor of the Gospel and the *Apostolos*.[80]

But where does this leave the *Antitheses* and the profile of Marcion as both theologian and editor of texts? Two recent attempts try to provide narratives to make historical sense of Marcion's gospel edition: both Markus Vinzent and Matthias Klinghardt argue that Marcion's Gospel holds the key to solving the Synoptic question and to arrive at a broader understanding of the emergence of the canonical gospels.[81] The research projects of both Vinzent and Klinghardt

---

78 See Roth 2015, 7–45. Roth rightly faults the reconstructions of Zahn und particularly Harnack for not strictly adhering to the methodological imperative of abandoning the criterion of a "Marcionite tendency" (25).

79 See Schmid 1995, 3–15.34; Lieu 2015, 206, 233, 242.

80 Schmid 2003, 149, quoted and endorsed by Roth 2015, 81. Vinzent, Klinghardt and BeDuhn concur. This is in effect not only an emancipation from Irenaeus and Tertullian, but also from the "Übervater" of modern Marcion studies, Harnack.

81 Vinzent 2014; Klinghardt 2015. These two studies are only the culmination of several earlier publications by each author.

(which renew similar attempts by earlier scholars) are very ambitious and it is clearly impossible to discuss and evaluate them in the short compass of this paper.[82] Here, I wish to limit myself to their construal of the relation between Marcion's *Antitheses* and Marcion's bible and thus, their profiling of Marcion's work.

According to Vinzent, Marcion published his Gospel/bible in 144 CE, the *Antitheses* serving as a preface to his bible edition. He had initially produced a gospel that was not meant to be published and was known only to friends and disciples.[83] But somehow—probably by students of Marcion—his gospel edition was circulated beyond his classroom and "was taken by several people, excerpted, copied, reworked, interpolated and made public, even before Marcion himself as author had published his original version." At this stage of the illicit publication of Marcion's Gospel, it became falsified, that is it "became judaized and harmonized with the Law and the Prophets and was put together with these Jewish Scriptures (held together if not published together, certainly in several volumes or codices)."[84] When Marcion published his own gospel, he

---

82   Since, as far as I have understood, both wish to develop certain important implications of their respective views in future publications, it would be unwise to consider them as already complete and consolidated in every detail. I must, however, indicate that, as of now, I do not share the optimism of either Vinzent or Klinghardt that their respective narratives (see below) regarding the origins of the Synoptic Gospels and the Gospel of Marcion can be confirmed by a novel interpretation of the heresiological tradition (mainly Tertullian). For a detailed critique of Klinghardt's hypothesis, see now Gramaglia 2017.

83   Vinzent 2014, 97, note 369, cites, amongst others, Galen, to show that books without titles were meant to be circulated among friends and disciples.

84   Vinzent 2014, 98 (both quotations). Vinzent bases his theory of an illicit publication and falsification of Marcion's gospel on a rather idiosyncratic interpretation of *Marc.* 4.4.2 (Vinzent 2014, 95). Tertullian writes: "A thing precedes its own modification, and an object its imitation. If this were not true, how absurd would it be that—if we have proved that our gospel is older, but Marcion's later—ours would have seemed to have been a fake even before it would have had an true object, and the gospel of Marcion would have been believed to have suffered imitation [i.e. by our gospel] before it would have even been edited (*aemulationem a nostro expertum quam est editum*) ..." Here Tertullian is simply highlighting the absurdity of the assumption that the earlier gospel (according to Tertullian, the Gospel of Luke) could possibly be considered a plagiarized and falsified version of the later gospel (i.e. the Gospel of Marcion). Neither a quotation from the *Antitheses* pointing out the plagiarism committed by the canonical gospels nor any further information about an unpublished early version of Marcion's Gospel and its pirating and falsification by judaizing opponents is to be gained from this passage that applies Tertullian's anti-heretical *praescriptio*; the same is true for Tertullian, *Praescr.* 38, also quoted by Vinzent 2014, 96. Vinzent restates his arguments in 2016, 323–325.

prefaced the *Antitheses* in order to defend his own (original) Gospel against the plagiarizers; he added the ten letters of Paul to back up his Gospel edition. The four gospels—Matthew, Mark and Luke and a first version of the Gospel of John were possibly produced before the period between 138 and 144 in reaction to the first draft of Marcion's Gospel (still without the Antitheses and the Pauline letters).[85]

If we take Vinzent's imaginative narrative at face value, it still claims a very close connection between the *Antitheses* and the edition of the Gospel: the *Antitheses* are the (critical and justificatory) preface to Marcion's bible edition. The original Gospel of Marcion, however, was not aligned with the doctrinal project of the *Antitheses* (which was dedicated to proving the separation of the gospel and the law), and which was conceived only at a second stage as a critical reaction against the plagiarism and falsification of the original gospel.[86] In dissociating the *Antitheses* from the original Gospel of Marcion in this way, Vinzent's narrative—irrespective of the host of objections that may be raised against it—manages to take account of the difficulties of clearly identifying a more or less uniform tendency of Marcion's Gospel text (as far as it can be recovered).[87]

Klinghardt shares the premise of Vinzent that the Gospel of Marcion is the key to the Synoptic question. But he is somewhat skeptical with the regard to the tightness of Vinzent's chronology (if I have understood it correctly, Vinzent suggests the possibility that the draft version of Marcion's Gospel and the response to it in the form of the three synoptic gospels and a first version of the Gospel of John may have emerged during a period of about six years) and proposes a different scenario.[88] According to Klinghardt, the pre-canonical gospels (i.e. the Gospel of Marcion, Mark, Matthew and John) emerged during the period between, roughly, 90 CE and 144 CE, with the gospel of Marcion cast in the role of the "Urevangelium."[89] In 144 CE, Marcion separated from the

---

85   Vinzent 2014, 99–100, 133–144.

86   This narrative, of course, flatly contradicts Tertullian, according to whom the Marcionites themselves claimed that the gospel had already been interpolated quite early, in the time of the emperor Tiberius, see above. See also Zwierlin 2015, 83.

87   It should be noted, just for the record, that Roth 2015 seems to argue cautiously for "the likely priority of a text very similar to our canonical Luke" (438). BeDuhn 2011 postulates a common "Urevangelium" from which both Marcion and Luke derive.

88   Klinghardt 2015, 388.

89   Klinghardt 2015, 383–388 is doubtful whether Marcion was the author of the gospel of Marcion—as Vinzent assumes. Klinghardt views Marcion rather as the first user of the Gospel of Marcion (388f.). Vinzent 2016, *passim*, seems to defend his position against Klinghardt.

Roman church; Klinghardt discusses possible reasons and seems to view the influence exerted by Cerdo as possibly a major cause. After the separation, the canonical edition—in which the Gospel of Luke joined the three other canonical gospels—was created in reaction to Marcion. When Justin mentions (ca. 150 CE) the *apomnêmoneumata apostolôn* (i.e. the gospels), he is referring to the canonical edition. Quoting Tertullian, *Marc.* 4.4.4, Klinghardt seems to view the *Antitheses* as Marcion's polemical response to the canonical edition: Marcion would have criticized not only the falsification of his gospel in the Gospel of Luke, but also the incorporation of it into a bible edition that comprised the gospel and the law and the prophets (i.e. the OT).[90] In Klinghardt's theory, the dissociation of the Gospel of Marcion from the *Antitheses* is almost complete. The Gospel is no longer an editorial project of Marcion whose doctrinal basis is laid in the *Antitheses*, but a text that Marcion[91] had used, transmitted and defended against the canonical edition which, faced with the Marcion's separation of the law and the gospel, tried to reassert the Jewish foundations of Christianity.[92]

If one abandons the traditional view of Marcion as the theologically motivated editor-cum-censor of the Gospel and the *Apostolos*, one is left with several questions: what are the purpose, scope, and contents of the *Antitheses*—the work of Marcion that according to Tertullian was most important in the eyes of his disciples? How are they related to Marcion's editorial work? And what are the extent and intention of this editorial work?

3 Conclusion

As we have seen, the ancient evidence about the life and works of Marcion presents us with several unresolved problems. Even key elements of modern scholarly accounts of Marcion—the date of 144 CE (whatever turning point in his life it is supposed to fix) and his profession as a *nauclerus*—seem dubious enough not to build too much on it. However, his activity as a Christian teacher in Rome under the emperor Antoninus Pius and his separation from the Roman church in one form or another seem to be well enough attested. Our knowl-

---

90   Klinghardt 2015, 35. For Zwierlein's critique of this interpretation of *Marc.* 4.4.4, see above, note 77.

91   Klinghardt 2015, 391: Marcion is seen as the conservative guardian of a tradition rather than as its reformer. As to determining the scope and profile of the gospel of Marcion, Klinghardt 2015, 359–362 leaves this task for future research.

92   Klinghardt 2015, 390.

edge also seems to provide sufficient reason to decisively abandon Adolf von Harnack's suggestive portrait of Marcion: Marcion was neither a prophet nor a reformer. Harnack, for whom Marcion was the "first modern Christian" (i.e. the first Neo-Protestant), was theologically over-invested in Marcion: this prevented him from seeing this second-century teacher in historical perspective.

However, if one rejects Harnack's portrayal of Marcion (as most recent research on Marcion clearly does, implicitly or explicitly), one is still left with the considerable challenge of putting together the diverse pieces of evidence offered by the ancient sources. As far as I can see we are left, as of now, with two Marcions: one is the editor of a gospel and ten letters of Paul, but at the present state of research, we are far from being able fully to assess and contextualize his editorial work and its impact. The other Marcion is a Christian teacher of the second century who—if one believes the doxographical *koinê*—propagated a theological dualism, distinguishing an utterly transcendent and benevolent God (and his Son) from an interventionist and irascible God (and his Christ) who functions as a demiurge and judge.

This splitting of Marcion into two is clearly an unsatisfactory state of affairs: only putting the two Marcions together will get us nearer to the historical Marcion. It seems plausible to assume that Marcion's theological dualism—even if partly dependent on philosophical conceptions—must have been grounded in exegetical argument. Tertullian reports several Marcionite exegeses—were they contained in the *Antitheses* or were they added as glosses to his edition of the biblical texts?[93]

At the present state of research, if we wish to make any progress, we have to work towards some sort of consensus first and foremost on Marcion the editor of the bible. This will be difficult enough, but perhaps it is possible to determine more precisely what is known and what is not known, and perhaps also to surmise what can be known and what will remain unknown unless we have more evidence. Regarding the second Marcion, the Christian teacher, it seems most promising to pursue and refine more recent attempts to situate his ideas and concepts in the rich spectrum of the discourses of first- and second-century philosophies (Jewish, Christian, pagan) about God and Man.[94] Harnack was probably wrong when he celebrated Marcion as a kind of theological singularity in the second century.

The return, however, to a research method that bases its reconstruction of Marcion's biblical texts on the application of the criterion of a "Marcionite ten-

---

93   Löhr 2010, 153 f.
94   See, e.g. Dungan 1974; Löhr 2010, 163–165 and, most impressively, Lieu 2015.

dency" seems impossible: for the time being, the methodological splitting of Marcion is likely to be the only safe option.

Bibliography

Aland, Barbara. 1992. "Marcion/Marcioniten." Pages 89–101 in *Theologische Realenzyklopädie* 22. Berlin/New York: De Gruyter.

BeDuhn, Jason D. 2011. *The First New Testament: Marcion's Scriptural Canon*. Salem, Ore: Polebridge.

Braun, René, ed./trad. 1990. *Tertullien: Contre Marcion*. Tome I. Sources chrétiennes 365. Paris: Éditions du Cerf.

Braun, René, ed./trad. 1991. *Tertullien: Contre Marcion*. Tome II. Sources chrétiennes 368. Paris: Éditions du Cerf.

Braun, René, ed./trad. 1994. *Tertullien: Contre Marcion*. Tome III. Sources chrétiennes 399. Paris: Éditions du Cerf.

Braun, René, ed./trad. 2001. *Tertullien: Contre Marcion*. Tome IV. Sources chrétiennes 456. Paris: Éditions du Cerf.

Braun, René, ed./trad. 2004. *Tertullien: Contre Marcion*. Tome V. Sources chrétiennes 483. Paris: Éditions du Cerf.

Clement of Alexandria. *Clemens Alexandrinus: Stromata Buch I–VI*. Edited by O. Stählin, new edition by L. Früchtel, 4th edition with supplements by U. Treu. Die griechischen christlichen Schriftsteller 52. Berlin: Akademie Verlag.

Deakle, David W. 2002. "Harnack & Cerdo. A Reexamination of the Patristic Evidence for Marcion's Mentor." Pages 177–190 in *Marcion and His Impact on Church History*. Edited by Gerhard May and Katharina Greschat. Berlin/New York: De Gruyter.

Dungan, David L. 1974. "Reactionary Trends in the Gospel Producing Activity of the Early Church: Marcion, Tatian, Mark." Pages 179–202 in *L'Évangile selon Marc: Tradition et rédaction*. Edited by Maurits Sabbe. Leuven: Leuven University Press.

Fredouille, Jean-Claude. 1981. *Tertullien: Contre les Valentiniens. Commentaire et Index*. Sources chrétiennes 281. Paris: Éditions du Cerf.

Gramaglia, Pier Angelo. 2017. *Marcione e il vangelo (di Luca): Un confronto con Matthias Klinghardt*. Torino: Accademia University Press.

Harnack, Adolf von. 1958. *Die Chronologie der altchristlichen Literatur bis Eusebius*. Erster Band, Leipzig: Hinrichs.

Harnack, Adolf von. 1985. *Marcion: Das Evangelium vom fremden Gott/Neue Studien zu Marcion*. Darmstadt: Wissenschaftliche Buchgesellschaft.

Hilgenfeld, Adolf. 1884. *Die Ketzergeschichte des Urchristentums*. Leipzig: Fues's Verlag (R. Reisland).

Hoffmann, R. Joseph. 1984. *Marcion: On The Restitution of Christianity*. Chico, Calif.: Scholars Press.

Klinghardt, Matthias. 2015. *Das älteste Evangelium und die Entstehung der kanonischen Evangelien*. Vol. i/ii. Tübingen: Francke Verlag.

Lampe, Peter. 1989. *Die stadtrömischen Christen in den ersten beiden Jahrhunderten*. Tübingen: Mohr Siebeck.

Lieu, Judith M. 2015. *Marcion and the Making of a Heretic*. Cambridge: Cambridge University Press.

Lipsius, Richard Adalbert. 1875. *Die Quellen der aeltesten Ketzergeschichte neu untersucht*. Leipzig: J.A. Barth.

Löhr, Winrich. 2002. "Did Marcion distinguish between a just god and a good god?" Pages 131–146 in *Marcion and His Impact on Church History*. Edited by Gerhard May and Katharina Greschat. Berlin/New York: De Gruyter.

Löhr, Winrich. 2010. "Markion." Pages 145–173 in *Reallexikon für Antike und Christentum* 24. Stuttgart: Hiersemann.

Löhr, Winrich. 2016. "Editors and Commentators. Some Observations on the Craft of Second Century Theologians." Pages 65–84 in *Pascha Nostrum Christus. Essays in Honour of Raniero Cantalamessa*. Edited by Pier Franco Beatrice and Bernard Pouderon. Paris: Beauchesne.

Mahé, Jean-Pierre. 1971. "Tertullien et l'Epistula Marcionis." *Revue des Sciences religieuses* 45:358–371.

Mahé, Jean-Pierre. éd./trad. 1980. *Tertullien: Contre les Valentiniens*. Tome i, Sources chrétiennes 280. Paris: Éditions du Cerf.

May, Gerhard. 2005. *Markion: Gesammelte Aufsätze*. Edited by Katharina Greschat and Martin Meiser. Mainz: Philipp von Zabern.

May, Gerhard and Katharina Greschat, eds. 2002. *Marcion and His Impact on Church History*. Berlin/New York: De Gruyter.

Moll, Sebastian. 2010. *The Arch-Heretic Marcion*. Tübingen: Mohr Siebeck.

Norelli, Enrico, ed. 2005. *Papia di Hierapolis: Esposizione degli Oracoli del Signore*. Milan: Paoline.

Refoulé, R.F., ed. 1957. *Tertullien: Traité de la prescription contre les hérétiques*. Sources chrétiennes 46. Paris: Éditions du Cerf.

Regul, Jürgen. 1969. *Die antimarcionitischen Evangelienprologe*. Freiburg: Herder.

Roth, Dieter T. 2015. *The Text of Marcion's Gospel*. Leiden: Brill.

Schmid, Ulrich. 1995. *Marcion und sein Apostolos: Rekonstruktion und historische Einordnung der marcionitischen Paulusbriefausgabe*. Berlin/New York: De Gruyter.

Schmid, Ulrich. 2003. "How Can We Access Second Century Gospel Texts? The Case of Marcion and Tatian." Pages 139–150 in *The New Testament Text in Early Christianity: Proceedings of the Lille colloquium, July 2000*. Edited by Christian-Bernard Amphoux and James Keith Elliott. Lausanne: Zèbre.

Schwartz, Eduard. 1908. *Eusebius Kirchengeschichte*. Leipzig: J.C. Hinrich.

Tsutsui, Kenji. 1992. "Das Evangelium Marcions. Ein neuer Versuch der Textrekostruktion." *Annual of the Japanese Biblical Institute* 18:67–132.

Vinzent, Markus. 2013. "Marcion the Jew." *Judaïsme Ancien/Ancient Judaism* 1:159–201.

Vinzent, Markus. 2014. *Marcion and the Dating of the Synoptic Gospels*. Leuven: Peeters.

Vinzent, Markus. 2016. *Tertullian's Preface to Marcion's Gospel*. Leuven: Peeters.

Zwierlein, Otto. 2015. *Die antihäretischen Evangelienprologe und die Entstehung des Neuen Testaments*. Mainz: Akademie der Wissenschaften und der Literatur.

CHAPTER 7

Justin Martyr as an Organic Christian Intellectual in Rome

Fernando Rivas Rebaque

The Apologists, whose development runs almost parallel to that of the Antonines and attained its greatest splendor in this same period, marked a profound innovation in early Christianity: never before had intellectuals played such an important role in this religious movement.[1] In order to investigate some of the elements that supported this innovation, I will use the concept of the "organic intellectual" introduced by the Italian thinker Antonio Gramsci in the early twentieth century, and I will focus on one of the most representative members of the Apologists, Justin.[2]

According to Gramsci, there are two types of intellectuals: organic and traditional. The organic intellectual is one created and established by a social group in order to achieve homogeneity and consciousness within economic, social, cultural and political fields. In certain cases, this intellectual is connected to emerging social movements.[3] By contrast, the traditional intellectual is an "employee" of the socially dominant group, someone who functions to maintain its social hegemony and political power through the creation of social and "spontaneous" consensus, to legitimate its rule and to discipline the groups that disagree with this power.[4]

---

1 Grant 1988, 28–132; Pouderon and Doré 1998; Young 1999; Fiedrowicz 2006, 47–300; Jacobsen 2009, 85–110.

2 Barnard 1967; Osborn 1973; Sanchez 2000; Parvis and Foster 2007; Parvis 2008; Skarsaune 2010.

3 "Ogni gruppo sociale, nascendo sul terreno originario di una funzione essenziale nel mondo della produzione economica, si crea insieme, organicamente, uno o piú ceti di intellettuali che gli danno omogeneità e consapevolezza della propria funzione non solo nel campo economico, ma anche in quello sociale e político ... Gli intellettuali 'organici' che ogni nuova classe crea con se stessa ed elabora nel suo sviluppo progressivo, sono per lo piú 'specializzazioni' di aspetti parziali dell'attività primitiva del tipo sociale nuovo che la nuova classe ha messo in luce", Gramsci 1969, 3–4.

4 "Gli intellettuali sono i 'commessi' del gruppo dominante per l'esercizio delle funzioni subalterne dell'egemonia sociale e del governo politico, cioè: 1) del consenso 'spontaneo' dato dalle grandi masse della popolazione all'indirizzo impresso alla vita sociale dal gruppo fondamentale dominante, consenso che nasce 'storicamente' dal prestigio (e quindi dalla fiducia)

© KONINKLIJKE BRILL NV, LEIDEN, 2020 | DOI:10.1163/9789004428010_009

The historical continuity of these traditional intellectuals renders their ideas characteristically natural, immutable and everlasting. Any group that wants to achieve social control must assimilate and conquer the ideology of traditional intellectuals. These stated goals are obtained with greater speed and efficiency if this group can produce its own organic intellectuals.[5] However, sometimes some intellectuals feel themselves independent of the social group to which they are connected. It is therefore necessary to distinguish between various levels or degrees of their belonging to this social group. Analyzed from these perspectives, Justin could be seen as one of thousands of intellectuals who swarmed though the Roman Empire during the second century, but who then, after his conversion,[6] became an organic intellectual of one of the Christian communities settled in Rome around the mid-century.[7]

Among the many questions that could be asked about Justin as an organic intellectual, I will consider only two: first, what led Justin to act as a Christian organic intellectual? And second: why did the Christian community accept intellectuals of this sort?

1   **What Led Justin to Act as a Christian Organic Intellectual?**

Regarding this first question, it should be noted that not all intellectuals of this time could aspire to enter within the small group of traditional intellectuals, some of which could be considered as members of the Second Sophistic,[8] or find a patron who would subsidize them. Many of them—especially if they had no contact with members of the upper stratum, had not studied at the most famous schools or had no fortune from their parents—were forced to work as freelancers in order to survive as teachers, like Justin, or in other similar jobs.[9]

---

derivante al gruppo dominante dalla sua posizione e dalla sua funzione nel mondo della produzione; 2) dell'apparato di coercizione statale che assicura 'legalmente' la disciplina di quei gruppi che non 'consentono' né attivamente né passivamente, ma è costituito per tutta la società in previsione dei momenti di crisi nel comando e nella direzione in cui il consenso spontaneo vien meno" (Gramsci 1969, 9).

5   Ibid. 7.
6   Skarsaune 1976; Girgenti 1990; Guerra 1992; Hofer, 2003; Aragione 2007.
7   Denning-Bolle 1987; Lampe 2003, 100–103; Parvis 2007.
8   Sirago 1989; Anderson 1993; Goldhill 2001; Whitmarsh 2004; id. 2005; Nasrallah 2005, 283–314, esp. 306–312.
9   Marrou 1948; Snyder 2000.

However, for many Christian intellectuals of the second century, things were easier because certain Christian communities, especially those established in the big cities (Rome, Alexandria, Ephesus or Antioch), became places of hospitality for some of these intellectuals. Such communities were very important for people who often came from distant countries and had no relatives or acquaintances to support them. These communities were also places where they could exercise their own talents, contact other intellectuals, compare their own knowledge with that of others and be recognized for their work. Apart from these communal spaces, these benefits would have been otherwise too difficult to obtain for most of them.[10]

These Christian intellectuals, who had to leave their families and their countries in order to study, could have found in Christian communities a substitute family and, in effect, an open and inclusive country, where differences of race and social status had been relativized by their being part of the same religious movement. In fact, the different *ekklesiai* functioned for such intellectuals as their community patrons, without some of the disadvantages and servility accompanying individual patronage.[11]

If we apply these ideas to Justin, we see that his role as a Christian organic intellectual allows us to make sense of certain topics, such as his geographical mobility, his stay in Rome, and the origin of his *alumni*.

Justin, like many other intellectuals of his time, travelled from Palestine (Samaria) to Asia Minor (Ephesus?) and then from Asia Minor to Rome—three important and significant places for Christian origins. Samaria is the place where the Hellenists went initially when they were expelled from Jerusalem and was probably the homeland of the Johannine movement. Although we have no historical record of Justin's stay in Asia Minor, his knowledge of theological exegesis, unique to Asia Minor, allows us to establish a relationship with this intensely Christianized area. In particular, it is quite probable that Justin was acquainted with Ephesus,[12] given the city's important Hellenistic cultural tradition and flourishing Christian community.[13] In Samaria, and especially in

---

10   *Alexandria*: Griggs 1990, 13–116; Jakab 2001; Martin 2003 and Mimouni 2003. *Rome*: La Piana, 1925, 201–277; Lüdeman 1979. *Antioch*: Grant 1972.

11   Eshleman 2012, 113–121.

12   Although the location of the *Dialogue with Trypo* in Ephesus appears in Eusebius of Caesarea (*Hist. eccl.* 4.8.6), it has not been historically demonstrated. However, some scholars maintain this place for the deep knowledge that Eusebius had of Justin's original text and the references to the gymnasium (Xystos of Ephesus?) in *Dial* 1.1; 9.3, see Archambault 1909, LXVIII–IX; Hyldahl 1966, 91–92, 97–98.

13   Schnabel 1999; Treblico 2004; Tellbe 2009, 111–129.

Ephesus (where Christian schools and teachers existed for a long time), Justin could establish a basis for his new faith and develop many of his own principles.[14]

Justin's stay in Rome may have had the same motivation as that of many intellectuals of his day: the benefits that Rome offered to intellectuals under the Antonines, especially to those who wrote in Greek.[15] These benefits were compounded by the fact that in this period, the Christian communities of Rome, where Justin was welcome, also spoke *koine* Greek.

Most of the students who attended Justin's school[16] would probably have come from Christian communities,[17] giving Justin his economic independence.[18] It was in these Christian communities that Justin's social network was established, in connection and competition with other Christian organic intellectuals of his time.[19] Such networks were common for this type of intellectual[20] and certainly explain theological debates, intellectual challenges and duels with both those inside and outside of the communities that characterized this time period.[21]

To defend his position Justin did not hesitate to present Christianity as "the true philosophy,"[22] to show Christ as teacher and philosopher,[23] and to

---

14 Justin could have received in Samaria many of his scriptural proofs, especially those closest to the Jewish Christian tradition, while may have learned more Hellenistic traditions in Ephesus. See Skarsaune 1987, 25–92; Rokeah 2002, 30–42; Bobichon 2007.

15 Petit 1974, 154–324; Grant 1994; Goodman 1997, 71–80, 149–158; Bowman, Garnsey and Rathbone 2008, 149–176; 875–942.

16 Ulrich 2012 and Georges 2012.

17 Cf. *Martyrium Iustinii* 3.4–8: five men (Chariton, Euelpistus, Hierax, Paion and Liberian) and one woman (Charito), in *The Acts of the Christian Martyrs* (ed. Musurillo), 44 f.; see Lampe 2003, 276–278.

18 Justin's autarchy (*Dial.* 58.1; 82.3) would be part of the *topos* of economic self-sufficiency of philosophers in Antiquity, unless we consider Marcus Pompeius (*Dial.* 141.6) as his patron, something quite difficult to prove.

19 Other Christian intellectuals: Simon the Samaritan (*1Apol.* 26.2), Marcion (*1Apol.* 26.5; 58); "some of these heretics are called Marcionites, some Valetinians, some Basilidians, and some Saturnilians" (*Dial.* 35.6) (translation of *1* and *2Apol.* is based on Minns and Parvis 2009).

20 See Eshleman 2012, 21–66 ("Inclusion and Identity"); Whitmarsh 2004, 90–130 ("Education: Strategies of Self-Making").

21 Therefore, his literary production differentiated between books for those outside (*1 and 2Apol.* [Pagans], *Dial.* [Jews, Jewish Christians]) and for those inside (*Treatise on Heresies*), with common elements.

22 Wilken 1970, 444; Allert 2002, 123–147; Dillon 2002; Wendel 2011, 127–142.

23 Cf. *1Apol.* 4.7; 12.9; 13.3; 15.5; 16.7; 19.6; 21.1; 32.2; *2Apol.* 7.5; *Dial.* 76.3; 101.2; 108.2. See Zanker 1995, 295s.

introduce himself as a philosopher[24] dressed in philosophical garb.[25] Hence the importance of his references to Socrates and certain other philosophers.[26] Some of these claims will be reflected later in early Christian art.[27]

Justin's role as a Christian organic intellectual can be seen especially in his passionate defense of the honor of Christianity and the promotion of its fame. For Justin, Christianity was his authentic family and his true homeland.[28] If some intellectuals of his time had acted as ambassadors to the imperial authorities on behalf of the cities to which they felt especially united,[29] Christian organic intellectuals not only put the word and pen in the service of Christianity, but even gave up their lives for the movement in which they had found the meaning of their existence and for which they felt a deep sense of loyalty (*eusebeia/pietas*).[30]

2 Why Did the Christian Communities Accept Intellectuals of This Sort?

The answer to the question of why the Christian communities accepted intellectuals of this sort is very simple: they needed them. The circumstances, as regards both the outside world and the internal life of the community, had changed greatly over the previous period. Solutions that had previously been effective, had now ceased to be so.

---

24 "Thus it is that I am now a philosopher" (*Dial.* 8.2); "a man [Trypho], accompanied by some friends, came up to me and said, 'Good morning, Philosopher'" (*Dial.* 1.1). The translation of *Dialogue with Trypho* is based on Slusser 2003. See Hyldahl 1966; Van Winden 1971; Lampe 2003, 272–274.

25 Urbano 2014, 184.

26 Cf. *1Apol.* 5.3–4; 46.3; *2Apol.* 3.6–7; 7.3–4; 10.4–8. See Young 1989; Fédou 1998; Skarsaune 1996.

27 Before portraying Christ as teacher, Justin has fashioned a christology that undergirds his teaching and philosophical agendas, continuing and appropriating an already venerable tradition: Christ surrounded by his disciples, showing the hierarchy between teachers and students, with his chair that soon will be occupied by the bishops. See Zanker 1995, 268.

28 The defense of this "family honor" makes sense of the *parrhesia* ("freedom and courage") with which the Apologists, Justin included (*1Apol.* 2–3), write to imperial authorities.

29 Schoedel 1989.

30 Chadwick 1965; Wilken 1970; Haddad 2010.

2.1   *In Connection with the Outside World*

In relation with the outside world, as long as the Christian community remained within the sociological model of sect (i.e. essentially inward-looking), the prophets, the elders and the teachers (the organic intellectuals of this time) were very helpful in building and maintaining community identity.[31]

However, at the beginning of the second century, when Christianity was changing sociologically into a denomination, with greater openness to the outside world, these organic intellectuals, who had focused primarily on the promptings of the Spirit and the study of Scripture,[32] were not able to cope with the new and powerful weapons used by the traditional intellectuals of the dominant culture. These new weapons were based fundamentally on the current *paideia* (oratory and philosophy).[33]

Organic Christian intellectuals could neither respond to the new charge against Christianity—that it was a *nova et malefica superstitio* subverting the roots of the dominant status quo—nor attract the cultured people or the members of the upper stratum. However, both cultured and the elite were necessary for the maintenance of the community in such a competitive (agonistic) society as that of Greco-Roman antiquity.[34]

Therefore, a new type of Christian intellectual was needed, one able to respond to the new situation that was developing. The new times required new exemplary models that would offer a more politically acceptable image of the community. And in the days of the Antonine emperors, who were themselves philosophers,[35] no figure enjoyed greater prestige than the philosopher.[36] So the Christian community opened its doors to people like Justin, who were edu-

---

31   Draper 1995; Clarke 2000, 145–208; Rivas Rebaque 2006.

32   Aune 1993.

33   Bowersock 1969; Swain 1996; Perkins 2009, 17–44.

34   Dorival 1998; Lampe 2003, 274–276; Vaage 2006; Urbano 2013, 6–21.

35   Birley 2008; McLynn 2009.

36   "There is a remarkable saying of a wise man concerning the pleasures of the table to the effect that, 'The first glass quenches thirst, the second makes merry, the third desire kindles, the fourth madness.' But in the case of a draught from the Muses' fountain the reverse is true. The more cups you drink and the more undiluted the draught the better it will be for your soul's good. The first cup is given by the master that teaches you to read and write and redeems you from ignorance, the second is given by the teacher of literature and equips you with learning, the third arms you with the eloquence of the rhetorician. Of these three cups most men drink. I, however, have drunk yet other cups at Athens—the imaginative draught of poetry, the clear draught of geometry, the sweet draught of music, the sharper draught of dialectic, and the nectar of all philosophy, whereof no man may ever drink enough" (Apuleius, *Flor.*, 20 [Butler 1909]). See Zanker 1995, 250–256.

cated (*pepaideumenos*) in high culture and they became the new Christian organic intellectuals, able to assimilate and conquer the dominant ideology of the traditional intellectual.[37]

Cross-culturalism was part of the lives of many of these Christian intellectuals, like Justin—born in Samaria, with its strong Roman influence, and educated in the Greek *paideia*.[38] This cross-cultural background helped Christianity start a complex process of hybridization between its roots (strongly marked by excessively local and foreign traditions) and the extended cultural traditions of the Empire (globally accepted in all places, with local characteristics).[39]

The Apologists, and particularly Justin, were intellectuals used to living on the margins. This social standing enabled them to "parasitize" the culture of their time so as to subvert it, with the usual mix of complicity and resistance that typically occurs in dependent or colonized cultures.[40] This particular mixture can be detected in Justin's ambivalence toward both imperial authority and philosophy: praise and criticism at the same time of both the political and the ideological foundations of the imperial system.[41]

This social and cultural context also allowed the Apologists to develop a series of frontier concepts, usually of a three-dimensional character, able to overcome the binary divisions hitherto predominant. From this time on, virtue would be found in the middle, in this unoccupied emptiness, because this new space (neither Jewish nor pagan) is the saving space where the imagined community will stand.[42]

Christians are going to be neither Barbarian nor Greek, but the third race, a *tertium quid*, a concept that Justin will apply to another field, that of knowl-

---

37 Malherbe 1963; Joly 1973, 9–71; Edwards 1991; Nahm 1992; Droge 2008; Thorsteinsson 2012a; Félix 2014.

38 "Justin, son of Priscus [Latin name] and grandson of Bacchios [Greek name] who both come from Flavia Neapolis in Syria Palaestina" (*1Apol.* 1.1). See Lyman 2003; Rhee 2005, 28–29; Nasrallah 2006; Lampe 2003, 261–272.

39 Bhabha 1994, 39–65; Young 1995, 20–28; Goldhill 2001,13; Boyarin and Burrus 2005; Lyman 2007.

40 Cf. *1Apol.* 54 (pagan mimicry); 59–60 (Plato, disciple of Moses); *Dial.* 2.1–2 and 7 (pagan philosophy versus prophetic true); *1Apol.* 53.1. See Osborn 1966; Helleman 2002; Crépey 2009; Pretila 2014.

41 "Yet we more than all people are your allies and fellow soldiers for peace" (*1Apol.* 12.1) and "for we warn you [Antoninus Pius] that you will not escape the coming judgement of God if you remain in wrong doing" (*1Apol.* 68.2). See Rhee 2005, 164–171 ("Christian Loyalty to the Empire").

42 Anderson 1983, 12–19; Moxnes, 2003, 12–15, 108–110.

edge.[43] Here, neither Greek reason (*logos*: *1Apol.* 68.1), nor Jewish scriptural techniques (*technê*) applied only to locate proofs (*Dial.* 58.1), will allow one to understand the hidden meaning of Scripture. The articulation of this *tertium quid* may only be done by the grace (*cháris*) that God gives to Justin himself (*Dial.* 9.1) and to certain Christians (*Dial.* 92.1).[44]

2.2   *In Connection with the Inner World of the Christian Community*

The emergence of this kind of organic intellectual was also favored by the internal needs of the communities themselves. The communities needed to compete not only with the distant "other" (pagans), but also with the close "other" (Jews), and—a novelty of the second century—the "other" from within (heretics). Hence the Apologists were required to battle, facing three separate and distinguishable directions.[45]

The Apologists, Justin especially, maintained a relatively respectful attitude to the outside (pagan) "other," at least as it regards social and written formalities.[46] The Apologists radically attacked arguments enabling not only the persecution of Christians, but also the moral and religious practices of the pagans,[47] against whom they utilized a strategy of terror (eternal punishment for those who did not convert).[48] However, they were careful not to burn their bridges or close the borders prematurely, because it was from the pagan world that they expected future Christians to come; and also because they basically shared the same *paideia* (although radically reformulated in the case of Christians).[49]

This element of respect was for the most part absent from their relationship with the close (Jewish) "other," with whom the Apologists shared the religious matrix (especially their biblical subculture).[50] It was just this closeness and similarity that made conflicts more virulent. This was due among other issues to the fact that Christians needed to prevent possible infiltrations into their ranks and to avoid being confused with the Jews, of whom the pagans had a neg-

---

43   Lieu 2004, 104–108, 257–266.
44   Pycke 1961; Joly 1973, 94–113; Wendel 2011, 97–102.
45   Bobichon 1999.
46   Munier 1988 and 1989; Thorsteinsson 2012b, 91–114.
47   Cf. *1Apol.* 9; *2Apol.* 12.5.
48   Cf. *1Apol.* 12.2–4; 17.4; 18.1–2; 21.6; 28.1; 45.6. See Joly 1973, 155–170 ("Le doux Justin").
49   Holte 1958; Price 1988.
50   Barnard 1964; De Vogel 1978; Droge 1987; Misiarczyk 1999; Presley 2014.

ative image. Moreover, both Jews and Christians were competing to attract the same public, as they had previously fought for the interest of the "God-fearing" or "proselyte" pagans.[51]

The organic intellectual played a central role in this conflict between Jews and Christians, as we can see in the case of Justin regarding two themes: his ambivalent view of Judaism and his reduction of the conflict to an "academic" level.[52]

The ambivalence with which Justin portrayed the imperial system is now applied to Judaism: praising it for its antiquity, but criticizing it for having failed to discover the hidden Messiah[53] and for remaining tied to obsolete laws and customs.[54] The same reconstruction that Justin had carried out with philosophy and *paideia*, he will now apply to the Hebrew Scriptures: he will accept them, but give them a different sense, accusing the Jews of not being faithful to them and of being unable to understand them.[55]

As for the second theme, the Apologists tried to focus the conflict on Jewish teachers. Thus, Justin accused them of having caused the division between Jews and Christians and of continuing to maintain hostilities.[56] In a similar way, the problems are set out in "academic" terms and presented only as a struggle of biblical interpretations among experts, something to which Apologists and Jewish teachers were accustomed.[57] Suggestive, in this sense, is the parallel between the emergence of the Christian Apologists and the strengthening of the role of the rabbis in Judaism, as if both were linked and needed each other.[58]

However, the competition with the close "other" (Jews), although it reached its peak in the early second century, was being gradually replaced from mid-century onwards by the fight with the inside "other" (heretics), in which Justin played a key role.[59]

Religious boundaries in the second century were porous, not only between the different groups (Jews, Christians, pagans), but also—and mainly—within

---

51   Remus 1986; Stanton 1998; Boyarin 2001.

52   Osborn 1973, 111–119; Lieu, 1996, 136–148; Horner 2001, 130–145; Eshleman 2012, 236.

53   Cf. *Dial.* 31–32; 36–38; 40; 48–108. See Higgins 1967; Trakatellis 1976; Misiarczyk 1999, 166–240; Lieu 1996, 124–129.

54   Cf. *Dial.* 11–12; 27–29. See Stylianopoulos 1975; Wilson 1995, esp. 258–284; Lieu 1996, 113–124.

55   Cf. *Dial.* 20.1.3; 27.2; 29.2; 32.4. See Shotwell 1965, 71–115; Martín 1977; Horner 2001, 147–165; Manns 1977, 130–152; Otranto 1987; Chilton 2007.

56   Cf. *Dial.* 9.1; 38.1–2; 48.2; 112.5; 117.3, 137.2. See Horner 2001, 130–136; Bobichon 2002; Lieu 1996, 129–132.

57   Aune 1966; Otranto 1976 and 1977; Misiarczyk 1999, 113–165; Skarsaune 2007.

58   Boyarin 2006, 37–73.

59   Cf. *1Apol.* 26; *Dial.* 35.2–6; 80.2–5. See Prigent 1964; Le Boulluec 1985, 37–91.

them. Hence the groups needed to maintain community identity and to control the definition of reality both inside and outside the group.[60] This task was more necessary for Christians because they had eliminated most of the ethnic boundaries that were still maintained by the Jews, making differentiation very difficult for the Christians.[61]

Missionary openness to the outside, with the inevitable mixture this produces, brought with it the risk of loss and confusion of identity. And the Apologists, as new "intelligentsia," were one of the groups responsible for mapping out who was outside and who was inside, what was truth and what was false.[62] They had the power of labeling and of constructing the right Christian identity (orthodoxy) against other false Christian identities (the heretics, from *heteros*, the "other"), who also made a claim to authenticity.[63]

Thus, in the same way that Justin had engaged with philosophy and Judaism, he will now engage with heretics:[64] salvation for Justin and orthodox Christianity will be found in the right balance between rigid continuity (Jewish Christian) and the discontinuity that broke with tradition (Marcion).[65]

This differentiation between orthodox and heretical groups became extremely complex, especially in large cities such as Rome, where there were multiple Christian communities that often coexisted with little (if not, indeed, odd and strange) contact with each other.[66] Many schools and Christian teachers,[67] all with pretensions of truth, were also very scattered, a condition greatly facilitated by the lack of a mono-episcopate until the late second century.[68] In this respect, the situation in Alexandria was very similar.[69]

---

60   Lieu 2004, 1–26; Perkins 2010; Iricinschi and Zellentin 2008, 1–27.

61   Lieu 2002, 49–68; id. 2004, 126–146; Eshleman 2012, 33.

62   Justin explicitly says that "they [the heretics] are not really Christians" (*1Apol.* 16.8), and he calls them "Christians only in name" (*1Apol.* 16.14). Vinzent 2008, esp. 397–401.

63   Ulrich 2009; Lieu 2004, 267.

64   Norris 1998, esp. 45–50; Royalty 2006; Choi 2010; Eshleman 2012, 217 ff.

65   Cf. *1Apol.* 26.4–8. See Räisänen 2005; Norelli 2009; Moll 2010, 147–152; Lieu 2015, 15–25, 293–322; Cherubini 2011.

66   Lampe 2003, 359–365, 383–393; Thomassen 2004; Vinzent 2008, 399–406.

67   Bardy 1932; Neymeyr 1989; Markschies 2002; Amata 2006; Vinzent 2008, 406–411.

68   In the middle of the second century many of the Christian *ekklesiai* were governed by the mono-episcopacy, which had focused functions previously performed by itinerant prophets and teachers. However, some cities, such as Alexandria and Rome, were led by a presbyterial and collegial government, with different presidents in each community (see *1Apol.* 65.3). This context made possible the emergence and survival of lay Christian teachers. See Maier 2002, 55–197 Pietri 2000, 420–434; Stewart 2014, 187–352.

69   Bardy 1937 and 1942; Tuilier 1982; Van den Broek 1995; Van den Hoek 1997; Le Boulluec 1999; Pietri 2000, 531–578 (Alain Le Boulluec, 'L'École d'Alexandrie'); Rivas Rebaque 2007.

Apart from these "policing" functions, the Apologists helped many of the illiterate classes (*idiotai*, who composed most of the Christian communities in this period) to connect with the esoteric knowledge, not only of Christianity itself, but also of the Jewish and pagan world.[70] This forced the different intelligentsia to remain in contact with one another, in most cases competitively (see Heidi Wendt's essay in this volume). Symptomatic of this situation are, for example, Justin's debates with the philosopher Crescens[71] and with the Jew Trypho.[72]

Another function of the Apologists was to bring their own written traditions, based primarily on Scripture, into contact with the oral traditions of previous organic intellectuals (prophets, teachers and elders),[73] and with Jewish[74] and pagan traditions.[75] This latter task required special preparation and expertise—another example of the three-dimensional vision of Justin. We can see that Justin became an expert in this type of exchange from his use of OT proof texts and the fluidity between the Gospel and the *Apomnêmoneúmata*.[76] In this way, the Apologists contributed to the creation of textual communities based on Scripture.[77]

3   Conclusions

The Apologists, who became the new organic intellectuals of Christian communities during the second century and adapted perfectly to this role, lost their usefulness at the end of the century, thereby becoming venerable relics or vanishing behind their writings, which became a literary genre functional for only certain contexts.[78]

However, social circumstances changed radically and, after the second century—for many, the best time of the Empire, given the prominence of the

---

70   In fact, Justin revalues the role of the *idiotai* in Christianity (*1Apol.* 39.3; 60.11; *2Apol.* 10.3). See Eshleman 2012, 103.
71   *2Apol.* 8.1–5. See Malherbe 1981; Thorsteinsson 2013.
72   Cf. Schneider 1962; Hirshman 1992/1993; Horner 2001, 147–165.
73   Barnard 1967, 54–74.
74   Rajak 1999.
75   Eshleman 2012, 28–31.
76   Cf. Piper 1961; Bellinzoni 1967; Osborn 1973, 120–138; Abramowski 1991, 323–335; Cosgrove 1982; Pryor 1992; Allert 2002, 188–220; Aragione 2004; Hill 2007.
77   Stock 1983 and 1990; Judge 2008.
78   Origen, with his *Adverus Celsum* and his *Hexapla*, represents the bridge between these two periods.

Antonine dynasty and its philosopher emperors—a new crisis arose in the third century with the Severi, who were basically occupied in the defense of the Empire. The character of the emperor would now be more authoritarian, and even militaristic; bad times for philosophy and culture, and for those who represented them.[79]

In addition, at the end of the second century and early third century, the bishops already presided over community celebrations such as the Eucharist and over the internal life of the community. Sometimes they functioned as judges within the Christian community and developed into the dominant social figures of Christian memory. Bishops played the role of patres familias and even as community patrons, in this way becoming convincing and resolute leaders for times of crisis.[80]

In fact, in the late second century, the bishops did not need the Apologists because the bishops could exercise most of the functions previously carried out by the Apologists. Trained in *paideia* and born into the upper stratum, the new bishops were able to exercise these functions (in public spaces) with greater competence than the Apologists (in private spaces), and they were better equipped for action and for governing people.[81]

Enjoying their situation as organic intellectuals, the Apologists had not been overly concerned about their own continuity, unlike the bishops and the rabbis with their succession narratives such as episcopal and rabbinic lists.[82] The Apologists had not generated doctrines (*didágmata*) that could become *traditio* or a *regula fidei*, and the plurality of their thought, their independence, and their segmentation into different schools (*didaskaleia*)[83] prevented the necessary homogeneity that could have served as a secure channel of transmission.[84]

In addition, there was no place for competition between the Apologists and the bishops because the Apologists were mere lay teachers, accustomed to private teaching with a small number of students in small schools. In the third century, the bishops, especially since the advent of the new Christian build-

---

79   Dal Covolo 1989; Dal Covolo and Rinaldi 1999; Pietri 2000, 256–265; Swain, Harrison and Elsner 2007, 401–418, 470–488.

80   Brent 1995, 458–540; Faivre 1977, 118–130; Saxer 2000, 777–816.

81   On differences, complementarities and conflicts between private and profane space (schools) and public and sacral space (*ekklesiai*) see Faivre 1992, 216–230; Snyder 2007; Eshleman 2012, 24–26; Rivas Rebaque 2015, esp. 112–120. The excommunication of Theodotus the Cobbler makes sense in this context (see Eusebius, *Hist. eccl.* 5.28).

82   Javierre 1967; Brent 1993; Eshleman 2012, 177–258, esp., 177 f.; 235 f.

83   See footnotes 67 and 69, also Pouderon 1998.

84   Van den Eynde 1933, 282–311; Kelly 1972, 62–99; Hanson 2006.

ing (*domus ecclesiae*), became the perfect orators used to speaking to crowds within the boundaries of a consecrated space.[85]

Therefore, history has preserved the works of only a few Apologists, who, in the third century and after, were converted by the collective memory into exemplary models. This was especially true for those Apologists who did not discuss the new church order or whose martyrdom had demonstrated absolute fidelity to Christianity.[86] In both respects, Justin was poised to assume a prominent role in Christian memory.

Bibliography

Abramowski, Luise. 1991. "The 'Memoirs of the Apostles' in Justin." Pages 323–335 in *The Gospel and the Gospels*. Edited by Peter Stuhlmacher. Grand Rapids, Mich.: Eerdmans.

Allert, Craig D. 2002. *Revelation, Truth, Canon, and Interpretation. Studies in Justin Martyr's Dialogue with Trypho*. Leiden: Brill.

Amata, Biagio. 2006. "Scuola." *Nuovo Dizionario Patristico e di Antichità christiane*, 1, cols 4813–4823. Edited by Angelo di Berardino. Genova/Milan: Marietti.

Anderson, Graham. 1993. *The Second Sophistic. A Cultural Phenomenon in the Roman Empire*. London/New York: Routledge.

Anderson, Benedict. 1983. *Imagined Communities. Reflections on the Origin and Spread of Nationalism*. London/New York: Verso.

Aragione, Gabriella. 2004. "Justin 'philosophe' chrétien et les 'Mémoires des Apôtres qui sont apellés Evangiles.'" *Apocrypha* 15:41–56.

Aragione, Gabriella. 2007. "Justin de Naplouse devient Justin Martyr (*1Apologie* 2, 4)." *Revue de théologie et de philosophie* 139:127–141.

Archambault, George. 1909. *Justin. Dialogue avec Tryphon*. Vol. 1. Paris: Alphonse Picard.

Aune, David E. 1966. "Justin Martyr's Use of the Old Testament." *Bulletin of the Evangelical Theological Society* 9:179–197.

Aune, David E. 1993. "Charismatic Exegesis in Early Judaism and Early Christianity." Pages 126–150 in *The Pseudoepigrapha and Early Biblical Interpretation*. Edited by James H. Charlesworth and Craig A. Evans. Sheffield: JSOT Press.

Bardy, Gustave. 1932. "Les écoles romaines au second siècle." *Revue d'histoire ecclésiastique* 28:501–532.

---

85   Countryman 1979; Brent 1995, 368.
86   The life (and the texts) of martyrs such as Ignatius, Polycarp, Justin, and Perpetua and Felicitas will acquire a special value in relation to the collective memory of Christianity.

Bardy, Gustave. 1937. "Aux origines de l'École d'Alexandrie." *Recherches de science religieuse* 27:65–90.

Bardy, Gustave. 1942. "Pour l'histoire de l'École d'Alexandrie." *Vivre et Penser* 2:80–109.

Barnard, Leslie W. 1964. "The Old Testament and Judaism in the Writings of Justin Martyr." *Vetus Testamentum* 14:395–406.

Barnard, Leslie W. 1967. *Justin Martyr: His Life and Thought.* Cambridge: Cambridge University Press.

Bellinzoni, Arthur J. 1967. *The Sayings of Jesus in the Writings of Justin Martyr.* Leiden: Brill.

Bhabha, Homi K. 1994. *The Location of Culture.* London/New York: Routledge.

Birley, Anthony. 2008. "Hadrian to the Antonines." Pages 132–194 in Bowman and Rathbone 2008.

Bobichon, Philippe. 1999. "Les enseignements juif, païen, hérétique et chrétien dans l'oeuvre de Justin Martyr." *Revue des Études Augustiniennes* 45:233–259.

Bobichon, Philippe. 2002. "Autorités religieuses juives et 'sectes' juives dans l'oeuvre de Justin Martyr." *Revue des Études Augustiniennes* 48:3–22.

Bobichon, Philippe. 2007. "Comment Justin a-t-il acquis sa connaissance exceptionelle des exégèses juives?" *Revue de théologie et de philosophie* 139:101–126.

Bowersock, Glen W. 1969. *Greek Sophists in the Roman Empire.* Oxford: Clarendon Press.

Bowman, Alan K., Peter Garnsey, and Dominic Rathbone, eds. 2008. *The Cambridge Ancient History, XI: The High Empire, A.D. 70–192,* 2nd ed. Cambridge: Cambridge University Press.

Boyarin, Daniel. 2001. "Justin Martyr Invents Judaism." *Church History* 70:427–461.

Boyarin, Daniel. 2006. *Border Lines. The Partition of Judaeo-Christianity.* Philadelphia: University of Pennsylvania Press.

Boyarin, Daniel and Virginia Burrus. 2005. "Hybridity as Subversion of Orthodoxy? Jews and Christians in Late Antiquity." *Social Compass* 52:431–441.

Brent, Allen. 1993. "Diogenes Laertius and the Apostolic Succession." *Journal of Ecclesiastical History* 44:367–389.

Brent, Allen. 1995. *Hippolytus and the Roman Church in the Third Century. Communities in Tension before the Emergence of a Monarch-Bishop.* Leiden: Brill.

Butler, Harold Edgeworth, trans. 1909. *The Apologia and Florida of Apuleius of Madaura.* Oxford: Clarendon Press.

Chadwick, Henry. 1965. "Justin Martyr's Defence of Christianity." *Bulletin of the John Rylands Library* 47:275–297.

Cherubini, Beatrice. 2011. "Remarques sur le personage Marcion dans l'interprétation de Justin Martyr: un pseudoprophète (ΨΕΥΔΟΠΡΟΦΗΤΗΣ)?" *Apocrypha* 22:233–252.

Chilton, Bruce. 2007. "Justin and Israelite Prophecy." Pages 77–87 in *Justin Martyr and His Worlds.* Edited by Sara Parvis and Paul Foster. Minneapolis: Fortress Press.

Choi, Michael J. 2010. "What is Christian Orthodoxy according to Justin's *Dialogue?*" *Scottish Journal of Theology* 63: 398–413.

Clarke, Andrew D. 2000. *Serve the Community of the Church. Christians as Leaders and Ministers.* Grand Rapids, Mich./Cambridge: Eerdmans.

Cosgrove, Charles H. 1982. "Justin Martyr and the Emerging Christian Canon. Observations on the Purpose and Destination of the *Dialogue with Trypho.*" *Vigiliae Christianae* 36:209–332.

Countryman, L. William. 1979. "The Intellectual Role of the Early Catholic Episcopate." *Church History* 48:261–268.

Crépey, Cyrille. 2009. "Marc Aurèle et Justin Martyr: deux discours sur la raison." *Revue d'histoire et de philosophie religieuses* 89:51–77.

Dal Covolo, Enrico. 1989. *I Severi e il cristianesimo: ricerche sull'ambiente storio-istituzionale delle origini cristiane tra il secondo e il terzo secolo* Rome: Libreria Ateneo Salesiano.

Dal Covolo, Enrico and Giancarlo Rinaldi, eds. 1999. *Gli imperatori Severi. Storia, archeologia, religione.* Rome: Libreria Ateneo Salesiano.

De Vogel, Cornelia J. 1978. "Problems Concerning Justin Martyr: Did Justin Find a Certain Continuity between Greek Philosophy and Christian Faith?" *Mnemosyne* 31:360–388.

Denning-Bolle, Sara J. 1987. "Christian Dialogue as Apologetic: The Case of Justin Martyr seen in Historical Context." *Bulletin of the John Rylands Library* 69:492–519.

Dillon, John. 2002. "The Social Role of the Philosopher in the Second Century C.E.: Some Remarks." Pages 29–40 in *Sage and Emperor: Plutarch, Greek Intellectuals, and Roman Power in the Time of Trajan.* Edited by Philip A. Stadter and Luc van der Stockt. Leuven: Press Universitaires.

Dorival, Gilles. 1998. "L' Apologétique chrétienne et la culture grecque." Pages 423–435 in *Les Apologistes chrétiens et la culture grecque.* Edited by Bernard Pouderon and Joseph Doré. Paris: Beauchesne.

Draper, Jonathan A. 1995. "Social Ambiguity and the Production of Text: Prophets, Teachers, Bishops, and Deacons and the Development of the Jesus Tradition in the Community of the *Didache.*" Pages 284–312 in *The Didache in Context. Essays on its Text, History, and Transmission.* Edited by Clayton N. Jefford. Leiden: Brill.

Droge, Arthur J. 1987. "Justin Martyr and the Restoration of Philosophy." *Church History* 56:303–319.

Droge, Arthur J. 2008. "Self-definition vis-à-vis the Graeco-Roman World." Pages 230–244 in *The Cambridge History of Christianity I: Origins to Constantine.* Edited by Margaret M. Mitchell and Francis M. Young. Cambridge: Cambridge University Press.

Edwards, Mark J. 1991. "On the Platonic Schooling of Justin Martyr." *Journal of Theological Studies* 42:17–34.

Eshleman, Kendra. 2012. *The Social World of Intellectuals in the Roman Empire. Sophists, Philosophers, and Christians. Greek Culture in the Roman World*. Cambridge/New York: Cambridge University Press.

Faivre, Alexandre. 1977. *Naissance d'une hiérarchie. Les premières étapes du cursus clerical*. Paris: Éd. Beauchesne.

Faivre, Alexandre. 1992. *Ordonner la fraternité. Pouvoir d'innover et retour à l'ordre dans l'Église ancienne*. Paris: Editions du Cerf.

Fédou, Michel. 1998. "La figure de Socrate selon Justin." Pages 51–66 in *Les Apologistes chrétiens et la culture grecque*. Edited by Bernard Pouderon and Joseph Doré. Paris: Beauchesne.

Félix, Viviana Laura. 2014. "Las filosofías en la teología de Justino Mártir." *Teología y vida* 55:435–448.

Fiedrowicz, Michael. 2006. *Apologie im frühen Christentum. Die Kontroverse um den christlichen Wahrheitsanspruch in den ersten Jahrhunderten*, 3rd ed. Paderborn/Munich/Vienna/Zürich: Schöningh.

Georges, Tobias. 2012. "Justin's School in Rome. Reflections on Early Christian 'Schools.'" *Zeitschrift für antikes Christentum* 16:75–87.

Girgenti, Giuseppe. 1990. "Giustino Martire, il primo platonico Cristiano." *Rivista di filosofia neo-scolastica* 2–3:214–255.

Goldhill, Simon, ed. 2001. *Being Greek under Rome. Cultural Identity, the Second Sophistic, and the Development of Empire*. Cambridge: Cambridge University Press.

Goodman, Martin. 1997. *The Roman World, 44 BC–AD 180*. London/New York: Routledge.

Gramsci, Antonio. 1969. *Gli intellettuali e l'organizzazzione della cultura*, 8th ed. Torino: Giulio Einaudi Editore.

Grant, Michael. 1994. *The Antonines. The Roman Empire in Transition*. London/New York: Routledge.

Grant, Robert M. 1972. "Jewish Christianity at Antioch in the Second Century." *Recherches de science religieuse* 60:97–108.

Grant, Robert M. 1988. *Greek Apologists of the Second Century*. London: SCM Press.

Griggs, C. Wilfred. 1990. *Early Egyptian Christianity from Its Origins to 451 CE*. Leiden/New York: Brill.

Guerra, Anthony J. 1992. "The Conversion of Marcus Aurelius and Justin Martyr. The Purpose, Genre, and Content of the First Apology." *Second Century* 9:171–187.

Haddad, Robert M. 2010. *The Case for Christianity. Saint Justin Martyr's Arguments for Religious Liberty and Judicial Justice*. Boulder, Colo.: Taylor Trade.

Hanson, Richard P.C. 2006. "Confessioni e simboli di fede." Pages 1154–1162 in *Nuovo Dizionario Patristico e di Antichità christiane*, I. Edited by Angelo di Berardino. Genoa/Milan: Marietti.

Helleman, Wendy E. 2002. "Justin Martyr and the Logos: an Apologetical Strategy." *Philosophia Reformata* 67:128–147.

Higgins, J.B. 1967. "Jewish Messianic Belief in Justin Martyr's *Dialogue with Trypho*." *Novum Testamentum* 9:298–305.

Hill, Charles E. 2007. "Was John's Gospel among Justin's Apostolic Memoirs?" Pages 88–94 in *Justin Martyr and His Worlds*. Edited by Sara Parvis and Paul Foster. Minneapolis: Fortress Press.

Hirshman, Marc. 1993. "Polemic Literary Units in the Classical Midrashim and Justin Martyr's *Dialogue with Trypho*." *Jewish Quarterly Review* 83:369–384.

Holte, Ragitak. 1958. "Logos Spermatikos, Christianity and Ancient Philosophy According to St. Justin's Apologies." *Studia Theologica* 12:109–168.

Hofer, Andrew. 2003. "The Old Man as Christ in Justin's *Dialogue with Trypho*." *Vigiliae Christianae* 57:1–21.

Horner, Timothy J. 2001. *Listening to Trypho. Justin Martyr's Dialogue Reconsidered*. Leuven: Peeters.

Hyldahl, Niels. 1966. *Philosophie und Christentum. Ein Interpretation der Einleitung zum Dialog Justin*. Copenhagen: Munksgaard.

Iricinschi, Eduard and Holger M. Zellentin, eds. 2008. *Heresy and Identity in Late Antiquity*. Tübingen: Mohr Siebeck.

Jacobsen, Anders-Christian. 2009. "Main Topics in Early Christian Apologetics." Pages 85–111 in *Critique and Apologetics: Jews, Christians and Pagans in Antiquity*. Edited by Anders-Christian Jacobsen, Jörg Ulrich, and David Brakke. Frankfurt am Main: Peter Lang.

Jakab, Attila. 2001. *Ecclesia alexandrina. Évolution sociale et institutionelle du christianisme alexandrine (IIᵉ et IIIᵉ siècles)*. New York: Peter Lang.

Javierre, Antonio M. 1967. *El tema literario de la sucesión en el judaísmo, helenismo y cristianismo primitivo*. Zürich: Pas.

Joly, Robert. 1973. *Christianisme et philosophie. Études sur Justin et les Apologistes grecs du deuxième siècle*. Brussels: Éditions de l'Université de Bruxelles.

Judge, Edwin A. 2008. "The Early Christians as a Scholastic Community." Pages 526–552 in *The First Christians in the Roman World: Augustan and New Testament Essays*. Edited by James R. Harrison. Tübingen: Mohr Siebeck.

Justin Martyr. *Dialogue with Trypho*. See Slusser 2003.

Kelly, John N.D. 1972. *Early Christian Creeds*, 3rd ed. London/New York: Continuum.

Lampe, Peter. 2003. *From Paul to Valentinus. Christians at Rome in the First Two Centuries*. Translated by Michael Steinhauser. Edited by Marshall Johnson. Minneapolis: Fortress Press.

La Piana, George. 1925. "The Roman Church at the End of the Second Century." *Harvard Theological Review* 18:201–277.

Le Boulluec, Alain. 1985. *La notion d'hérésie dans la littérature grecque: IIᵉ–IIIᵉ siècles, 1. De Justin à Irénée*. Paris: Études Augustiennes.

Le Boulluec, Alain. 1999. "Aux origins encore de l'école d'Alexandrie." *Adamantius* 5:8–36.

Le Boulluec, Alain. 2000. "L'École d'Alexandrie." Pages 531–578 in Pietri and Le Boulluec 2000.

Lieu, Judith M. 1996. *Image and Reality. The Jews in the World of the Christians in the Second Century*, Edinburgh: T&T Clark.

Lieu, Judith M. 2002. *Neither Jew nor Greek? Constructing Early Christianity*. London: T&T Clark.

Lieu, Judith M. 2004. *Christian Identity in the Jewish and Graeco-Roman World*. Oxford: Oxford University Press.

Lieu, Judith M. 2015. *Marcion and the Marking of a Heretic. God and Scripture in the Second Century*. Cambridge: Cambridge University Press.

Lüdeman, Gerd. 1979. "Zur Geschichte des ältesten Christentums in Rome." *Zeitschrift für die neutestamentliche Wissenschaft und die Kunde der älteren Kirche* 70:86–114.

Lyman, Rebecca. 2003. "The Politics of Passing: Justin Martyr's Conversion as a Problem of 'Hellenization.' " Pages 34–54 in *Conversion in Late Antiquity and the Early Middle Ages: Seeing and Believing*. Edited by Kenneth Mills and Anthony Grafton. Rochester: University of Rochester Press.

Lyman, Rebecca. 2007. "Justin and Hellenism. Some Postcolonial Perspectives." Pages 160–168 in *Justin Martyr and His Worlds*. Edited by Sara Parvis and Paul Foster. Minneapolis: Fortress Press.

Maier, Harry O. 2002. *The Social Setting of the Ministry as Reflected in the Writings of Hermas, Clement and Ignatius*. Waterloo: Wilfrid Laurier University Press.

Malherbe, Abraham J. 1963. "Apologetic and Philosophy in the Second Century." *Restoration Quarterly* 7:19–32.

Malherbe, Abraham J. 1981. "Justin and Crescens." Pages 312–327 in *Christian Teaching: Studies in Honor of LeMoine G. Lewis*. Edited by Everett Ferguson. Abilene: Abilene Christian University.

Manns, Fréderic. 1977. *Essais sur le Judéo-Christianisme*. Jerusalem: Franciscan Printing Press.

Markschies, Christoph. 2002. "Lehrer, Schüler, Schule: Zur Bedeutung einer Institution für das antike Christentum." Pages 97–120 in *Religiöse Vereine in der römischen Antike: Untersuchungen zu Organisation, Ritual und Raumordnung*. Edited by Ulrike Egelhaaf-Gaiser, Alfred Schäfer, and Jörg Rüpke. Tübingen: Mohr Siebeck.

Marrou, Henri Irénée. 1948. *Histoire de l'éducation dans l'Antiquité*. Paris: Éditions du Seuil.

Martin, Annick. 2003. "Aux origins de l'Alexandrie chrétienne: topographie, liturgie, institutions." Pages 105–121 in *Origeniana octava. Origen and the Alexandrian Tradition. Papers of the 8th International Origen Congress. Pisa, 27–31 August, 2001*. Edited by Lorenzo Perrone. Leuven: Leuven University Press.

Martín, José Pablo. 1977. "Hermenéutica en el cristianismo y en el judaísmo según el 'Diálogo' de Justino." *Revista Bíblica* 39:327–344.

McLynn, Frank. 2009. *Marcus Aurelius: Warrior, Philosopher, Emperor*. London: Bodley Head.

Mimouni, Simon Claude. 2003. "À la recherche de la communauté chrétienne d'Alexandrie aux Ier–IIe siècles." Pages 137–175 in *Origeniana octava. Origen and the Alexandrian Tradition. Papers of the 8th International Origen Congress. Pisa, 27–31 August, 2001*. Edited by Lorenzo Perrone. Leuven: Leuven University Press.

Minns, Denis and Paul Parvis, eds. 2009. *Justin, Philosopher and Martyr: Apologies*. Oxford: Oxford University Press.

Misiarczyk, Leszek. 1999. *Il midrash nel 'Dialogo con Trifone' di Giustino Martire*. Plock: Instytut Wydawniczy.

Moll, Sebastian. 2010. *The Arch-Heretic Marcion*. Tübingen: Mohr Siebeck.

Moxnes, Halvor. 2003. *Putting Jesus in His Place. A Radical Vision of Household and Kingdom*. Louisville/London: Westminster John Knox Press.

Munier, Charles. 1988 and 1989. "La méthode apologétique de Justin le Martyr." *Revue de sciences religieuses*. 62:90–100 and 63:227–239.

Musurillo, Herbert, ed. 1972. *The Acts of the Christian Martyrs*. Oxford: Oxford University Press.

Nahm, Charles. 1992. "The Debate on the 'Platonism' of Justin Martyr." *Second Century* 9:129–151.

Nasrallah, Laura. 2005. "Mapping the World: Justin, Tatian, Lucian, and the Second Sophistic." *Harvard Theological Review* 98:283–314.

Nasrallah, Laura. 2006. "The Rhetoric of Conversion and the Construction of Experience. The Case of Justin Martyr." Studia Patristica 40:467–474.

Neymeyr, Ulrich. 1989. *Die christlichen Lehrer im zweiten Jahrhundert: Ihre Lehrtätigkeit, ihr Selbstverständnis und ihre Geschichte*. Leiden: Brill.

Norelli, Enrico. 2009. "Marcione e la costruzione dell'eresia come fenomeno universale in Giustino Martire." *Rivista di storia di cristianesimo* 6:363–388.

Norris, Richard A. 1998. "Heresy and Orthodoxy in the Later Second Century." *Union Seminary Quarterly Review* 52:43–59.

Osborn, Eric Francis. 1966. "Justin's Response to Second Century Challenges." *Australian Biblical Review* 14:37–54.

Osborn, Eric Francis. 1973. *Justin Martyr*. Tübingen: Mohr Siebeck.

Otranto, Giorgio. 1976. "Metodo delle citazioni bibliche ed esegesi nei capitoli 63–65 del 'Dialogo con Trifone.'" *Vetera Christianorum* 13:83–113.

Otranto, Giorgio. 1977. *Esegesi biblica e storia in Giustino (Dial. 63–84)*. Bari: Istituto di Literatura Cristiana Antica.

Otranto, Giorgio. 1987. "La terminología esegetica in Giustino." *Vetera Christianorum* 24:23–43.

Parvis, Paul. 2008. "Justin Martyr." *Expository Times* 120:53–61.

Parvis, Sara. 2007. "Justin Martyr and the Apologetic Tradition." Pages 115–127 in *Justin*

Martyr and His Worlds. Edited by Sara Parvis and Paul Foster. Minneapolis: Fortress Press.

Parvis, Sara and Paul Foster, eds. 2007. *Justin Martyr and His Worlds*. Minneapolis: Fortress Press.

Perkins, Judith. 2009. *Roman Imperial Identities in the Early Christian Era*. London/New York: Routledge.

Perkins, Pheme. 2010. "Schism and Heresy. Identity, Cracks, and Canyons in Early Christianity." Pages 227–238 in *The Routledge Companion to Early Christian Thought*. Edited by D. Jeffrey Bingham. London/New York: Routledge.

Petit, Paul. 1974. *Histoire Général de l'Empire Romain*. Paris: Éditions du Seuil.

Pietri, Luce and Alain Le Boulluec, eds. 2000. *Histoire du christianisme 1: Le nouveau peuple. Des origines à 250*. Paris: Desclée.

Piper, Otto A. 1961. "The Nature of the Gospel According to Justin Martyr." *The Journal of Religion* 41:155–168.

Pouderon, Bernard. 1998. "Réflexions sur la formation d'une élite intellectuelle chrétienne au IIe siècle: les 'Écoles' d'Athènes, de Rome et d'Alexandrie." Pages 237–269 in *Les Apologistes chrétiens et la culture grecque*. Edited by Bernard Pouderon and Joseph Doré. Paris: Beauchesne.

Pouderon, Bernard and Joseph Doré, eds. 1998. *Les Apologistes chrétiens et la culture grecque*. Paris: Beauchesne.

Presley, Stephen O. 2014. "A Loftier Doctrine: The Use of Scripture in Justin Martyr's Second Apology." *Perichoresis* 12:185–200.

Pretila, Noël Wayne. 2014. *Re-Appropriating "Marvellous Fables": Justin Martyr's Strategic Retrieval of Myth in 1 Apology*. Cambridge: James Clarke.

Price, Richard M. 1988. "'Hellenization' and Logos Doctrine in Justin Martyr." *Vigiliae Christianae* 42:18–23.

Prigent, Pierre. 1964. *Justin et l'Ancient Testament. L'argumentation scripturaire du traité de Justin Contre toutes les hérésies comme source principale du Dialogue avec Tryphon et de la Première Apologie*. Paris: Éd. Gabalda.

Pryor, John W. 1992. "Justin Martyr and the Fourth Gospel." *Second Century* 9:153–169.

Pycke, Nestor. 1961. "Connaissance rationelle et connaissance de grace chez Saint Justin." *Ephemerides Theologiae Lovanienses* 37:52–85.

Räisänen, Heikki. 2005. "Marcion." Pages 100–124 in *A Companion to Second-Century Christian "Heretics."* Edited by Anti Marjanen and Petri Luomanen; Leiden: Brill.

Rajak, Tessa. 1999. "Talking at Trypho: Christian Apologetic as Anti-Judaism in Justin's *Dialogue with Trypho the Jew*." Pages 59–80 in *Apologetics in the Roman Empire. Pagans, Jews, and Christians*. Edited by Mark Edwards, Martin Goodman, and Simon Price. Oxford: Oxford University Press.

Remus, Harold. 1986. "Justin Martyr's Argument with Judaism." Pages 59–80 in *Anti-*

Judaism in Early Christianity, 2. Separation and Polemic. Edited by Stephen H. Wilson. Waterloo: Wilfrid Laurier University Press.

Rhee, Helen. 2005. *Early Christian Literature. Christ and Culture in the Second and Third Centuries.* London/New York: Routledge.

Rivas Rebaque, Fernando. 2006. "Los profetas (y maestros) en la *Didajé*: cuadros sociales de la memoria de los orígenes cristianos." Pages 181–203 in *Los comienzos del cristianismo.* Edited by S. Guijarro Oporto. Salamanca: Universidad Pontificia de Salamanca.

Rivas Rebaque, Fernando. 2007. "La escuela de Alejandría: los contextos en la primera inculturación de la fe." Pages 49–99 in *Contexto y nueva evangelización.* Edited by Gabino Uríbarri. Madrid/Bilbao: Desclée de Brower.

Rivas Rebaque, Fernando. 2015. "De la casa a la basilica. Espacio social y vida comunitaria en el cristianismo primitivo (ss. I–IV)." *Salmanticensis* 62:103–137.

Rokeah, David. 2002. *Justin Martyr and the Jews. Jewish and Christian Perspectives.* Leiden: Brill.

Royalty, Robert M. 2006. "Justin's Conversion and the Rhetoric of Heresy." Studia Patristica 43:509–514.

Sanchez, Sylvain J.G. 2000. *Justin, apologiste chrétien. Travaux sur le Dialogue avec Tryphon.* Paris: Gabalda.

Saxer, Victor. 2000. "Les progrès de l'organisation ecclésiastique de la fin du IIe siècle au milieu du IIIe siècle [180–250]." Pages 777–816 in Pietri and Le Boulluec 2000.

Schnabel, Eckhard J. 1999. "Die ersten Christen in Ephesus. Neuerscheinungen zur frühchristlichen Missionsgeschichte." *Novum Testamentum* 41:349–382.

Schneider, H.P. 1962. "Some Reflections on the Dialogue of Justin Martyr with Trypho." *Scottish Journal of Theology* 15:164–175.

Schoedel, William R. 1989. "Apologetic Literature and Ambassadorial Activities." *Harvard Theological Review* 82:55–78.

Sirago, Vito A. 1989. "La seconda sofistica come espressione culturale della classe dirigente del II sec." Pages 36–74 in *Aufstieg und Niedergang der römischen Welt* II.33.1. Berlin: De Gruyter.

Skarsaune, Oskar. 1976. "The Conversion of Justin Martyr." *Studia Theologica* 30:53–73.

Skarsaune, Oskar. 1987. *The Proof from Prophecy: A Study in Justin Martyr's Proof-Text Tradition. Text-Type, Provenance, Theological Profile.* Leiden: Brill.

Skarsaune, Oskar. 1996. "Judaism and Hellenism in Justin Martyr. Elucidated from His Portrait of Socrates." Pages 585–611 in *Geschichte—Tradition—Reflexion: Festschriften für Martin Hengel zum 70. Geburtstag,* vol. 3. Edited by Hubert Cancik, Herman Lichtenberger, and Peter Schäfer. Tübingen: Mohr Siebeck.

Skarsaune, Oskar. 2007. "Justin and His Bible." Pages 51–74 in *Justin Martyr and His Worlds.* Edited by Sara Parvis and Paul Foster. Minneapolis: Fortress Press.

Skarsaune, Oskar. 2010. "Justin and the Apologists." Pages 121–136 in *The Routledge Companion to Early Christian Thought*. Edited by D. Jeffrey Bingham. London/New York: Routledge.

Shotwell, Willis A. 1965. *The Biblical Exegesis of Justin Martyr*. London: SPCK.

Slusser, Michael, ed. 2003. *St. Justin Martyr: Dialogue with Trypho*. Translated by Thomas B. Falls. Revised by Thomas P. Halton. Selections from the Fathers of the Church 3. Washington, DC: Catholic University of America Press.

Snyder, H. Gregory. 2000. *Teachers and Texts in Ancient World. Philosophers, Jews and Christians*. London: Routledge.

Snyder, H. Gregory. 2007. "'Above the Bath of Myrtinus': Justin Martyr's 'School' in the City of Rome." *Harvard Theological Review* 100:335–362.

Stanton, Graham N. 1998. "Justin Martyr's Dialogue with Trypho: Group Boundaries, 'Proselytes' and 'Godfearers.'" Pages 263–278 in *Tolerance and Intolerance in Judaism and Christianity*. Edited by Graham N. Stanton and Guy G. Stroumsa. Cambridge: Cambridge University Press.

Stewart, Alistaire C. 2014. *Office and Order in the First Christian Communities*. Grand Rapids, Mich.: Baker Academic.

Stock, Brian. 1983. *The Implications of Literacy: Written Language and Models of Interpretation in the Eleventh and Twelfth Centuries*. Princeton: Princeton University Press.

Stock, Brian. 1990. *Listening for the Text: On the Uses of the Past*. Baltimore: Johns Hopkins University Press.

Stylianopoulos, Theodore. 1975. *Justin Martyr and the Mosaic Law*. Missoula, Mont.: Scholars Press.

Swain, Simon. 1996. *Hellenism and Empire. Language, Classicism and Power in the Greek World, AD 50–250*. Oxford: Clarendon Press.

Swain, Simon, Stephen J. Harrison and Jas Elsner, eds. 2007. *Severan Culture*. Cambridge: Cambridge University Press.

Tellbe, Mikael. 2009. *Christ-Believers in Ephesus. A Textual Analysis of Early Christian Identity Formation in a Local Perspective*. Tübingen: Mohr Siebeck.

Thomassen, Einar. 2004. "Orthodoxy and Heresy in Second-Century Rome." *Harvard Theological Review* 97:241–258.

Thorsteinsson, Runar M. 2012a. "By Philosophy Alone: Reassessing Justin's Christianity and His Turn from Platonism." *Early Christianity* 3:492–517.

Thorsteinsson, Runar M. 2012b. "The Literary Genre and Purpose of Justin's *Second Apology*: A Critical Review with Insights from Ancient Epistolography." *Harvard Theological Review* 105:91–114.

Thorsteinsson, Runar M. 2013. "Justin's Debate with Crescens the Stoic." *Zeitschrift für antikes Christentum* 17:451–478.

Trakatellis, Demetrius C. 1976. *The Pre-Existence of Christ in the Writings of Justin Martyr*. Missoula, Mont.: Scholars Press.

Treblico, Paul. 2004. *The Early Christians in Ephesus from Paul to Ignatius*. Tübingen: Mohr Siebeck.

Tuilier, André. 1982. "Les évangélistes et les docteurs de la primitive église et les origins de l'école (*didaskaleion*) d'Alexandrie." Studia Patristica 17/2:738–749.

Ulrich, Jörg. 2009. "Apologetics and Orthodoxy." Pages 209–229 in *Critique and Apologetics: Jews, Christians and Pagans in Antiquity*. Edited by Anders-Christian Jacobsen, Jörg Ulrich, and David Brakke. Frankfurt am Main: Peter Lang.

Ulrich, Jörg. 2012. "What Do We Know about Justin's 'School' in Rome?" *Zeitschrift für antikes Christentum* 16:62–74.

Urbano, Arthur P. 2013. *The Philosophical Life. Biography and the Crafting of Intellectual Identity in Late Antiquity*. Washington, DC: Catholic University of America Press.

Urbano, Arthur P. 2014. "Sizing up the Philosopher's Cloak: Christian Verbal and Visual Representations of the *Tribōn*." Pages 176–194 in *Dressing Judeans and Christians in Antiquity*. Edited by Kristi Upson-Saia, Carly Daniel-Hughes, and Alicia J. Batten. London/New York: Routledge.

Vaage, Leif E., ed. 2006. *Religious Rivalries in the Early Roman Empire and the Rise of Christianity*. Waterloo: Wilfrid Laurier University Press.

Van den Broek, R. 1995. "The Christian School of Alexandria in the Second and Third Century." Pages 39–47 in *Centers of Learning and Location in Pre-Modern Europe and the Near East*. Edited by J.W. Drijvers and A. McDonald. Leiden: Brill.

Van den Eynde, Damien. 1933. *Les normes de l'énseignement chrétien dans la littérature patristique des trois premiers siècles*. Gembloux: J. Duculot.

Van den Hoek, Anneweis. 1997. "The 'Cathechetical' School of Early Christian Alexandria and Its Philonic Heritage." *Harvard Theological Review* 90:59–87.

Van Winden, J.C.M. 1971. *An Early Christian Philosopher. Justin's Dialogue with Trypho. Chapters One to Nine*. Leiden: Brill.

Vinzent, Markus. 2008. "Rome." Pages 297–412 in *The Cambridge History of Christianity I: Origins to Constantine*. Edited by Margaret M. Mitchell and Francis M. Young. Cambridge: Cambridge University Press.

Wendel, Susan J. 2011. *Scriptural Interpretation and Community Self-Definition in Luke-Acts and the Writings of Justin Martyr*. Leiden: Brill.

Whitmarsh, Tim. 2004. *Greek Literature and the Roman Empire. The Politics of Imitation*. Oxford: Oxford University Press.

Whitmarsh, Tim. 2005. *The Second Sophistic*. Oxford: Oxford University Press.

Wilken, Robert. 1970. "Toward a Social Interpretation of Early Christian Apologetics." *Church History* 34:437–458.

Wilson, Stephen G. 1995. *Related Strangers: Jews and Christians, 70–170 C.E.* Minneapolis: Fortress Press.

Young, Francis. 1999. "Greek Apologists of the Second Century." Pages 81–104 in *Apolo-*

getics in the Roman Empire. Pagans, Jews, and Christians. Edited by Mark Edwards, Martin Goodman, and Simon Price. Oxford: Oxford University Press.

Young, M.O. 1989. "Justin, Socrates, and the Middle-Platonists." Studia Patristica 18:161–166.

Young, Robert, ed. 1995. *Colonial Desire: Hybridity in Theory, Culture, and Race*. London: Routledge.

Zanker, Paul. 1995. *The Mask of Socrates. The Image of the Intellectual in Antiquity*. Translated by A. Shapiro. Berkeley/Los Angeles/Oxford: University of California Press.

CHAPTER 8

Tatian *Theodidaktos* on Mimetic Knowledge

Miguel Herrero de Jáuregui

1   A Christian Rhetor in Rome

The last decade has been surprisingly prolific in the reconsideration of Tatian's figure. The times are past in which he was despised, in comparison with other Apologists more inclined to recognize some valuable aspects of Hellenism, as a short-sighted anti-Greek fanatic, whose only merit was the painstaking (but ultimately worthless for moderns) chronology to show the priority of Hebrews over Greeks, which had been the only reason for preserving his single extant work, the *Oratio ad Graecos*.[1] The reasons for this re-evaluation are twofold. On the one hand, the deconstruction of the typical portrait of Tatian as a "heretic" coined by Irenaeus and later authors has allowed readers to see his work from a new perspective that does not aim primarily to find "proto-Gnostic" elements *in nuce*.[2] On the other hand, a synchronic analysis that puts Tatian in relation to the contemporary rhetorical schools in the period of the so-called Second Sophistic has illuminated his argumentative techniques (and also his theological conceptions) as deeply grounded in Greek rhetorical thinking. His very anti-Greek stance responds itself to the Hellenic ways of thought that are apparent in some illustrious Greek contemporaries like Philostratus, Lucian, or Dio Chrysostom.[3] Moreover, Tatian's bitter style must be valued as

---

1   Cf. Nasrallah's starting line ("nobody likes Tatian"), with some ancient and modern revealing judgements (2010, 65). This quite unique hatred against a second-century author is still current today, as in Petersen's unsympathetic portrait of him: "unpleasant, rigid, uncompromising personality … cock-sure of himself, an evangelist pouring on the brimstone … incapable of enjoying (or not interested in) the good things of life: wine, women (or men) and song" (2008, 134–137).

2   Lampe 2003, Hunt 2006; Koltun-Fromm 2008. States of the question and bibliography in Nesselrath 2016, Crawford 2018 and Wyrwa 2018, to which the excellent, but not-much-cited study of Aragione 2015a should be added. English translations are taken from Whittaker 1982, with some changes of my own that mainly adapt it to the improved text of Nesselrath 2016.

3   Karadimas 2003, 38: "[Tatian's] rhetoric is not only a means used to explain, defend, and spread efficiently the new faith, or even to attack its opponents, it also participates essentially in the formation and final formulation of a number of doctrines of his faith." Cf. other 'horizontal' studies of Tatian's ideas in relation to his pagan contemporaries: Nasrallah 2010

an idiosyncratic striving for originality against the background of more conventional writers who duly follow trodden paths marked by anthologies of pagan texts for apologetic use. The *Oratio* abbreviates precisely in those aspects which others treat at most length (e.g. the scandalous pagan myths illustrated by long quotations from the Greek poets) and instead gives preference to less well-known topics. Clearly, Tatian had in mind other models like the philosophical diatribe, which were for him more attractive than the usual apologetic denunciation of paganism.

This novel approach may also illuminate his outlook regarding the topic of this volume, i.e. the significance and role of teachers in Rome in the second century CE. The *Oratio*, though written in Greek, was probably composed in Rome and expresses Tatian's judgements not only on Greek teachers and doctrines in general, but also on Justin and on his rival the Roman philosopher Crescens (19.2). Though some scholars think that it was written at a later stage after Tatian had returned to Syria, it seems intended primarily for an audience familiar with the Roman atmosphere, who would be able to appreciate some details: the sanctuaries of Jupiter Latiaris and Diana at Aricia are the only ones to be explicitly mentioned in the account of his conversion at the gates of Rome, where his new life begins (29.1, commented below); the mention of Greek statues in "the city of the Romans" (35.1) follows a section on statues of women which decorated the Campus Martius.[4] However, even if Tatian had composed the definitive version after he left Rome, parts of the *Oratio* vividly reflect his Roman experience, and in any case, the overall argumentation is embedded in the general discussions of his time in the main cities of the Empire, not only among Christian apologists, but also among pagan intellectuals.

As we shall see, his ideas on the relative importance of teaching and on the primacy of textual interpretation over any other source of true learning are based on his reflections on some key concepts of the rhetorical and literary theories of his time, particularly *mimesis*. As the so-called Apologists often do, Tatian rejects basic dimensions of Greek philosophical and religious thought, while at the same time appropriating them in a more or less modified version for the Christian camp. But also in this field he holds a very original place

---

on perceptions of art, Lössl 2010 on *logou dynamis*, and Crawford 2015 on concepts of order; more generally on Christians as part of the *intelligentsia* of the age, Eshleman 2013.

4   The debate on the date and place of composition has often been tainted by the question around the orthodoxy of the *Oratio*: those who stress continuity with Justin's teachings tend to prefer an earlier dating in Rome, while those who see heretic and Gnostic elements tend to argue for a later Syrian date. Once these constraints are overcome, the question is still open: Aragione argues for a Roman location (2015a, 36–41), Nesselrath for a Syrian one (2016, 15–17).

among this generation of Christian writers: he is the only one to give preference to *mimesis* and related concepts instead of the usual apologetic topics (anthropomorphism of the gods, mystic rites, use of allegory, etc.).[5] Therefore, a study of his thought on these matters will offer us a unique vision that differs from commonplaces and inherited arguments. The fact that Tatian's figure and theories did not earn much success among his Roman contemporaries and later Christians must not blind us against appreciating the profound originality of his thought in these matters.

2   *Mimesis* and *Thauma*

Studies on Tatian have paid surprisingly little attention to *mimesis*, a concept emphatically rejected in the first paragraph of the *Oratio*, in which he tells the Greeks that they must not believe they are superior to barbarians, for all aspects of their wisdom have been invented by foreigners. In conclusion, "stop calling inventions your imitations" (1.1: παύσασθε τὰς μιμήσεις εὑρέσεις ἀποκαλοῦντες). This opening announces the demonstration of chronological priority which he will carry out in the last part of the discourse. Just as the Greeks have taken magic from the Persians and writing from Phoenicians, they have imitated the religious revelation of the Bible and turned it into superstitious idolatry, in a sort of intellectual falsification, as he will state in the closing section (40.2: *parakharattein*). Tatian uses the metaphor of a false currency because for him, Greek wisdom, under a cover of basic similarity, is not only secondary, but a completely illegitimate diversion from the original.[6] Thus the first paragraph lays out a conceptual key that crosses the whole work, i.e. the downgrading of Greek *mimesis* as opposed to authentic knowledge.

This is of course rhetoric, but not "empty rhetoric." As Tim Whitmarsh has repeatedly underlined, *mimesis* is a fundamental concept in the intellectual

---

5   E.g., in a single paragraph (*Orat.* 21) he deals with two topics that occupy many pages in Justin's *Apology*, Athenagoras' *Legatio*, Theophilus' *Ad Autolycus*, or Clement's *Protrepticus*: Christ's human form can be compared to his advantage with the Greek anthropomorphic gods; allegory is not legitimate to justify myths. Theogonic myths are briefly reviewed in *Or.* 8 and 10. Mystic rites deserve only a brief mention in 29.1, with two untypical examples. By contrast, in none of the works of these four authors is there a special interest in *mimesis, thauma,* or *pathos,* key concepts in the *Oratio* as argued in this paper.

6   Cf. Aragione 2015a, 285. Nesselrath 2016, 186, n. 604, shows that Clement of Alexandria followed this Tatianic image in his outlaying of the "plagiarism of the Greeks" (*Strom.* 1.87.2). More in general, Kleingünther 1933 and Thraede 1962 on the importance of the *heuretes* in Greek tradition and Christian apologetics.

world of the second century, whereby the Greeks feel legitimized to imitate creatively the classical authors and style.[7] Plato's harsh attack on *mimesis* as a false reflection of the real truth in the *Republic* was compensated for by Aristotle's vindication on the pedagogic value of *mimesis* as a way of attaining real knowledge. The respectable link between *mimesis* and learning has a classical defence in the *Poetics*: it is through *mimesis* that we achieve our first understandings (*matheseis*) as children, and later we tend to like mimetic art because we find pleasure in learning (*manthanein*) since, thanks to mimetic works of art, we learn by comparing them to nature. In spite of occasional reappraisals of Plato's hostility, the Aristotelian line of thought, followed and re-elaborated by authors who were otherwise much influenced by Plato, like Plutarch, pseudo-Longinus, Dionysius of Halicarnassus, and others, was a basic pillar of Greek intellectual identity in early Imperial Age.[8]

Therefore, Tatian's sharp rejection of *mimesis* is not just one more instance of the priority argument so common in Jewish and Christian apologetics. Neither is it similar to Justin's use of the term as the key of his explanation of the similarity between pagan and Christian rituals and myths—i.e. demonic imitation that aims to confound men by forging idolatrous caricatures of the true religion.[9] Tatian is going much farther: he is attacking the basis of the Hellenic culture of his time, which he (rightly) sees as grounded in *mimesis*. The consequences of the rejection of imitation for our subject are clear: dependence on a previous teacher, which is at the heart of Hellenic pedagogy, is rejected as an inferior kind of adulterated knowledge, incapable of arriving at the original truth. In his initial review of philosophers, Plato is dismissed as an imitator of previous wise men: "I laugh, too, at Pherecydes' old wives' tales, and the doctrine inherited from him by Pythagoras, and Plato's imitation of the latter, even if some think otherwise" (*Or.* 3.5).[10] Though used to attack Plato, the

---

7   Whitmarsh 2001, 29–90. Further authors have followed this path for specific works, e. g. Zadorojnyi 2012 for Plutarch's *Lives*.

8   Plat. *Resp.* 602d–603e, 605a–c; Arist. *Poet.* 1448b, *Rhet.* 1370a. Plut. *Quom. adol. poet. aud. deb.* 14b–37b, *Aem. Paul.* 1.2; Ps-Long. *De subl.* 13; Dion. Hal. *De imitatione* (fragments edited by Usener-Radermacher).

9   Yoshiko Reed 2003. Cf. e. g. Justin, *1Apol.* 54.4, 55.1, 60.10, 64.1, 66.4. In Justin, *mimesis* is not intrinsically evil, only when practiced by demons: Christians should imitate God (*1Apol.* 10.1).

10   *Orat.* 3.5: γελῶ καὶ τὴν Φερεκύδους γραολογίαν καὶ τοῦ Πυθαγόρου τὴν περὶ τὸ δόγμα κληρονομίαν καὶ τοῦ Πλάτωνος, κἄν τινες μὴ θέλωσι, τὴν περὶ τούτου μίμησιν. Schwartz's emendation τούτους, though followed by Marcovich and Whittaker (but rejected by Trelenberg 2012, 92 and Nesselrath 2016, 120), seems wrong: Cic. *Tusc.* 1.38–39 establishes the ordination Pherecydes-Pythagoras-Plato, making Plato the disciple only of Pythagoras (concerning the doctrine of reincarnation).

Platonic heritage in his negative concept of *mimesis* is clear. A single mimetic step implies an insurmountable distance from the original, and therefore, the more intermediate levels there are, the farther from the truth one is. This of course applies to all pagan wisdom, itself a corrupted *mimesis* of the barbarian one, even at the most ancient layers. All the care that Plutarch and others had invested in justifying the pedagogic value of texts like, for instance, the lives of great men, which would foster imitation of their virtue in the readers' minds, is brushed aside. This radical judgement of *mimesis* as leading to error not only falls upon pagan culture, but also affects a well-established Christian tradition of imitation, not only of Christ (not mentioned in the entire *Oratio*), but also of earlier exemplary Christians.[11] And it brings us to a crucial matter, Tatian's own indebtedness to his teacher, Justin.

Tatian has been traditionally considered Justin's disciple and even the revisionist tide of the last years has not shattered this axiom. Tatian's intellectual dependence on Justin is indeed beyond any doubt.[12] This is a point in which diverse ancient witnesses agree, starting with Irenaeus, who says that Tatian was his auditor (*akroates*), and after Justin's death he boasted in being a teacher (*didaskalos*), as if inheriting his school. This keeping Tatian "orthodox" while Justin lived and making him heretic afterwards (and linked to Encratites and Marcionites) resembles too neatly an heresiological portrait, but it probably springs from the fact that Tatian stayed with Justin in Rome and after his death took up his position as intellectual leader of the same group.[13]

However, in the light of his vision of pagan teachers, we should inquire whether Tatian considered himself a "disciple," and how he may have understood Justin's role in regard to himself. As is well known, he calls Justin "the most admirable" (18.6: ὁ θαυμασιώτατος Ἰουστῖνος). However, the undoubtedly praising adjective points to the realm of *mimesis*: "wonder" (*thauma*) is a feeling of admiration and awe felt, for instance, at those works of art that are strikingly

---

11   Moss 2010.

12   Already Bellinzoni said: "it is now apparent that the concept of a gospel harmony did not originate with Tatian; indeed, he was a *pupil* in a *school* in which gospel harmonies were apparently commonplace. What is new in Tatian's *Diatessaron* and what is not found in Justin's writings is a full gospel harmony rather than one of limited scope and the incorporation into a gospel harmony of the Gospel of John" (1967, 142). In spite of the necessary refining of the terms, "pupil" and "school," intellectual dependence is clear. The studies of Hanig 1999, Hunt 2006 and above all Trelenberg 2012 have proved beyond any possible doubt Tatian's indebtedness to Justin's conceptions. Cf. also n. 21 below.

13   Iren. *Haer.* 1.28. Cf. similar statements (probably expanding on Irenaeus) in Eusebius *Hist. eccl.* 4.29, and Epiphanius, *Pan.* Cf. Koltun-Fromm 2008 on the heresiological agenda of these testimonies; a good summary of the question in Foster 2010.

similar to nature (i.e. mimetic), and to cause such emotion is a key aspiration, for example, in Greek novels.[14] Achieving the *thauma* of the audience is a cornerstone of rhetoric and scientific taste for public display in the period of the Second Sophistic.[15] And Tatian, consistent with his rejection of *mimesis* as abysmal distancing from truth, scorns Greek works of art, mysteries, and all the mimetic works that the Greeks think worth of *thauma*, as is patent in several passages of the *Oratio*. We will examine them before ascertaining how far this is consistent with his praising of Justin as *thaumasiotatos*.

Tatian mocks individuals celebrated in pagan literature as models for the living: "is it not absurd to wonder (θαυμάζεσθαι) at Nestor, made feeble and sluggish by age, admiring him for trying to fight on equal terms with young men?" (32.4). He also derides the works of art admired by his contemporaries: he denounces claims that the statue of the cannibal tyrant Phalaris is worthy of admiration (34.1: ὡς τις ἀνὴρ θαυμαστὸς δείκνυται). Likewise, the statue of a woman who bore thirty children "is a work considered a marvel and worth observing" (34.3: ὡς θαυμαστὸν ἡγεῖσθαι καὶ κατανοεῖν ποίημα). For Tatian, the aesthetic beauty of the statue does not cover her incontinence, so any admiration that it causes is misleading.[16]

The same harshness accrues to *thauma* that arises, not in front of monuments or books, but in the spectacles of theatre (the prototypical instance of *mimesis*), which he denounces as a place where spectators are fouled and falsely educated in deception (22.1–7):

> Of which kind are your teachings (διδάγματα)? [...] I saw a certain man on many occasions; and seeing him I was amazed, and then my amazement was replaced by contempt, as I saw how he was one man inside, and outwards he pretends to be what he is not (ἰδὼν ἐθαύμασα καὶ μετὰ τὸ θαυμάσαι κατεφρόνησα πῶς ἔσωθεν μέν ἐστιν ἄλλος, ἔξωθεν δὲ ὅπερ οὐκ ἔστι ψεύδεται) [...] I refuse to stand and gape (κεχηνέναι) at a chanting crowd, and I do not want to feel any emotion because someone is gesticulating and writhing in an unnatural way (τῷ νεύοντι καὶ κινουμένῳ παρὰ φύσιν οὐ βούλομαι συνδιατίθεσθαι). Is there any kind of wonder left for you to devise? They blow through their noses and use foul language, they move with

---

14 Whitmarsh 2001, 86–87.

15 Cf. Von Staden 1997 for shared elements between Galen's *epideixis* and that of contemporary rhetors (particularly p. 51 on *thauma*).

16 For Tatian's critique of artistic works cf. Nasrallah 2010, 65–79. Nesselrath 2016 ad loc. points out that the woman could be the Eutychis mentioned by Pliny *Nat.* 7.34 (2016, 175, also for the superiority of the variant ἡγεῖσθαι over the usual ἡγεῖσθε).

indecent movements (κινοῦνται δὲ κινήσεις ἃς οὐκ ἐχρῆν) ... your daughters and your sons behold them giving lessons (σοφιστεύοντας) in adultery on the stage. Admirable places, indeed, are your lecture-rooms (ἀκροατήρια), where every base action perpetrated by night is proclaimed aloud, and the hearers (ἀκροατάς) are regaled with the utterance of infamous discourses! Admirable, too, are your mendacious poets, who by their fictions beguile their hearers (ἀκροωμένους) from the truth.

Even within so traditional a topic as the condemnation of theatre, Tatian in this passage is extremely careful to make his terminology consistent with his overall condemnation of teaching based on impressive emotions: the verb συνδιατίθημι means "to be sympathetically affected together";[17] χάσκω (gaping) will be also used for the mouth-opening of the actor in a later reminder of this attack (24.1); and the verbs σοφιστεύω and the nouns ἀκροατήρια and ἀκροατάς (on which the participle ἀκροωμένους depends) mix up the spectators of theatre with the audiences and disciples of sophists and philosophers who go to auditions to learn. The actor bases his success in generating in the audience a collective emotion which transports those who listen to a mimetic disposition towards his acting. This, says Tatian, has the same (worthless) value as lectures of philosophers and poets, i.e., just leading through emotional *mimesis* towards deception.

Immediately afterwards, Tatian's critique of the philosophers as recipients of *thauma* grows even stronger, when he accuses them of imitating animals in their obsessive will to impress (25.1–2): "What great and wonderful things (τί μέγα καὶ θαυμαστόν) are your philosophers doing? They leave bare one of their shoulders; they let their hair grow long; they cultivate their beards; their nails are like the claws of wild beasts [...] You, sir, behaving like a dog—you have no knowledge of God and have sunk to imitating irrational animals (τὸν θεὸν οὐκ οἶδας καὶ ἐπὶ τὴν ἀλόγων μίμησιν μεταβέβηκας)." This last sentence not only shows the topical accusation (specially against Cynics) of leaning towards beasts instead of towards the divine, but also the conceptual opposition between "knowing" and "imitating," keeping the former for God and the latter for animals. Philosophers, therefore, with all their pride in rationality, are no better than actors, for they are only concerned with causing *thauma* through *mimesis*.

However, there is one last use of *thauma* in the *Oratio* which is not applied to the Greeks but to Tatian himself. When he announces the launching of his

---

17   Cf. *LSJ*, s. v. In medical texts it is identified with συμπάσχω, which links it to the root of
      pathein, belonging, as we shall see, to the same conceptual cluster. Aristotle says (fr. 15
      Rose) that the ultimate goal of the mysteries is to achieve not *mathein*, but *pathein* and
      diatethenai (on the opposition *mathein/pathein* cf. n. 30 below).

chronological argument, he says (31.1–2): "We shall find (εὑρήσομεν) that our history is not only earlier than Greek culture, but even than the invention of writing. As witnesses I will not take members of our own household, but will rather employ Greek supporters. The former option would be senseless (ἄγνω-μον), for we ourselves would not accept it, but if the latter come off it will be wonderful (θαυμαστόν), when I will be resisting you with your own weapons and getting from you proofs that are above suspicion." Not only does he use Greek authors for his chronological proof,[18] he also aims to fill the Greeks with *thauma*. Tatian has just criticized as a typical trait of Greek argumentation the aim to impress and to instil wonder, and he now uses this strategy himself. Likewise, some paragraphs before (26.5–8) he has accused grammarians of being "at the beginning of all Greek chattering" and asked them "why do you start a war on the letters?" whereas now he takes pride in doing exactly the same for the Christian side (i.e. showing the Biblical prophets are prior to any Greek literacy). Using the weapons that one has denied to the adversary is typical of Christian apologetic literature and more generally of all polemics. However, he still underlines one key difference between his own work and the pagan *thaumata*. The *thauma* that he will cause is derived from a previous labour of *heuresis*, and is not the proof of truth, but its result, merely useful for the effect of persuasion.

Given such a marked and insistent use of the root, it cannot be merely accidental when he uses the epithet *thaumasiotatos* for Justin in this same work (18.6). Tatian is of course comparing him favourably to philosophers, poets, and the rest of pagan teachers. The superlative acknowledges that Justin is, unlike the philosophers, worthy of true *thauma* and imitation.[19] Since it is said as an introduction to a quotation of Justin's judgement on the demons, it also implies admiration for his doctrine. Justin is a teacher who "announces the truth" (19.1: κηρύττων τὴν ἀλήθειαν)—and indeed Tatian's likening himself to Justin in deserving Crescens' hostility is a proof of such *mimesis*,[20] which is evidenced also by the fact that some lines before, Tatian has referred to himself also as an "announcer of the truth" (17.1: κήρυκα τῆς ἀληθείας). However, a reader

---

18   The absence of Jews makes clear that the list he uses is of Greek origin; cf. Droge 1989, 88. The quality of his Greek sources is another distinctive trait of Tatian in comparison with other apologists.

19   This is not incompatible with Marcovich's supposition (1995, 2) that *thaumasiotatos* means that Justin had already endured martyrdom, as in *Mart. Pol.* 5.1, 16.2. Nesselrath takes it as self-evident (2016, 6, 15).

20   If the manuscript reading in *Or.* 19.2 καὶ ἐμὲ ὡς is right. Eusebius' reading μεγάλῳ, accepted by Marcovich and Trelenberg (2012, 136), would take out Tatian's ego from the sentence, but as Nesselrath points out, it is more plausible that Eusebius deleted Tatian's association to Justin's martyrdom than that it was inserted in the manuscript (2016, 150).

of the *Oratio* is aware that the adjective *thaumasios* conveys an emotion that one cannot trust by itself: it is not in *thauma* alone where the proof of truth lies. Therefore, we can ascertain that Tatian surely admired Justin, and read his works, and imitated his oral and written style, took many thoughts from him, and possibly may have called himself his *akroates* and even inherited some of his students.[21] Yet we should not equate all this, at least, without careful thought and cautious quotation marks, as "disciple" in the modern sense, for Tatian does not make his access to true knowledge depend on one person, but, as we shall see, on an anonymous, God-given, text.

3 Legitimate Mimesis

Consistent with his downplaying of personal elements that are persuasive as causing *thauma* or fostering *mimesis*, in his exhortation, he does not appeal to miracles or to the example of Christ, or of any virtuous man.[22] He appeals only to the truth of Christian texts, which are the only true source of *mathein*. Even when alluding to Christian preaching, his reference is always the divinely-inspired text. For instance, he says that Christians take their doctrine "not from the tongue, or from probabilities, or from a sophistic ordination of ideas, but using the words of a more divine voice" (12.9). In the famous passage on his conversion by finding the Scriptures (29.1), to which we shall return later, he calls himself *theodidaktos*, taught by God. Thanks to the sole dependence on the text, there are no human intermediations that can only degrade the divine teaching.[23] The fragments of Tatian's other works transmitted in quotations and allusions, as well as his *Diatessaron*, show him as fully committed to Scriptural interpretation.[24] The God-given texts are the link that allows the dis-

---

21   Cf. note 12 above; Trelenberg 2012, 195–203; Nesselrath 2016, 15–16.

22   McGehee rightly says: "although Tatian might have refused to buttress his argument with miracles because he anticipated a sceptical audience, it is possible that he considered 'proof through miracles' as no proof at all" (2004, 158). However, this lack of appealing to miracles is not, as he intends, because it did not fit in the protreptic genre (cf. Clem. Alex. *Protr.* 1.9.2–10.1), but rather because miracles were the kind of *thaumata* that he despises as proof of pagan truth. However, McGehee's suggestion of linking it to the protreptic genre is convincing, and a further proof of Tatian's adapting models of contemporary pagan literature.

23   Petersen 2008, 130: "Tatian's conversion (at least as he describes it) is essentially an intellectual exercise, not a charismatic experience. He is not evangelized; there is no catharsis; there is no emotion involved."

24   E.g., Eus. *Hist. eccl.* 5.13.8: "Tatian prepared a book on *Problems*, in which he undertook to set out what was unclear and hidden in the divine scriptures." It is usually supposed to be

tance between God's truth and man to be covered by just one single direct step, instead of an innumerable mimetic chain of steps hiding the original truth. Of course, the transition between God and text, however direct it may be, is also mimetic. But direct teaching from God is the single instance in which *mimesis* is acceptable for Tatian.

Likewise, in this role as an expounder of texts, the teacher is mimetic of God's role. In fact, in the *Oratio* there is only one passage where *mimesis* at the human level will be accepted as purveying a positive result, i.e., that in which Tatian compares his own actions to those of the Logos. He wants to explain the creation of matter by God, undiminished by such creation, and likens it to his own preaching—it is relevant that the analogy is drawn as a secondary point in an argument about matter, because it means that it is interiorized and taken as self-evident (5.5–6): "I speak and you hear: yet surely when I address you I am not myself deprived of speech through transmission of speech, but by projecting my voice my purpose is to set in order the disorderly matter in you. Just as the Word begotten in the beginning in turn begot (καθάπερ ὁ λόγος ἐν ἀρχῇ γεννηθεὶς ἀντεγέννησε) our creation by fabricating matter for himself, so I too, in imitation of the Word, having been begotten again (οὕτω κἀγὼ κατὰ τὴν τοῦ λόγου μίμησιν ἀναγεννηθεὶς) and obtained understanding of the truth, am bringing to order the confusion in kindred (συγγενοῦς) matter."[25] The vocabulary of generation is carefully ordered so that Tatian's speaking is shown to be of lesser category, and we should bear in mind that this is a demonstrative example rather than a theological statement; but still, Tatian shows a proud consciousness of his own participation in God's creation through his speaking. Just as he is *theodidaktos* through the text, so should the audience be if they follow his teaching.

For Tatian, therefore, there is a legitimate *mimesis*, when it derives directly from God, and an illegitimate one when it derives from some other entity. This distinction between two kinds of *mimesis* can be projected back to the very beginning of creation, of which Tatian gives a summarized account in order to

---

an attempt to smooth contradictions in the Scriptures, just as the *Diatessaron* (Petersen 1994, 26). His famous attack on pagan allegory in *Orat.* 21.1 ("don't allegorize myths and gods, for if you try to do that, your divinity is lost for you and for us") is not followed by any defence of the method for the Christian Scripture (cf. instead Orig. *Cels.* 4.17, 4.48–51). We may suppose he opposed the allegorical method also for the Bible, for all his accounts are quite literalistic.

25   Cf. Crawford 2015: "this creates a nice contrast between Tatian, who is imitating the divine Λόγος, and those Greek philosophers whom, as he says later in the *Oratio*, are imitating ἄλογοι creatures." The pair of opposites *logos/alogos* also runs through the work, and as others (e.g., unity vs. multiplicity), often encroaches on the polarities examined here.

explain why men can be resurrected and immortalized or condemned. It starts with the creation of man as imitation of God's image (7.1): "The celestial Word, made Spirit from the Father and Word from power of the Word, in the likeness of the Father who begot him made man an image of immortality" (κατὰ τὴν τοῦ γεννήσαντος αὐτὸν πατρὸς μίμησιν εἰκόνα τῆς ἀθανασίας τὸν ἄνθρωπον ἐποίη-σεν). According to the Platonic model, that initial *mimesis* carried out by the heavenly Logos achieves a legitimate image of the divine model.

In contrast, mimetic acts carried out by other entities (daemons or humans) only adulterate the image they seek to model. And it is precisely in this chain of illegitimate images that man lost his primordial immortality and fell into corruption. For God also created angels, and one of them rebelled and had imitators (7.4–5): "one that was first-born and therefore more intelligent was followed (συνεξηκολούθησαν) and made God by men, even though he had tres-passed God's law; and the force of the Logos denied sharing its life with the head of the error and to his followers (συνακολουθήσαντας). And the creature made in the image of God (ὁ μὲν κατ᾽ εἰκόνα τοῦ θεοῦ γεγονώς), when the more powerful spirit departed from him, became mortal, while because of his trans-gression and rebellion the first-born was appointed a demon, along with those who had imitated his example and his imaginations (τοῦτον οἱ μιμησάμενοι τού-του τε τὰ φαντάσματα) became an army of daemons and, through their free will, were abandoned to their own folly".[26]

The followers in rebellion imitate the first-born rebellious angel and are degraded to mortals just as he was degraded to the status of a daemon. Cor-respondingly, the men who follow God through his Logos will imitate him and recover immortality. In the description of his teaching, Tatian, re-born through imitation of the Logos, becomes an agent of this recovery. The account of the primordial rebellion is close to Justin's demonology, but the severe condemna-tion of *mimesis* of evil as a voluntary decision (hence its likening to "following") is Tatian's own contribution, springing surely from his awareness of the impor-tance of such concepts in contemporary rhetoric.[27]

---

26   *Orat.* 7.5: I follow the text and punctuation suggested for this passage by Nesselrath (2016, 49, 126).

27   Cf. the study of Lössl 2010 on *logou dynamis*, a theological notion present in this passage which springs from rhetorical theory. Similarly, cf. Crawford 2015 on the concept of order in *Or.* 5.5–6, quoted above.

4 Pathos

This double value of *mimesis* offers an interesting analogy to another concept associated with the same field of *thauma*, usually translated as "passion" or "affection" (*pathos/pathema*). In the common Greek philosophical tradition, which in this aspect was immediately followed by Christianity, passions (*pathe/pathemata*) are considered as negative and degrading.[28] And as is usual in Christian apologetic writings, Tatian accuses the Greek gods of being "subject to fate, along with their ruler Zeus, having been dominated by the same human passions" (8.2: τοῖς αὐτοῖς πάθεσιν οἷσπερ καὶ οἱ ἄνθρωποι κρατηθέντες). In a vicious circle, these daemon-gods "impel their disciples to imitate them" precisely in such passions, through the negative kind of *mimesis* (8.2: τοὺς ἀκούοντας ἐπὶ τὰ ὅμοια προύτρέψαντο). Demons are the cause of illness and suffering, and pagan remedies like medicine or philosophy can do nothing against them (17.3): "suffering is not cured by remedies against suffering (πάθος οὐκ ἔστι δι' ἀντιπαθείας ἀπολλύμενον), and the madman is not cured through the use of amulets. They are attacks of the demons, and they take as helpers he who is ill, or he who claims to be in love, or he who hates and he who wants revenge." Afterwards, he advises the pagans after condemning the avarice and love of war inspired upon them by divination and demons (19.9): "if you are above the passions you will despise everything in the world. Such people are we; do not abhor us, but reject the demons and follow the only God (τῶν παθῶν ἂν ὑπάρχῃς ἀνώτερος, τῶν ἐν τῷ κόσμῳ πάντων καταφρονήσεις. τοιούτους ἡμᾶς ὄντας μὴ ἀποστυγήσητε, ἀλλὰ παραιτησάμενοι τοὺς δαίμονας θεῷ τῷ μόνῳ κατακολουθήσατε)." Passions impel men to follow demons, so following God, as Christians do, means liberating oneself from this chain of demonic *mimesis*.

This is, so far, not very novel. But in the *Oratio* there is one striking exceptional case of *pathos* in the account of the separation of human soul from the divine spirit, which is nevertheless repairable (13.4–6):

> The Spirit became originally the soul's companion, but gave it up when the soul was unwilling to follow it (ἔπεσθαι μὴ βουλομένην αὐτῷ). The soul kept a spark, as it were, of the spirit's power, yet because of its separation it could no longer see things that are perfect, and so in its search for God went astray and fashioned a multitude of gods, following the demons and their hostile devices (τοῖς ἀντισοφιστεύουσι δαίμοσι κατακολουθοῦσα). God's

---

28 E.g. Athenag. *Leg.* 22.4, Clem. Alex. *Protr.* 32.1, Orig. *Cels.* 1.137. Cf. Herrero de Jáuregui 2019 on Christian condemnation of divine *pathemata*.

spirit is not given to all, but dwelling among some who behaved justly and being intimately connected with the soul it revealed by predictions to the other souls what had been hidden. The souls which were obedient to wisdom (αἱ μὲν πειθόμεναι ⟨τῇ⟩ σοφίᾳ) attracted to themselves the kindred spirit, but those which were disobedient and rejected the servant of the suffering God (αἱ δὲ μὴ πειθόμεναι καὶ τὸν διάκονον τοῦ πεπονθότος θεοῦ παραιτούμεναι) were clearly shown to be enemies of God rather than his worshippers.

The participle πεπονθότος is usually referred to the passion of Christ, even though Christ would be the *diakonos* rather than "the suffering God."[29] Yet in whichever way we take it, it shows that God's Spirit is able to put itself at the level of man and therefore go through *pathein* (it is important to note that the distinction between "suffering" and "passion" is in the translation, not in the Greek). God will still not be subject to passions, but he allows his *diakonos* to be victim of the human passions and suffer. It is a concession to the weak nature of the human soul, which, having once gone astray by not being willing to follow the Spirit, is unable to recognize God. As a device of persuasion, God is willing to descend to the realm of man and even share the sphere of *pathein*, so that pious souls will be able to recognize him. Since humans can only be persuaded through *pathein*, God can provide it.

Again, this descent of God to the level of man in order to facilitate human access to him has an analogy, indeed mimetic, in Tatian's depiction of his own role among humans. Approaching the end of his *Oratio*, he says (35.3): "Do not get impatient with our culture and involve yourselves in fatuous and scurrilous controversy against us, saying: "Tatian is going to be better than the Greeks and the countless hordes of philosophers with his newfangled barbarian doctrines!" For what hardship is it for men who have shown themselves ignorant to be confuted now by one who is now of equal experience (ἀμαθεῖς ὑπὸ ἀνθρώπου νῦν ὁμοιοπαθοῦς)? And how can it be absurd, according to your own wise man, to "grow old always learning something?"

The connexion between *mathein* and *pathein*, the roots of the two terms in opposition, would undoubtedly sound familiar to those educated in classical rhetoric and literature, as Tatian was, even more so when it is just preceding a famous quotation of Solon, who was famously associated with Croesus' learn-

---

29 Hanig thinks it is opposed to Justin's *apathes* God (1999, 62 f.). Karadimas 2003: n. 160: "we cannot know for certain what he meant." It seems to have caused some problems to earlier interpreters: Marcovich emended it (most implausibly) to πεποιηκότος and it is absent from one secondary manuscript (v).

ing through suffering (*pathei mathos*).[30] The association of both terms recalls, in the first place, Tatian's rejection of *pathein*-based wisdom (like that of mystery cults) in favour of true doctrine.[31] But it is, again, much more than a mere rhetorically clever wordplay; it conveys Tatian's deep consciousness of his role.

Homoiopathes is a term with venerable roots in Plato (*Tim* 45c) and the New Testament (Acts 14:15, James 5:17), used to designate "humans of the same condition." Justin uses it in that sense (*2 Apol.* 1.1, *Dial.* 93.3) and also for Christ as suffering like us (*Dial.* 48.3, 57.3). Tatian strategically places the adverb *nûn* to allude to the "horizontal" and "vertical" dimensions of the term at the same time: he is now a man of the same condition as the rest, but they should follow him before it is too late (as it was for Croesus, Solon's quotation seems to recall), for at some point, he will not "share passions" with them any more. This passage is purposefully drawing a certain analogy between God, who descended to the realm of human *pathos*, and Tatian, who, having been immersed in *pathos* like the Greeks, leads them now out from *amathia* to knowledge. Tatian is again describing himself as mimetic of the Logos when he joins men in their *pathos* to take them out of it. And he is able and willing to establish "pathetic" relations with the rest of men (e.g., by using rhetoric for persuasive means), just as he was willing to provoke *thauma* with his chronological endeavor.

The notions of *mimesis*, *thauma*, and *pathos* belong to the same conceptual cluster, opposed to that informed by ideas of *heuresis* and *mathesis*: in short, impressive emotional effects vs. true doctrine. The former leads men to error, except when it is God himself who is using these emotional elements to approach men—and by analogy, when Tatian (or Justin or any good teacher for that matter) is imitating God in this teaching of impressionable men. Since the first degree of *mimesis*, that between man and God, is accepted, there can be an analogical impulse making certain men helpers of other men immersed in passion in order to liberate themselves and reach knowledge. Justin may have been such a man for Tatian, and Tatian aspires to be one for others. They are like

---

30   The dichotomy *pathein/mathein* was very popular in the philosophical and literary debates of classical times (cf. Dörrie 1938). In the Imperial age it must have been a traditional *topos*, especially in relation to Croesus, who understood Solon's advice too late (e.g., Clement of Alexandria, *Protr.* 3.43.4: σωφρόνησον ὕστατον γοῦν, ὦ Κροῖσε, τῷ πάθει μεταμαθών). It seems also at work (in a weaker way) in *Or.* 12.10: "those of you who are willing should be eager to learn (μανθάνειν); you who do not reject the Scythian Anacharsis even now must not think beneath you (ἀναξιοπαθήσητε) to find instruction (παιδεύεσθαι) from those who follow barbarian code."

31   Cf. Aristotle, fr. 15 Rose (transmitted by Synesius, *Dion* 8, applying the dichotomy to Egyptian monks who lacked doctrine): "the initiates must not learn, but experience and be brought into a condition" (τοὺς τελουμένους οὐ μαθεῖν τί δεῖν, ἀλλὰ παθεῖν καὶ διατεθῆναι).

those souls that, since they "behaved justly," received the spirit in order to utter prophecies (13.5). This descent to the world of *pathos*, where the pure reason of the text does not arrive, is the role of the teacher for him, along with Scriptural exegesis.

Tatian has often been accused of being a disorderly writer, since the compositional principles of the *Oratio* are not always evident, but his internal consistency in this regard is undeniable: his association within the same conceptual cluster of the notions of *pathos*, *mimesis* and *thauma* is perceivable in different layers of the *Oratio*. For instance, this is the reason why his critique of the philosophers is based fundamentally on petty *ad hominem* jabs rather than on doctrinal discussions. He attacks them as figures incapable of inspiring others, as if they were the heroes and gods of Greek myths, which are equally criticized. He puts them in the same bag as statues, actors, or mystery cults, paradigmatic of the *pathos*-based wisdom which he has denounced. In his portrait, the teachings of the philosophers found their authority on *pathos* and *mimesis*, and therefore all their *didaxein* is by essence mimetic and spurious. In the *Oratio*, Justin's advantage over them is not justified by his superior doctrine, about which there is no word, but by his truer condition of "worthy of admiration," Tatian's advantage over pagan teachers, instead, comes from his self-proclaimed condition as "herald of the truth" (17.2), who has direct access to the truth from above and proclaims it without any intermediation.

5   Tatian as Anti-Heraclitus

In effect, Tatian's knowledge of the truth comes directly from God. As we saw, Justin is praised as a Christian model worthy of admiration, but Tatian does not claim to be his disciple. On the contrary, he explicitly states that he has no teacher. He calls his own soul "taught by God," *theodidaktos*, in the famous account of his conversion to Christianity just before entering Rome after his many travels (*Or.* 29). *Theodidaktos* is a term coined in Paul's First Letter to the Thessalonians (4:9), "you have been taught by God how to love," which is then used by the Apologists to mean divine inspiration and God-given wisdom, frequently in relation to the Scripture.[32] Tatian is, characteristically, the

---

32   E.g., *Ep. Barn.* 21.6, Clement of Alexandria, *Strom.* 1.98.4, 2.48.4, 6.166.4; Athenagoras, *Leg.* 11.1, 32.4; Theophilus *Autol.* 2.9. Clement in *Protrepticus* 11.112.2 defines Christians as disciples (*mathetai*) of God/Christ.

only one to use it for himself.³³ However, it is not just a touch of pride, but a cornerstone of his self-envisioning as an authorized voice to speak among the Christians and to the Greeks, and also of his conception of the way in which truth is attained and transmitted.

A closer look at the passage shows the care with which he composes his self-portrait. As is well known, Tatian adapts a traditional tale of conversion, which was also used by Justin, of the man who after having sought truth everywhere, finds it in Christianity.³⁴ But at the same time, the passage seems purposefully drawn as a contrast, at a very detailed level, to Heraclitus, who had been criticized earlier as arrogant, presumptuous, and obscure. Let us recall both passages, which show clear correspondences (marked with the relevant Greek words):

> *Oratio* 3.1: I would not accept Heraclitus and his boast "I taught myself" (ἐμαυτὸν ἐδιδαξάμην) because he was self-taught (αὐτοδίδακτον) and arrogant (ὑπερήφανον), nor do I think much of his trick in hiding (κατακρύψαντα) his work in the temple of Artemis (ἐν τῷ τῆς Ἀρτέμιδος ναῷ), in order to achieve publication later in a mysterious way (μυστηριωδῶς). For the pundits say that the tragedian Euripides went down and read it, and from memory little by little, revealed the obscurity of Heraclitus in a serious way (τὸ Ἡρακλείτειον σκότος σπουδαίως). His manner of death showed up his ignorance (ἀμαθίαν).

> *Oratio* 29: Therefore, having seen these things and also taken part in mysteries (μυστηρίων) and having scrutinized the rituals conducted everywhere by effeminate homosexuals and found (εὑρὼν) that among the Romans, their Zeus Latiaris took pleasure in men's gore and bloodshed by manslaughter and that Artemis (Ἄρτεμιν), not far from the great city, practiced arts of the same sort and that different demons in different places were busily encouraging wrong-doing, when I was by myself I began to seek (κατ᾽ ἐμαυτὸν γενόμενος ἐζήτουν) by what means I could discover the truth (τἀληθὲς ἐξευρεῖν). While I was engaged in serious thought (περινοοῦντι δέ μοι τὰ σπουδαῖα) I happened to read some barbarian writings (συνέβη γραφαῖς τισιν ἐντυχεῖν), older (πρεσβυτέραις) by comparison

---

33   The reason that the adjective qualifies the soul, rather than Tatian himself, apart from giving a more modest tone to the expression, is the consistency with his theory of the privileged illuminated souls, like those of the prophets, as formulated in *Or.* 13.

34   Nasrallah 2005. The same *topos* is used in the Eusebian account of Clement's conversion to Christianity after having been initiated into the Greek mysteries (*Praep. ev.* 2.2.64).

with the doctrines of the Greeks, more divine (θειοτέραις) by comparison
with their errors. The outcome was that I was persuaded by these (μοι
πεισθῆναι ταύταις συνέβη) because of the lack of arrogance (τὸ ἄτυφον) in
the wording, the artlessness (τὸ ἀνεπιτήδευτον) of the speakers, the easily
intelligible (εὐκατάληπτον) account of the creation of the World, the foreknowledge of the future, the remarkable quality of the precepts and the
doctrine of a single ruler of the Universe. My soul was taught by God (θεο-
διδάκτου δέ μου γενομένης τῆς ψυχῆς) and I understood that some parts had
a condemnatory effect, while others freed us from many rulers and countless tyrants, giving us not something we had never received, but what we
had been prevented from keeping by our error.

While Tatian is *theodidaktos*, Heraclitus is *autodidaktos*; while Tatian retires to
investigate how he can discover truth, Heraclitus "teaches himself";[35] while
Tatian humbly states that he found the Scriptures by chance, Heraclitus is
proud of his own self-teaching; while Heraclitus' book is obscure and has purposefully hidden meanings, the Scriptures are humble and easily intelligible;
while Heraclitus needs Euripides to interpret him in a serious way (σπου-
δαίως),[36] Tatian's serious effort to find the truth is directly answered by the
Scripture (περινοοῦντι δέ μοι τὰ σπουδαῖα). And of course, while Heraclitus is
ultimately ignorant and his text confusing, the Scriptures make Tatian discover
truth, as they are more ancient and more divine. The opposition is also emphasized using the goddess Artemis as point of reference for paganism:[37] while
Heraclitus hid his book in her sanctuary at Ephesus and hence gave his edition
a mystic allure, Tatian's conversion comes after being disgusted by discovering
(εὑρών: e.g. unveiling the secret of) the last of the mysteries he participates in,

---

35   The text misquotes Heraclitus fr. 101 DK: ἐδιζησάμην ἐμεωυτόν. However, it is noticeable that
      Heraclitus' original "I investigate myself" is closer to Tatian's account of his own "research"
      (*zetein*). The misquotation is probably original, since it aims to support the charge of *auto-
      didaktos*. It is perhaps significant as a reminiscence that the *Epistle of Barnabas* (21.6)
      explains *theodidaktoi* as those who "investigate what the Lord inquires" from them and
      do it "so that they find" it in the day of Judgement (ἐκζητοῦντες τί ζητεῖ κύριος ἀφ' ὑμῶν
      καὶ ποιεῖτε, ἵνα εὕρητε ἐν ἡμέρᾳ κρίσεως). The same two verbs that Tatian associates in this
      passage to *theodidaktos*, *zetein* and *heuriskein*, are present here.

36   This is the manuscript reading, retained by Trelenberg, Aragione and Nesselrath. Whit-
      taker and Marcovich accept Schwartz's conjecture τοῖς σπουδαίοις, which would introduce
      a mystic idea of "the initiated who make the effort to understand." The conjecture seems
      unnecessary.

37   Artemis' relevance as the last stand of paganism may be influenced, as in other Christian
      texts, by the fact that she is the only pagan deity to be mentioned in Acts (19:24–41) as rival
      of Christianity. Cf. Herrero de Jáuregui forthcoming.

that of Artemis (Diana) at Aricia, at the gates of Rome. The contrast is so carefully drawn that it seems to go farther than the usual contraposition between Christian and Pagan "scriptures."[38] In a way, by choosing Heraclitus as a pendant in classical times, but as an anti-model rather than as a model, Tatian follows in a typically subversive way a usual trend of the authors of the Second Sophistic to pick up a great figure from classical times as a reference (e.g., Arrian as the "new Xenophon"): in this case, as an antipodal reference.[39] Among the possible reasons to choose Heraclitus as antagonist, we may think of the Logos-centered content of his book or the obscurity and sententiousness of Tatian's own style.

6 Conclusion: Tatian's Theodidactics

In opposition, therefore, to Heraclitus' self-teaching, or to those who have received mimetic knowledge from others, Tatian's true teaching comes directly from God via the Scripture. This primacy of the text over the teacher, to use Gregory Snyder's terms, is a clear feature of his thought, consistent with the polarity *heuresis/mimesis* that dominates the text from the start, each one with its associated notions and encroaching on other fundamental oppositions like *logos/alogos*. Regarding another crucial polarity in second-century Rome, that of dispersion-centralization theorized by Einar Thomassen, this Scripture-centered theology which downplays the role of teachers puts Tatian closer to the former pole—with the result that later authors with more affinity for doctrinal authority ranked him among Gnostics and Heretics.[40] They also accused him of "exaltation at being a teacher," but, as we are seeing, this exaltation, easy to perceive in the *Oratio*, was justified for Tatian precisely in the fact that teachers had a minor role to play, except for ordering the minds of their audience by giving them adequate access to the divine text. There is scarcely any place in his worldview for the individual charisma of the teacher, which would be a dangerous source of human *mimesis*. It is always subordinated to the true *heuresis* that can only be found in the Scripture. In spite of his rhetorical boasting in

---

38　E.g. Origen *Cels.* 1.18: "And challenging a comparison of book with book, I would say, 'Come now, good sir, take down the poems of Linus, and of Musæus, and of Orpheus, and the writings of Pherecydes, and carefully compare these with the laws of Moses—histories with histories, and ethical discourses with laws and commandments.'"

39　Cf. Whitmarsh 2001, 27. In *Or.* 33 he draws a comparison (33.2: συγκρίναντες) between famous Greek women, led by Sappho, and Christian women to show how superior and more philosophical the latter are: cf. Aragione 2015b.

40　Snyder 2000 on text/teacher; Thomassen 2004 on dispersion vs. centralization.

the *Oratio*, doubtless the cause of many later accusations against Tatian's purported arrogance, this is most probably what he did throughout his life through a painstaking demonstrative work that aimed to attain pure *heuresis*.

In effect, Tatian's doctrine of "theodidactics" based on Scripture is clearly the basis of his life work which he produced back in Syria, after he left Rome, disappointed with his fellow Christians. The *Diatessaron*, whose study is an entire discipline of scholarship by itself, is a unique and momentous attempt to establish a single unified account of Jesus' life and teachings by harmonizing the four Gospels. There is little doubt that Tatain's obsession with the absence of contradictions in God's revelation, and his conviction that in the correct reading of the Scripture lies the key to immediate knowledge of God, gave him the impulse to take up this enterprise. As we have seen, there is a good deal of consistency between the apologetic and the theological parts of the *Oratio* in their consideration of the transmission of truth, and it is plausible that, as in the case of the *Diatessaron*, a similar desire for consistency characterized other lost works by Tatian.

A proof of such consistency is that the same range of meanings that we have examined in *mimesis* and related concepts in the *Oratio* can be also found in another term, *homoiosis*, that is a fundamental notion both in Platonic philosophy and Christian theology.[41] Tatian quotes three times Genesis 1:16 as the standard definition of man: "man is image and likeness of God" (*Or.* 12.1 and 15.3–4: εἰκὼν καὶ ὁμοίωσις), and therefore he must tend to the divine to be true to this pristine nature. However, men have also a certain *homoiosis* with the daemons, who were also created by God, and if he imitates them he falls into the wrong kind of likeness that leads them into the trap of sin, idolatry and condemnation.[42] On the other hand, the prophets philosophized like Moses (40.2: Μωυσέα καὶ τῶν ὁμοίως αὐτῷ φιλοσοφούντων). Therefore, *homoiosis* is a natural state that offers the necessary conditions to achieve *mimesis*, be it legitimate or illegitimate. The basic notion that similar elements are naturally attracted lies behind this fundamental anthropology that, at the same time, links all men in one community of shared *homoiosis* in which pagans have the option of acting like Christians (24.3: κατὰ τὸ ὅμοιον), just as Tatian was *homoiopathes* with the

---

41   The likeness to God (ὁμοίωσις Θεῷ) is a central concept of Imperial Platonic philosophy
      and will be received in Christian theology. Cf. the classical monograph of Merki 1952, the
      recent study of Lavecchia 2006, and a summary with other bibliography in Gerson 2013,
      299, n. 37. It was often linked to *mimesis* also in aesthetic theory (cf. Whitmarsh 2001, 73
      on Dionysius of Halicarnassus).

42   The passages which dwell on relations of *homoiosis* between daemons and men in the
      Oratio are 8.2 (τοὺς ἀκούοντας ἐπὶ τὰ ὅμοια προὐτρέψαντο), 14.2 (τῶν ὁμοίων ἐπικρατεῖν), 14.5
      (τὴν σύστασιν, ὁμοίαν), 16.5 (τοῖς ὁμοίοις αὐτοῖς) 16.6 (τὴν ὁμοίαν αὐτοῖς ὕλην πολεμοῦσιν).

Greeks and then converted. Likewise, man can be an *eikon* of God (7.1, 7.5, 10.4), and treat his own body with utmost rigor and respect as a living temple, or he can become an *eikon* for statues, like that of the tyrant Phalaris (33.5, 34.1).[43]

To conclude. Tatian's position on the transmission of knowledge is based on a central idea that ran counter to the usual admiration for teachers and teaching institutions in the Empire of the second century: illegitimate mimetic wisdom comes from teachers who just aim to cause wonder (*thauma*), and has passion (*pathos*) as its only achievement, instead of the direct knowledge (*mathesis*) of truth through the Scripture that leads to likeness (*homoiosis*) to God. This central idea of "theodidactics," with its implications about Christian and pagan teachers, not only pervades the entire *Oratio*, but is also consistent with all other evidence about Tatian's work. It is natural, therefore, to think that the initial opposition *mimesis/heuresis* was not just a rhetorical contraposition that supports his chronological argument, but a central tenet of Tatian's thought.

Appendix 1: Adam's Condemnation

Let us close this analysis of how truth is (re)discovered and transmitted only through legitimate *mimesis* of God in the *Oratio* with the examination of two obscure testimonies that become more significant in the light of Tatian's "theodidactics." Irenaeus says that Tatian was the first Christian to deny Adam's salvation (*Adv. Haer.* 3.23.1–8): "the ones called Encratites, issuing from Saturninus and Marcion, preached abstinence from marriage ... they likewise deny the salvation of him who was the first formed (Adam). But this last idea was recently invented among them, when a certain Tatian first introduced this blasphemy. He was an auditor of Justin ... and exalted at the prospect of being a teacher, and puffed up as if he were superior to everyone else, he created a unique doctrine. Like those who follow Valentinus, he expounded an account of invisible Aeons; and like Marcion and Saturninus, he said marriage was corruption and fornication. But denying the salvation of Adam was his own doing."

This "heresy" is attributed solely to Tatian with unusual firmness, and we do not know where it may have been formulated. Irenaeus himself seems to link it to the Encratite and Marcionite condemnation of sex, as if there lay the key to Adam's sin. Some scholars have detected instead an emphasis on

---

43   Clement of Alexandria, *Protr.* 10.98 dwells extensively on the inverse relation between the statues of gods as *eikones* of men, and man as *eikon* of God. Cf. Herrero de Jáuregui 2019, 252–257. On Clement's development of some of Tatian's ideas, cf. notes 6 and 32 above.

free will that might be considered proto-Pelagianism. Leaving aside teleological schemes, it is true that the doctrine of Adam's condemnation is consistent with the doctrine of free will and just punishment briefly established in *Oratio* 7.1.[44] It is also, however, linked to the idea of "theodidactics." The ignorant person, the *amathes*, can be saved and led to true knowledge through learning (*manthanein*). His error is due to his following through a chain of illegitimate acts of *mimesis*, the false examples and doctrines of other men or demons. But Adam had been the most *theodidaktos* of all, since he had direct access to God, and he purposefully followed the Devil in exercise of his own free will. Like the fallen angel (*protogonos* in the *Oratio*) he has no possible salvation after he sinned. Adam's individual guilt is then transmitted to other men through *mimesis*, but can be repaired for them since their free will has been less complete. This is a Christian (Tatian's) interpretation of another very important subject for the second-century philosophers, both pagan and Christian, i.e., the transmission of an ancestor's faults to their descendants.[45] When error and sin are a matter of intellectual knowledge, the primordial faults and their transmission are necessarily linked to the transmission of knowledge, i.e., to concepts like *mimesis* and inheritance (*kleronomia*) like those used in Plato, Pythagoras, and Pherecydes.

However, Tatian's individual liberation of the mimetic chains of transmitted error has an enormous price. As "newly born" (*Oratio* 5.3: ἀναγεννηθείς) after his conversion, Tatian's soul is *theodidaktos*, and in this way his own position is akin to Adam's. Once he has directly seen the truth, any fall into sin can be a fatal error comparable to that of the *protogonos* demon, or to Adam's. Perhaps a good deal of Tatian's purported rigidity springs from this terrifying conviction.

Appendix 2: Rhodon vs. Apelles

A second text that deserves comment is one of the few extant fragments from Rhodon, who according to Eusebius had been taught in Rome by Tatian (*Hist. eccl.* 5.13.7). In Rhodon's re-creation of the dialogue with his rival, the Marcionite Apelles, he says: "I laughed when I recognized him, for while he said he was a teacher, he did not know how to prove his teaching" (ἐγὼ δὲ γελάσας κατέγνων αὐτοῦ, διότι διδάσκαλος εἶναι λέγων, οὐκ ἤδει τὸ διδασκόμενον ὑπ' αὐτοῦ κρατύνειν). In effect, Apelles failed to justify his belief in the single divine prin-

---

44   Petersen 2008, 151. The link with *Oratio* 7.1 was already established by Barnard 1968.
45   Plutarch dedicated a whole treatise, *De sera numinis vindicta*, to the transmission of ances-tral fault to the descendants, which was later reappraised by Proclus. Cf. Gagné 2013, chapters 1 and 2.

ciple, and "he said that he did not know, but he was simply inclined to think in this way" (μὴ γινώσκειν ἔλεγεν, οὕτως δὲ κινεῖσθαι μόνον). Asked again by Rhodon, he said "that he could not establish how there is one uncreated God, but he believed it" (μὴ ἐπίστασθαι πῶς εἷς ἐστιν ἀγένητος θεός, τοῦτο δὲ πιστεύειν). In this *kineisthai* alleged by Apelles, usually translated as "inclination," some (German) scholars have seen the influence of Stoic thought, e.g. Poseidonius.[46] However, we must remember that Apelles' words are transmitted by Rhodon, and that he may be projecting his own perspective of his rival's view in order to deride him—as Tatian does without scruple in the *Oratio* and all the apologists and polemicists do in their works. Now let us remember that, in the *Oratio*, *kinesis* is exclusively compared in the most pejorative way to the spasmodic movements of the actor who aims to cause misleading *thauma* (22.2: κινουμένῳ παρὰ φύσιν ... κινοῦνται δὲ κινήσεις ἃς οὐκ ἐχρῆν). As this dialogue with Apelles shows, the preference for doctrine and demonstration over sheer emotion as the backbone of true knowledge was a principle that Rhodon shared with Tatian, and following his teacher's rhetoric, he may have attributed the (failed) argument of *kinesis* to Apelles in a polemical writing. The Tatianic ring of his "laughing at a so-called teacher" is unmistakable.

Acknowledgements

I am grateful to Greg Snyder for the revision of my English, and to the anonymous reader for his/her fruitful suggestions to improve several aspects of the original paper.

Bibliography

Aragione, Gabriella. 2015a. *Taziano. Ai Greci*, Milan: Paoline.
Aragione, Gabriella. 2015b. "'Ne raillez pas nos femmes philosophes.' La description des comportements féminins et sa fonction identitaire dans le *Discours aux Grecs* de Tatien." Pages 37–51 in *L'identité à travers l'éthique Nouvelles perspectives sur la formation des identités collectives dans le monde gréco-romain*. Edited by Katell Berthelot, Ron Naiweld and Daniel Stökl Ben Ezra. Turnhout: Brepols.
Barnard, L.W. 1968. "The Heresy of Tatian—Once Again." *Journal of Ecclesiastical History* 19:1–10.

---

46   Theiler 1964, 143; May 1994, 155; Greschat 2000, 80.

Bellinzoni, Arthur J. 1967. *The Sayings of Jesus in the Writings of Justin Martyr.* Leiden: Brill.

Crawford, Matthew R. 2015. "'Reordering the Confusion': Tatian, the Second Sophistic, and the Diatessaron." *Zeitschrift für Antikes Christentum* 19.2:209–236.

Crawford, Matthew R. 2018. "Tatian." *Brill Encyclopedia of Early Christianity Online*, General Editor David G. Hunter, Paul J.J. van Geest, Bert Jan Lietaert Peerbolte. Leiden: Brill.

Dörrie, Heinrich. 1938. *Leid und Erfahrung: Die Wort und Sinn-Verbindung pathein-mathein im griechischen Denken.* Mainz: F. Steiner.

Droge, Arthur J. 1989. *Homer or Moses? Early Christian Interpretations of the History of Culture.* Tübingen; Mohr Siebeck.

Eshleman, Kendra. 2013. *The Social World of Intellectuals in the Roman Empire: Sophists, Philosophers, and Christians.* Cambridge: Cambridge University Press.

Foster, Paul. 2010. "Tatian." Pages 15–35 in *Early Christian Thinkers: The Lives and Legacies of Twelve Key Figures.* Edited by Paul Foster. London: SPCK.

Gagné, Renaud. 2013. *Ancestral Fault in Ancient Greece.* Cambridge: Cambridge University Press.

Gerson, Lloyd P. 2013. *From Plato to Platonism.* Ithaca: Cornell University Press.

Greschat, Katharina. 2000. *Apelles und Hermogenes: Zwei Theologische Lehrer Des Zweiten Jahrhunderts.* Leiden: Brill.

Hanig, Roman. 1999. "Tatian und Justin. Ein Vergleich." *Vigiliae Christianae* 53:31–73.

Herrero de Jáuregui, Miguel. 2019. "Xenophanes redivivus? L'anthropomorphisme des dieux d'Homère dans la littérature apologétique chrétienne." Pages 235–260 in *Les dieux d'Homère II. Anthropomorphismes.* Edited by Renaud Gagné and Miguel Herrero de Jáuregui. Liège: Presses Universitaires de Liège.

Herrero de Jáuregui, Miguel. forthcoming. "Great is Artemis of the Ephesians! The cults of Artemis as icon of Graeco-Roman paganism." In *Diana, Artemis and Related Cults in Ancient Greece and Italy.* Edited by Giovanni Casadio and Patricia A. Johnston. Cambridge: Scholar's Press.

Hunt, Emily J. 2003. *Christianity in the Second Century. The Case of Tatian.* London: Routledge.

Karadimas, Dimitrios. 2003. *Tatian's Oratio Ad Graecos: Rhetoric and Philosophy/Theology.* Stockholm: Almqvist & Wiksell.

Kleingünther, Adolf. 1933. *Πρῶτος εὑρετής.* Leipzig: Dieterich.

Koltun-Fromm, N. 2008. "Re-Imagining Tatian: The Damaging Effects of Polemical Rhetoric." *Journal of Early Christian Studies* 16:1–30.

Lampe, Peter. 2003. *From Paul to Valentinus: Christians At Rome in the First Two Centuries.* Translated by Michael Stenhauser. Edited by Marshall D. Johnson. Minneapolis: Fortress Press.

Lavecchia, Salvatore. 2006. *Una via che conduce al divino: la homoiosis theo nella filosofia di Platone.* Milan: Vita e Pensiero.

Lössl, Josef. 2010. "Zwischen Christologie und Rhetorik: Zum Ausdruck 'Kraft des Wortes' (λόγου δύναμις) in Tatians 'Rede an die Griechen'." Pages 129–147 in *Logos der Vernunft-Logos des Glaubens: Festschrift Edgar Früchtel zum 80. Geburtstag.* Edited by F.R. Prostmeier and H. Lona. Berlin: De Gruyter.

Marcovich, Miroslav. 1995. *Tatian. Oratio ad Graecos.* Berlin: De Gruyter.

May, Gerhard. 1994. *Creatio ex Nihilo. The Doctrine of 'Creation out of Nothing' in Early Christian Thought.* Translated by A.S. Worrall. Edinburgh: T&T Clark.

McGehee, Michael. 1993. "Why Tatian Never 'Apologized' to the Greeks." *Journal of Early Christian Studies* 1:143–158.

Merki, Hubert. 1952. Ὁμοίωσις Θεῷ: *Von der platonischen Angleichung an Gott zur Gottähnlichkeit bei Gregor von Nyssa.* Freiburg in der Schweiz: Paulusverlag.

Moss, Candida. 2010. *The Other Christs: Imitating Jesus in Ancient Christian Ideologies of Martyrdom.* Oxford: Oxford University Press.

Nasrallah, Laura. 2006. "The Rhetoric of Conversion and the Construction of Experience: The Case of Justin Martyr." Pages 467–474 in *Studia Patristica: Papers presented at the 14th International Conference on Patristic Studies held in Oxford 2003.* Edited by F. Young, M. Edwards, P. Parvis. Leuven: Peeters.

Nasrallah, Laura. 2010. *Christian Responses to Roman Art and Architecture: The Second-Century Church Amid the Spaces of Empire.* Cambridge: Cambridge University Press.

Nesselrath, Heinz-Günther. 2016. *Gegen falsche Götter und falsche Bildung. Tatian, Rede an die Griechen.* Tübingen: Mohr Siebeck.

Petersen, William L. 1994. *Tatian's Diatessaron: Its Creation, Dissemination, Significance, and History in Scholarship.* Leiden: Brill.

Petersen, William L. 2008. "Tatian the Assyrian." Pages 125–158 in *Companion to Second Century Christian Heretics.* Edited by Antti Marjanen and Petri Luomanen. Leiden: Brill.

Snyder, H. Gregory. 2000. *Teachers and Texts in in the Ancient World: Philosophers, Jews, and Christians.* London: Routledge.

Theiler, Willy. 1964. *Die Vorbereitung des Platonismus.* Berlin: Weidmann.

Thomassen, Einar. 2004. "Orthodoxy and Heresy in Second Century Rome." *Harvard Theological Review* 97:241–256.

Thraede, Klaus. 1962. "Das Lob des Erfinders." *Rheinisches Museum* 105:158–186.

Trelenberg, Jörg. 2012. *Tatianos. Oratio ad Graecos.* Tübingen: Mohr Siebeck.

Yoshiko Reed, Annette. 2004. "The Trickery of the Fallen Angels and the Demonic Mimesis of the Divine: Aetiology and Polemics in the Writings of Justin Martyr." *Journal of Early Christian Studies* 12:141–171.

Van Staden, Heinrich. 1997. "Galen and the 'Second Sophistic.'" *Bulletin of the Institute of Classical Studies. Supplement* 68:33–54.

Whitmarsh, Tim. 2001. *Greek Literature and the Roman Empire.* Oxford: Oxford University Press.

Whittaker, Molly. 1982. *Tatian*: Oratio ad Graecos and Fragments. Oxford: Clarendon Press.

Wyrwa, Dietmar. 2018, "Tatian." Pages 817–824 in *Philosophie der Kaiserzeit und der Spätantike*. Die Philosophie der Antike 5. Edited by Christoph Riedweg, Christoph Horn, and Dietmar Wyrwa. Basel: Schwabe.

Zadorojnyi, Alexei V. 2012. "Mimesis and the (plu)past in Plutarch's *Lives*." Pages 175–198 in *Time and Narrative in Ancient Historiography: The 'Plupast' from Herodotus to Appian*. Edited by Jonas Grethlein and Christopher B. Krebs. Cambridge: Cambridge University Press.

CHAPTER 9

Shoemakers and Syllogisms: Theodotus "the Cobbler" and His School

H. Gregory Snyder

If we imagined a scenario in which a literate, second-century Roman like Aulus Gellius dropped into the local cobbler's shop and there found the proprietor and a few friends comparing manuscripts on a worktable among the awls, eyelets, and scraps of leather, we might think that he would have been somewhat surprised. Taken as a class, shoemakers would not seem to be likely candidates for the high literacy required to write and collate manuscripts. And we might think it would have been equally surprising for our literate intellectual to learn that the Christians were parsing syllogisms and dedicating themselves to the study of logic and textual criticism. Though followers of the Christ cult had edged on to the social radar by the late-second century, most people acquainted with the group would not have expected to find them working through the fine points of Aristotelian logic or discussing Galen's most recent public dissection at the Temple of Peace. In light of these reasonable assumptions about literacy and social class, the surprising case of Theodotus, leather-worker, logician, text-critic, and school founder, merits a close look. It also provides an opening to explore one particular instance of a school-like group in the city of Rome.

In fact, as I hope to show in this paper, our literate Roman might have looked upon this manuscript-collating, logic-chopping cobbler with appreciation, recognizing in him a type of teacher/philosopher known to us from stories about Socrates and his contemporary, Simon the Cobbler. Stories about cobbler-philosophers are frequently found in the literature, to the point where the cobbler-philosopher becomes enough of a convention to draw the satirical eye of Lucian. I propose that Theodotus "the Cobbler" fashioned his image in light of this widely-known cultural trope, and that this social profile makes him distinct from other Christian teachers and intellectuals such as Justin Martyr.

As the alleged originator of adoptionism, Theodotus figures reliably—if briefly—in histories of early Christian theology.[1] According to the earliest sources that mention him, he invented the heresy that Christ was merely human.

---

1 E.g., Heine 2004, 204–205.

And while his doctrinal stance has drawn a good bit of scholarly attention, there is surprisingly little on Theodotus as a teacher and on the paradoxical social profile he occupies, as a leatherworker, philosopher, and textual critic.[2] My aim in this paper is not to ascertain what his beliefs were, nor is it to reconstruct the historical details about Theodotus and his successors. Rather, the goal is to understand the social and cultural outlines of a teacher like this and plausibly situate him in the landscape of religious experts and entrepreneurs in late second-century Rome. How do we understand Theodotus and the group of followers he attracted, a group that persisted, it seems, through at least three generations of teachers and students? How shall we compare this "school" to other such groups in the city? This set of questions has not been adequately addressed.

What little is known about Theodotus the Cobbler comes from a source known as *The Little Labyrinth*, which was written by an unknown Christian author that Eusebius quotes and places in the Severan period (193–211).[3] This anonymous writer (henceforth, "Anonymous") addressed himself to the teachings of a certain Artemon, who taught that Christ was a "mere man" before his adoption as the Son of God. The author of *The Little Labyrinth* says that Artemon and his followers claimed this teaching was the majority opinion "until the time of Victor," a bishop in Rome from 189–198, but that the truth had been corrupted under Victor's successor Zephyrinus. Apparently, the followers of Artemon were claiming that Victor shared their opinion in this matter and that this belief had been commonplace before Victor's time. Anonymous objects:

> How then is it possible that after the mind of the church had been announced for so many years that the generation before Victor can have preached as these say? Why are they not ashamed of so calumniating Victor when they know quite well that Victor excommunicated (ἀπεκήρυξεν τῆς κοινωνίας) Theodotus the Cobbler (ὁ σκυτεύς) the founder and father of this insurrection which denies God, when he said that Christ was a mere man? For if Victor was so minded towards them as their blasphemy teaches, how could he have thrown out (ἀποβάλλω) Theodotus who invented this heresy?[4]

---

2 See Walzer 1949, 75–86; Lampe (2003, 344–348) covers the "Theodotians" generally; Ehrman 1993a, 51–52; Ehrman 1993b, 46–51.

3 *Hist. eccl.* 5.28. This estimation on the part of Eusebius cannot be taken at face value, given that the treatise (λόγος) is anonymous. John Fitzgerald (Fitzgerald 1998) gives a thorough treatment of the issues of authorship and date; he dates *The Little Labyrinth* to the 240s or early part of the 250s.

4 Eusebius, *Hist. eccl.* 5.28 (tr. Lake 1.519). I employ Lake's translation throughout, though mind-

This comment by the anonymous, unnamed critic of Artemon allows us to situate Theodotus the Cobbler in Rome as a contemporary of Victor, at the end of the second century. "Anonymous" maintains that the heresy of the otherwise unknown Artemon follows in the same stream of tradition as that of Theodotus.[5]

One further piece of information comes to us from Hippolytus, who mentions that Theodotus was a native of Byzantium.[6] If true, he is yet another Greek-speaking immigrant from the east, like Valentinus (Alexandria), Marcion (Pontus), and Justin (Judaea), all of whom made their way to Rome. But there is no way of knowing when Theodotus first came to Rome or set himself up as a teacher.[7] Events in and around Byzantium were especially turbulent in the last decade of the second century, at the time surrounding the ascension of Severus. His rival claimant to the throne, Pescennius Niger, made Byzantium a base of operations, and the heavily fortified city held out even after Niger decamped for the East. After a determined resistance, the city fell in 194 to Severus, who demolished the walls, deprived the city of its privileges, and confiscated the property of its citizens.[8] Perhaps the rising tide of events would have encouraged emigration before the crisis, or in the wake of it, brought flotsam and jetsam to the West. Perhaps Theodotus had relocated to Rome twenty years prior and had been pursuing his craft and his work as a teacher for many years. But given the history of the city as a holdout against Severus, it raises the possibility that Hippolytus, by attaching "Byzantium" to Theodotus at the time of his writing in the early third century, meant to do more than simply provide information about point of origin: it may have carried with it the implicit charge of rebellion. Perhaps it is not a coincidence that Anonymous accuses Theodotus of "insurrection" (ἀποστάσις).[9]

Writing much later, Epiphanius also treats Theodotus at some length. He does not know whether the sect still exists in his day, but bases his comments on

---

ful of and sometimes altering formulations too much indebted to traditional patristic categories.

5 While the two groups may share certain Christological beliefs, they are not necessarily genetically connected. Given that heresiologists tend to defame their targets by lumping them together with other known "heretics," we cannot assume that Artemon is connected in any way with the followers of Theodotus.

6 *Refutatio Omnium Haeresium* 7.35: ὢν Βυζάντιος (ed. Marcovich, 318; 7.23 in the Ante-Nicene Fathers edition) and 10.23 (ed. Marcovich, 401; 10.19 ANF).

7 Ehrman (1993a, 52) asserts that Theodotus "came to Rome from Byzantium in the days of Pope Victor (189–198 CE)," but nothing in the sources precludes an earlier arrival.

8 Dio Cassius 75.14.3; In 75.10–14, Dio relates more details about Byzantium and the siege.

9 *Hist. eccl.* 5.28.6 (ed. Lake, 518).

certain "written works" known to him. On his account, Theodotus was a "cobbler by trade, but very learned in argument" (σκυτεὺς τὴν τέχνην, πολυμαθὴς δὲ τῷ λόγῳ).[10] He came to Rome in the aftermath of a persecution—"I cannot say which one"—in which he had been arrested along with other Christians. Unlike them, he denied Christ, and for reasons of shame moved to Rome, whereupon being recognized by the Christians there, he was charged with "falling away from the truth, in spite of "being a man of great learning (ἀνὴρ πολυμαθής)." By way of response, he claimed that he did not deny God, but the man Christ, and thereafter, went about collecting texts as "an excuse for his defection." Some of this represents polemical extrapolation on the part of Epiphanius, but he does go on to quote from a document that preserves exegetical arguments used by Theodotus to argue for the merely human nature of Christ, and this appears to be a legitimate source, independent of *The Little Labyrinth*. But first, let us focus on what can be known about Theodotus himself, and the image of the "learned cobbler."

On three occasions, the anonymous source quoted by Eusebius describes Theodotus as "ὁ σκυτεύς," which Lake renders as "the Cobbler."[11] Richard Walzer reads the term as "leather merchant," perhaps because Theodotus' high literacy level and social associations seem more appropriate to an upscale businessman than to a simple craftsman or shopkeeper.[12] A leather merchant who procured and sold hides for army use (shields, shoes, tents, armor, saddlery) might have indeed made a comfortable living.[13] Anonymous goes on to tell a story that touches on the group's finances:

> There was a certain confessor, Natalius, not long ago but in our time. He was deceived by Asclepiodotus and by a second Theodotus, a banker (τρα-πεζίτης) These were both disciples of Theodotus the cobbler (θεοδότου τοῦ σκυτέως μαθηταί) who was first removed from the fellowship (ἀφορισθέν-

10   Epiphanius, *Pan.* 54.1 (ed. Karl Holl 317); English translation in Williams 2013.
11   Eusebius *Hist. eccl.* 5.28 (ed. Lake, 1.519). LSJ (s.v. σκυτεύς) equates it with σκυτοτόμος, but the references given do not mention shoes; the word is used in a list of crafts, e.g., Xenophon, *Mem.* 4.2.2: "... coppersmiths, carpenters, workers in iron, cobblers (σκυτεύς), and painters were all busy making weapons of war, so that you might have thought that the city was really a war factory"; nothing here limits the meaning to "cobbler" instead of the more generic "leather worker" or "leather cutter." Leather goods for an army might include tents and saddlery as well as boots. Especially germane in this regard is Epictetus *Disc.* 1.19.19, in which τοῦ Καίσαρος σκυτεύς can hardly mean "leather merchant of the Emperor."
12   Walzer 1949, 75; Frend (1984, 344) adopts Walzer's "leather merchant."
13   C. Julius Alcimus, a "supplier to shoemakers" (*comparator mercis sutoriae*; CIL 5.5927) employs 62 freedmen and freedwomen (Lau 1967, 152).

τος τῆς κοινωνίας) by Victor, who, as I said, was then bishop, for this way of thinking, or rather of not thinking. Natalius was persuaded by them to be called bishop of this heresy with a salary, so that he was paid a hundred and fifty denarii a month by them.[14]

Charges of taking money for church duties is standard polemic and should be viewed critically, but if true, this would indicate a significant degree of financial capacity on the part of the group.[15] At first blush, this seems inconsistent with a point of origin in a cobbler's shop. But Asclepiodotus and the banker Theodotus belong to the second generation of Theodotus the Cobbler's school, and by this time, the school may have attracted well-to-do patrons. In any event, I find no place in the literature where the term σκυτεύς necessarily carries the more elevated sense of "leather merchant."[16] Moreover, to call Theodotus a leather merchant rather than a cobbler obscures a most crucial fact: there is a long and widely known connection between philosophers and shoemakers. The appellation, "Theodotus the Cobbler" carries a distinct and special valence that should not be missed.

On the one hand, the cobbler was often taken as a classic example of a menial craftsman. On numerous occasions, when describing the ideal society, Plato uses the cobbler as an archetypal artisan.[17] In a later time period, Pliny the Elder tells the story of the famous painter Apelles:

> It was under these circumstances, they say, that he was censured by a shoemaker (*sutor*) for having represented the shoes with one shoe-string too little. The next day, the shoemaker, quite proud at seeing the former error corrected, thanks to his advice, began to criticize the leg; upon which Apelles, full of indignation, popped his head out, and reminded him that a shoemaker should give no opinion beyond the shoes, a piece of advice which has equally passed into a proverbial saying ("let not the shoemaker judge beyond the sandal": *ne supra crepidam sutor iudicaret*).[18]

---

14   *Hist. eccl.* 5.28 (ed. Lake, 521).

15   An average civilian worker might earn 25 denarii per month; skilled quarrymen at Mons Claudianus (in Egypt) earned a maximum of 47 denarii a month plus rations. A Roman legionary infantryman in the second century earned 300 denarii per annum (Cuvigny 1996, 139–145).

16   The Suda (s.v. σκυτοτόμος) equates it with σκυτοτόμος and "thong-cutter" (λωροτόμος) which emphasizes the manual labor aspect of the term. In *Rep.* 601, Plato uses σκυτεύς and σκυτοτόμος interchangeably and in quick succession.

17   Plato, *Rep.* 333a, 369d (σκυτοτόμος), 370d, 397e, 374b, 434a, 443c, 598b, 601a, 601c.

18   Pliny the Elder, *Nat.* 35.36. The story is perhaps influenced by the comment of Socrates,

The proverb suggests that while the shoemaker may indeed possess expertise within the boundaries of his craft, he should not stray outside those boundaries.

It is this very typicality of the craft that makes the image of the shoemaker a favorite of the satirists. Nothing is more objectionable than a shoemaker getting above his station, either by striving or by chance. Martial is especially galled by a slave cobbler who has inherited his owner's estate:

> You used to stretch ancient hides with your teeth and bite an old shoe sole rotten with mud: now you possess the Praenestine realm of your patron, gone before his time ... But my foolish parents taught me my ABC. What use to me are grammarians and rhetors? Break your puny pens and tear up your little books, Thalia, if a shoe can give all that to a cobbler (*sutor*).[19]

Sardonically, Martial juxtaposes his own estate as literate but impecunious intellectual to that of a cobber, whose simple craft carries him to the very feet of the emperor. Literacy has failed to yield the fruit it promised, while illiteracy has been no impediment, and the cobbler, of all the craftsmen, makes for the sharpest contrast to the literate intellectual. A job that involves handling and gnawing on muck-encrusted shoes is the lowest employment imaginable, quite opposite to the privileges (supposedly) afforded by literacy—hence the sharp effect of the epigram. Epictetus also employs the figure of the cobbler in a story about the unexpected twists of fate:

> Epaphroditus had a shoemaker (σκυτεύς) whom he sold because he was good for nothing. This fellow by some good luck was bought by one of Caesar's men, and became Caesar's shoemaker. You should have seen what respect Epaphroditus paid to him ...[20]

Once the owner and the social superior, the master has now become the client, paying calls and fawning on his former slave, and a slave *cobbler* to boot; a most repulsive outcome. Galen too, finds it objectionable that cobblers (as well as

---

that craftsmen who are confidant within their particular τέχνη tend to think themselves wise in other matters as well (*Apol.* 22).

19   *Ep.* 9.73 (tr. Shackleton-Bailey). The same scenario, where a cobbler receives an estate, is portrayed twice by Lucian in *The Cock* (§ 12 and 15).

20   *Disc.* 1.19.19.

carpenters, dyers, and bronze workers) presume to practice medicine.[21] And Celsus disparages Christians by observing:

> They leave their fathers and schoolmasters, and along with the women and little children who are their playfellows to the wooldresser's shop, or to the cobbler's, or to the washerwoman's shop, that they may attain to perfection.[22]

Cobblers, then, come naturally to mind when intellectuals and elites look for examples of low professions.

Not surprisingly, what Martial and Epictetus find objectionable—the sudden inversion of status—Lucian stages as a comedy in *Cataplus*, or Voyage to the Underworld, where he juxtaposes the shoemaker (σκυτοτόμος) Micyllus with the cruel and rapacious ruler Megapenthes, who keeps sneaking off from the band of newly-deceased, underworld travelers in an attempt to return to the upper world. Micyllus relishes the precipitous downfall of the tyrant, and the sudden erasure of all the distinctions that seemed to matter in life:

> Bless me, how dark it is! ... All complexions are alike here, no question of beauty, greater or less. Why, the cloak I thought so shabby before passes muster here as well as royal purple; the darkness hides both alike ...[23]

His chipper attitude mystifies Hermes, who ferries the band over the River Styx:

> *Her.* Why, Micyllus, have *you* never an Oh or an Ah? It is quite improper that any shade should cross the stream, and make no moan.
> *Mi.* Get along with you. What have I to do with Ohs and Ahs? I'm enjoying the trip!
> *Her.* Still, just a groan or two. It's expected.
> *Mi.* Well, if I must, here goes.—Farewell, leather, farewell! Ah, Soles, old Soles!—Oh, ancient Boots!—Woe's me! Never again shall I sit empty from morn till night; never again walk up and down, of a winter's day, naked, unshod, with chattering teeth! My knife, my awl, will be another's: whose, ah! whose?
> *Her.* Yes, that will do. We are nearly there.[24]

---

21   Galen, *De Methodo Medendi* 1.1.2 (ed. Kühn 10.5.9).
22   *Contra Celsum* 3.55 (Chadwick 1953, 166).
23   *Catapl.* 22 (tr. Fowler).
24   *Catapl.* 20 (tr. Fowler).

In high spirits, Micyllus falls in with Cyniscus, a Cynic philosopher, who is also taking well to his new life among the shades. Cyniscus' only desire is to make things as difficult as possible for Megapenthes. Because of their hard circumstances and similar outlook, both cobbler and philosopher share a common attitude. Both forms of life conduce to similar outcomes: when Rhadamanthus inspects their bodies for besmirching marks of sin, he finds nothing on either Cynic or cobbler.

This chummy fraternizing between cobbler and philosopher is not Lucian's innovation: cobblers and philosophers have a long association in philosophy and literature. A foundational figure in this regard was Simon the Cobbler, who supposedly hosted Socrates in his workshop in the Athenian Agora:

> Simon was a citizen of Athens and a cobbler (σκυτοτόμος). When Socrates came to his workshop (ἐργαστήριον) and began to converse, he used to make notes of all that he could remember.[25]

Diogenes Laertius goes on to tell how Pericles and other aristocrats used to drop by this shop for conversation, and how, when Pericles wished to put him on retainer, Simon declined, saying that he preferred to keep his job and along with it, his self-sufficiency and his freedom of speech.[26] Plutarch also mentions Simon the Cobbler as a conversation partner of Socrates and Pericles.[27]

While these notices about Simon come relatively late, they are not implausible. Xenophon never mentions Simon, but he informs us that Socrates used to frequent the shops and storefronts around the Agora, and describes an interaction with Euthydemus, a handsome youth who fancied himself rather too highly because he had acquired a great many "writings of poets and famous sophists." Because he was still too young to enter the Agora, he goes to the saddlery shop (ἡνιοποιεῖον) and it is in this leather-working shop where he encounters Socrates and his friends.[28] The orator Lysias makes a similar remark in a speech addressed to the citizens of Athens: "Each of you is in the habit of dropping by different shops: perfumers, barbers, leather-workers (σκυτοτο-μεῖον), generally, those nearest the Agora" (Lysias, 24.10). There is even archaeological evidence for the existence of a cobbler's shop with a proprietor named

---

25   Diog. Laert. 2.122; see also Goulet 1997, 119–125; Sellars 2003, 207–216.
26   Diog. Laert. 2.122–123.
27   Plutarch, *Maxime cum principibus* (*Mor.* 776B).
28   Xen. *Mem.* 4.2.1.

Simon on the corner of the Agora: bone eyelets, hobnails, and a kylix-style bowl with ΣΙΜΟΝΟΣ inscribed on its base.[29]

The connection between cobblers and philosophers crops up again in a story about Crates (ca. 360–280 BCE), one of the foundational figures of Cynicism. The anecdote derives from one of his students, Zeno of Citium, who became the patriarch of the Stoic school of philosophy. Some of Crates' followers, Zeno among them, were in a cobbler's shop belonging to a certain Philiscus, listening to Crates read aloud from Aristotle's *Protrepticus*. In that treatise, Aristotle compliments Themison, the dedicatee of the work, as being especially equipped for the study of philosophy in light of his wealth and easy circumstances. Philiscus attends to the reading but keeps on stitching. Crates pauses to address him, "it seems to me, Philiscus, that I should write a *Protrepticus* for you, since I see that you have more advantages for being a philosopher than the man for whom Aristotle wrote."[30] For Crates, at least, a life spent practicing a humble but useful craft qualifies a person for philosophical pursuits. A related point is made by Plutarch, in his treatise, *That the Philosopher Ought to Converse with Rulers*, where the figure of Simon is used as an example of the class of philosopher who shuns relations with the powerful in order to avoid any dependency or obligation that would limit his freedom of speech.[31]

Similar references occur in later cynic literature. In the so-called Cynic epistles, pseudepigraphic letters written under the names of students of Socrates and dating (probably) from the second century CE, Simon occurs again as a character and even as a correspondent.[32] "Antisthenes" writes to "Aristippus," chiding him for paying court to the Sicilian tyrant Dionysius. In his sarcastic reply, Aristippus describes the wretched life he endures, eating and drinking extravagantly, dallying with three beautiful courtesans supplied by Dionysius. He advises Antisthenes to consult with Simon the shoemaker (σκυτοτόμος), "in whom you have someone who is greater in wisdom than anyone ever was or will be and converse with him." The tradition preserves a response, ostensibly from Simon, that runs as follows:

> I hear that you ridicule our wisdom in the presence of Dionysius. I admit that I am a shoemaker and that I do work of that nature, and in like manner I would, if it were necessary, cut straps once more for the purpose of

---

29 Thompson 1960, 34–40.
30 Stobaeus, *Flor.* 95,21 (ed. von Arnim, 63–64).
31 Plutarch, *Maxime cum principibus* (*Mor.* 776B).
32 On the date, see Malherbe 1977, 27–31.

admonishing foolish men who think that they are living according to the teaching of Socrates when they are living in great luxury.[33]

"Aristippus" writes back in a seemingly conciliatory but still insouciant tone, in which he professes to admire Simon:

> I do admire and praise you, since, though you are but a shoemaker (σκυ-τικός), you are filled with wisdom and used to persuade Socrates and the most handsome and noble youths to sit with you ...[34]

He even invites Simon to decamp for Sicily, in particular, to Syracuse, where "straps (ἱμάντες) are held in honor, and other leather goods." At any rate, Simon should cut ties with Antisthenes, who counsels all the Athenians to go barefoot and begging, advice "that is contrary to your craft."

And finally, Simon turns up outside of Cynic and Socratic sub-literatures. He is mentioned as an example of someone who managed to rise above his lowly origins in Aelius Theon's *Progymnasmata*, a training manual for teachers, most probably deriving from Alexandria in the first century CE.[35] He also makes frequent appearances in the commentary literature on Aristotle, where he is described as a student of Socrates, serving as a case study in predication: Simon may be good, and Simon may be a leatherworker, but it does not necessarily follow that Simon is therefore a good leather worker.[36] And we have seen Lucian make use of Micyllus the cobbler as the boon companion of a Cynic philosopher, a cobbler whose life of hard knocks makes him a practical philosopher. In fact, the connection between cobblers and the name "Simon" is sufficiently established that Lucian can use the name for one of his cobblers that vaults from rags to riches by inheriting an estate.[37]

And when it comes to exploring background elements in the case of the Christian philosopher Theodotus, there is yet another important strand to consider, namely the example of the Apostle Paul, a tent-maker along with Prisca and Aquila, his Jewish co-workers (σκηνοποιός; Acts 18:3). The term is quite unusual and does not occur in earlier literature, but since tents were

---

33   *Cynic Epistles*, 251 (tr. Stowers).

34   *Cynic Epistles*, 251 (tr. Stowers).

35   Older and corrupt editions of the work referred to "Heron" the shoemaker, but recent manuscript discoveries confirm that "Simon" should be read; see Patillon and Bolognesi 1997, 111; also Kennedy 1998, 476–480.

36   For references, see Goulet 1997.

37   Lucian, *The Cock*, 15.

typically made of leather, Paul qualifies as a leather-worker. But as we have seen, "leather-worker" often overlaps significantly with "cobbler." In Rufinus' Latin translation of Origen's commentary on Romans, when Paul, Prisca and Aquila are described as *artifices tabernaculorum* (a quotation of Acts 18:3), the unusual expression is explained: "that is, a cobbler" (*hoc est, sutor*).[38] And Theodoret utilizes the phrase, "the writings of the leatherworker" (τὰ τοῦ σκυ-τοτόμου συγγράμματα) as a way of referring to Paul's letters, making an apparent equation between the trades of leatherworker and tent-maker.[39]

How then shall we understand the appellation "Cobbler" that Anonymous applies to Theodotus? Three possibilities present themselves. First, it may be that the term carried within it a polemical jab of the sort Martial would have made: "Theodotus the *Cobbler* ... that gnawer on shoe leather." But it is most unlikely and arbitrary to suppose that Anonymous would have simply manu-factured and applied the name out of the blue by way of insult if Theodotus did not have some actual connection to the trade. Second, it is possible that Theodotus simply chanced to be or was at some point a cobbler who happened to possess the remarkably high literacy necessary to collate manuscripts, or to stand at the head of a group of people who did, and that "cobbler" was applied because he was, in fact, a cobbler. But this seems to be a simplistic reading of the evidence: taking a wink for a mere blink, as Clifford Geertz says in his account of "thick description." It is far more likely, I would argue, that the surname "Cobbler" has been claimed by Theodotus himself with conscious reference to the rich literary and philosophical connotations of the term—anchored in the figure of Simon, a disciple of Socrates, supposedly the first person to write a Socratic dialogue—affiliated with the free-speaking, self-sufficiency of the Cynics. In addition, it seems highly likely that Theodotus also drew on the precedent of the Apostle Paul, another literate leatherworker, whose followers copied, gathered, and distributed written texts. As such, the appellation "Cob-bler" is a part of Theodotus' own self-presentation. By using it, Theodotus lays claim to a particular niche in the philosophical spectrum and appeals to those who would have appreciated that tradition.

Theodotus has thus situated himself and his work in a distinctly differ-ent cultural niche than the barefoot cynics racketing around marketplaces or well-heeled dandies such Aulus Gellius and his friends. He can also be distin-guished from Justin, who seems to have presented himself as a professional

---

38   *Patrologia Graeca* 14.1279 (ed. Migne). The reference is from Hock 1980, 20. It is difficult to
      say whether this explanatory remark goes back to Origen or to Rufinus' Latin translation.
39   *Graecarum affectionum curatio* § 80 (PG 83.945). John Chrysostom, in his fourth homily on
      2 Timothy, also refers to Paul as a σκυτοτόμος (PG 62.622).

teacher, taking apparent pride in the public display of his philosopher's cloak, and engaging in public disputation with opponents like the Cynic philosopher Crescens.[40] Like the original Simon the Cobbler in ancient Athens, Theodotus may have been a stay-at-home philosopher, rooted primarily in his workshop, if he followed the *modus operandi* implicit within the title, "the Cobbler."

If Paul is included in the intellectual ancestry of Theodotus and his group, a few further questions arise naturally. Traditional accounts of church history make Theodotus the founder of adoptionism. But Paul himself can be recruited to that line of thought, for example, Rom. 1:7: "descended from David according to the flesh and declared to be the Son of God with power according to the spirit of holiness by resurrection from the dead" (Rom. 1:4). In Acts 13:32–33, Paul, describing the resurrection of Jesus, is made to say (quoting Psalm 2), "you are my Son; today I have begotten you." It may be that Theodotus and his students would have seen themselves standing in the tradition of Paul, both theologically, and in terms of lifestyle. Paul, we know, took pride in his self-sufficiency and financial independence. "We worked night and day so as not to burden you," says Paul (1 Thess. 2:9). Theodotus may have understood himself in similar terms.

A full investigation of the term "cobbler" requires a look not simply at the literary evidence, which, in the case of the satirists like Martial and Juvenal, is deeply colored by elitist prejudice, but also at the physical evidence for the social status of cobblers. This material adds important elements to the picture gained from the literature. No doubt many cobblers were of slender means, like the fictional Micyllus, but a different picture can be gained from the funeral stele of Gaius Julius Helius, a shoemaker who kept a shop by the Porta Fontinalis; the stone dates to 120–130 CE (Fig. 9.1).

The inscription (*CIL* 6.33914) reads:

> Gaius Julius Helius, shoemaker at the Porta Fontinalis, while still living, made this for himself, his daughter Julia Flaccilla, his freedman Gaius Julius Onesimus, and for their freed slaves.[41]

---

40   Though Thorsteinsson (2013) argues that Crescens is better classed among the Stoic rather than Cynic philosophers.

41   *CIL* 6.33914: C(aius) Iulius Helius sutor a / Porta Fontinale fecit sibi et / Iuliae Flaccillae fil(iae) et C(aio) Iulio / Onesimo liberto libertabusque / posterisque eorum v(ivo) f(ecit). John Bodel was kind enough to point out to me a few mistakes in some of the published transcriptions and translations of this inscription, in particular, the mention of "freed-women" (libertas). For treatments of the monument: Lanciani 1892, 273–275; Petersen 2009, 182–184.

FIGURE 9.1
Funeral stele of Julius Helius

The stele is topped by a rounded pediment featuring two shoe lasts, one with the outlines of a military sandal (*caliga*); Helius must have been a specialist in this type of shoe. Because the portrait is very like many other "freedman" portraits, Helius has often been taken as an ex-slave, anxious to mark his rise in the world with an ostentatious burial monument. At any rate, his daughter Julia was born free, and Helius had sufficient means to own and to liberate Onesimus, and Julia and Onesimus both have their own freed slaves. Helius thus makes himself out as a kind of patriarch of at least three generations of descendants.[42] "Sutor" holds pride of place in the inscription, and while Martial or

---

42   Mayer 2012, 117.

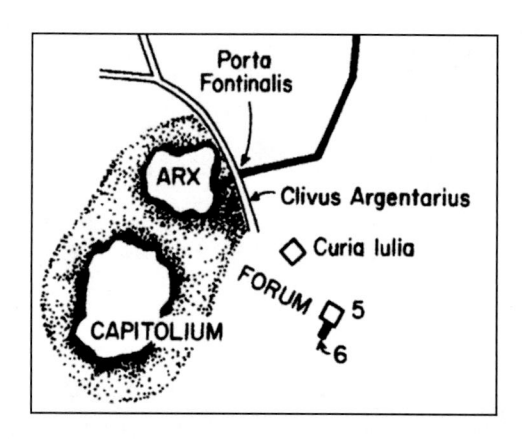

FIGURE 9.2
Location of the Porta Fontinalis

Juvenal deride the profession, Helius appears to take pride in his craft and the means it has provided him to sponsor a relatively deluxe funeral monument. His face is stern, but with the faintest hint of a contented smile in the mouth slightly upturned on the right. A large and hairy mole decorates the lower left lip. The realistic facial features of an older man make for an interesting contrast with the beefy torso, bordering on buxom, that supports it. By conflating such real and ideal features, the portrait mimics Republican-age portraits in which an aged head sits atop a young, athletic body: an attempt to project an idealized blend of mature wisdom and manly vigor.[43] In its stylistic pretensions, Helius' attempt to join the portrait company of Roman aristocrats might have seemed to some like another case of a cobbler getting above himself.

The monument makes a statement about the image Helius wishes to project; it also says something about his financial means and the possible level of achievement for a cobbler. The stele, carved of Carrera marble, is of good quality. The location of his shop is also significant. It lies by the Porta Fontinalis, where the Clivus Argentarius passed through the Servian wall, located on the shoulder of the Capitoline Hill, just to the north and east of the Julian Forum (Fig. 9.2).[44]

The central location lies just around the corner from the Roman Forum and the Curia Julia. If the dating of Helius' epitaph can be trusted (120–130 CE), he occupied this spot perhaps during and shortly after the major renovation to the

---

43   See Petersen 2015, 447–448.

44   The map is taken from Bodel 1998, 54. Piso had built certain structures connecting his private houses directly over the Porta Fontinalis, structures that were to be destroyed as per order of the Senate. This new information may be added to the discussion of Richardson 1992, 303.

FIGURE 9.3 Detail of the sarcophagus of the cobbler T. Flavius Trophimus

area resulting from the installation of Trajan's Forum (dedicated in 113 CE).[45] It would indeed have been a mark of distinction and no little expense to maintain a shop in this neighborhood.

And there is other evidence of surprisingly affluent cobblers, based on their funeral monuments: the monumental tomb of a shoemaker in Nuceria, just to the east of Pompeii; Atilius Artemas in Ostia; another cobbler of the same name in Nuceria, no doubt from the same family; also T. Flavius Trophimus, also from Ostia, whose sarcophagus shows a cobbler and his slave at work (Fig. 9.3). The stele dates from the Trajanic period. Also from Ostia, a female cobbler (*sutrix*) Septimia Stratonice (Fig. 9.4). Still other examples can be produced.[46] It would be a mistake to assume that the majority of shoemakers had such means, but if these monuments may serve as a guide, we need not take the disparaging

---

45   It is remarkable that the remains of a few shops still survive in precisely this area: as one proceeds down the remains of the Clivus Argentarius, starting at the point where the modern Via di S. Pietro in Carcere veers off to the right, walking down the old basalt cobbles towards the Chiesa dei Santi Luca e Martina, a row of shops is visible on the left, still intact, with the remains of a few others on the right. See Coarelli 2007, 105. As Coarelli observes, "all these structures must date to Trajan's reconstruction." The reader can even "walk" past them with the help of Google maps by searching on "Clivo Argentario" and utilizing the street view feature. The name Clivus Argentarius dates back only to the Middle Ages.

46   E.g., the *sutor caligarius* C. Atilius Iustus, whose monument is now held in Milan. See Spagnolis 2000, 66.

FIGURE 9.4
Funeral stone of the
sutrix Septimia Strato-
nice

comments of the satirists at face value when estimating the social level and economic capacity of shoemakers.

And Helius is not the only *sutor* in this part of the city. In Fig. 9.5, the Clivus Argentarius can be seen in the lower left hand corner. Proceeding along the Clivus Argentarius, just past the approximate site of Helius' shop, a staircase can be seen descending into the Julian Forum. Crossing through the Julian Forum, passing into the Forum Transitorium of Nerva, one finds the beginning of the street known as the Argiletum (in the upper right-hand portion of Fig. 9.5) which, according to Martial, was "thronged by many a cobbler."[47] The Vicus Sandalarius that branches off from the Argiletum takes its name from the concentration of cobbler shops.[48]

The area had this specific character at least since the time of Augustus, who set up a compital altar here, with a statue going under the name of Apollo Sandalarius (Suet., *Aug.* 57). The altar still survives, as do the names of some of the *vicimagistri* who presided over it. Helius, therefore, is located not too far from a district that has long been populated by other shoemakers.

---

47   *Ep.* 2.17.
48   See Coarelli 1999, 189. The map detail is from Grande and Scagnetti 2000.

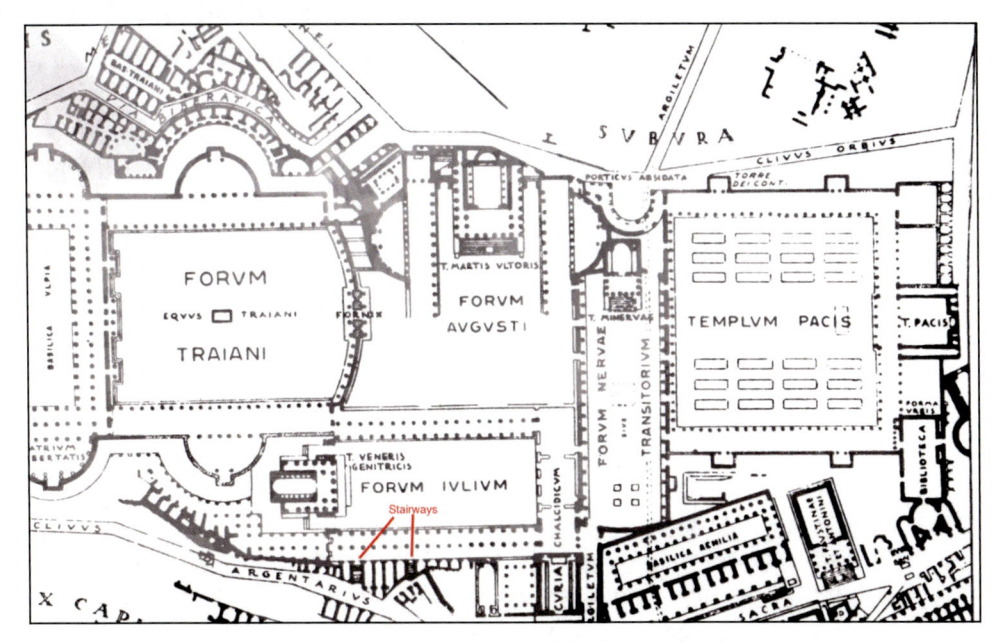

FIGURE 9.5 Imperial fora, showing the proximity of Helius' shop on the Clivus Argentarius to the Argiletum

The shops in the Argiletum, which runs through Subura, may have been somewhat more modest than that of C. Helius.

And as it turns out, this district of the Sandaliarion and the Argiletum is more than just a center for shoemakers: it is also the bookstore district of ancient Rome, as we know from remarks of Martial, Galen, and Aulus Gellius.[49] The story where Galen describes an argument he witnessed while walking through the Sandaliarion is well-known. One of the disputants had just bought a book by Galen on the assumption that it was genuine, while the other maintained it was a forgery. Galen suddenly emerges from the crowd to pronounce the text as a forgery and to congratulate the skeptic for his good Greek education that allowed him to spot counterfeit texts.[50] And Galen can be found in the neighborhood on other occasions. He encountered his rival, Martianus the Erasistratean, in the Sandaliarion and fell into a dispute about a text of Hippocrates.[51] He staged public lectures and dissections at the Temple of Peace,

---

49   Martial (*Ep.* 1.2, 1.3, 1.117); Aulus Gellius (*NA* 18.4). See White 2009, 271.
50   *Libr. Propr.* 1 (19.8–9K).
51   "On his way down to the Sandaliarion" (*Praecog.* 4 = 14.620 Kühn). References to Galen's movements can be found in Mattern 2013.

right at the head of the Argiletum.[52] He also stored many of his books in a supposedly fireproof warehouse near the Temple of Peace that was destroyed in
the great fire of 192.

The combination of the leatherworking shops and bookstores in this area
may not be accidental: most books in the ancient world, after all, were written
on parchment, and the tools and expertise for preparing and cutting leather
would naturally lend themselves to that stage in the production of books. The
commercial networks dedicated to the acquisition of leather products for shoemakers would conceivably be able to serve bookmakers and booksellers as
well. And the Horrea Chartaria, the paper warehouse, was also in this district,
close to the Temple of Telluris (see Fig. 9.6), according to the fourth-century
regionary catalogue of city buildings.[53]

All of this brings us back around to Theodotus and his school. It would be
a mistake to presume a high level of literacy among cobblers generally, but
there is ample precedent in a variety of literatures, testifying to the socially
recognized figure of philosophically oriented cobblers, who practice their craft
and their philosophy within the precincts of their shops. And so, rather than
internal tension, there is actually a certain synergy within the phrase, "learned
cobbler." And the archaeological evidence gives us reason to believe in a cobbler who might have had the wherewithal to maintain a space where people
could have met for study and conversation.[54]

It is, of course, impossible to locate Theodotus within the city as to his res-
idence. However, if we were to make an informed guess, what better place
could be found for a leather-working, book-making, Galen-admiring group
like Theodotus' than the district around the Sandaliarion and the Argiletum,
"thronged by many a cobbler?"

While this matter of actual physical location must remain purely conjec-
tural, it is possible to find a place for Theodotus and his group in the social and
cultural environment of ancient Rome: that of the leather-working shop owner,
whose cultural and intellectual ancestry included Simon the cobbler, the host
of Socrates and author of dialogues, also owing a debt to the self-sufficiency and
independence of the Cynics—though not their itinerant and rootless ways. It

---

52 *Puls. Diff.* 1.1 (8.494–5K).
53 See Richardson 1992, 192.
54 What would the rent have been for one of the *tabernae* by the Porta Fontinalis, or for a shop
    along the Argiletum or the Sandaliarion? Figures are extremely hard to come by. Sueto-
    nius (*Julius Caesar* 38), observers that Caesar remitted annual rents to everyone who paid
    less than 2000 sesterces per year—presumably as a kind of welfare aimed at those with
    lower incomes—roughly equivalent to roughly 40 denarii/month. A shop on the ground
    floor of a deluxe neighborhood would doubtless have cost more.

FIGURE 9.6 Location of the Vicus Sandaliarius (lower left corner)

also owes something to the Apostle Paul and his habits of working, teaching, and writing. I maintain that Theodotus self-consciously situated himself and his school within these traditions.

And so, if we go back to where we began, with Aulus Gellius paying a visit to that cobbler shop, he might have been momentarily surprised to find a shoemaker poring over books in his *taberna*: this would have been exceptional behavior for a cobbler. Exceptional, but not impossible: Gellius would, we can be sure, have been able to call up Simon the Shoemaker as a precedent, along with other points of cultural contact as a way of making sense of this cobbler and his books.

Bibliography

Bodel, John. 1999. Punishing Piso. "The Senatus Consultum de Cn. Pisone Patre: Text, Translation, Discussion." *American Journal of Philology* 120: 43–63.

Coarelli, Filippo. 2007. *Rome and Environs; an Archaeological Guide*. Translated by James Clauss and Daniel Harmon. Berkeley, Calif.: University of California Press.

Coarelli, Filippo. 1999. "Vicus Sandaliarius." Page 189 in *LTUR* vol. 5.

Cuvigny, Hélène. 1996. "The Amount of Wages Paid to the Quarry-Workers at Mons Claudianus." *The Journal of Roman Studies* 86: 139–145.

Cynic Epistles. See Malherbe 1977.

Ehrman, Bart. 1993a. *The Orthodox Corruption of Scripture*. New York: Oxford University Press.

Ehrman, Bart. 1993b. "The Theodotians as Corruptors of Scripture. Pages 46–51 in *Biblica et Apocrypha, Orientalia, Ascetica*." Edited by Elizabeth Livingstone. Papers presented at The Eleventh International Conference on Patristic Studies, Oxford, 1991. Leuven: Peeters.

Epiphanius. *Panarion*. Edited by Karl Holl. Griechischen christlichen Schriftsteller 31. Leipzig: J.C. Hinrichs'sche Buchhandlung.

Eusebius. 1980. *The Ecclesiastical History*. Edited and translated by Kirsopp Lake. Cambridge, Mass.: Harvard University Press.

Fitzgerald, John. 1998. "Eusebius and *The Little Labyrinth*." Pages 120–146 in *The Early Church in its Context; Essays in Honor of Everett Ferguson*. Edited by Abraham Malherbe, Frederick Norris, and James Thompson. Supplements to Novum Testamentum 90. Leiden: Brill.

Frend, W.H.C. 1984. *The Rise of Christianity*. Philadelphia: Fortress Press.

Goulet, R. 1997. "Trois cordonniers philosophes." Pages 119–125 in *Studies in Plato and the Platonic Tradition*. Edited by M. Joyal. Aldershot: Ashgate.

Grande, Giuseppe and Francesco Scagnetti. 2000. "Roma Urbs Imperatorum Aetate." Rome: Quasar.

Heine, Ronald. 2004. "Articulating Identity." Chapter 18 in *The Cambridge History of Early Christian Literature*. Cambridge: Cambridge University Press.

Hippolytus. *Refutatio Omnium Haeresium*. Edited by Miroslav Marcovich. Patristische Texte und Studien 25. Berlin: Walter de Gruyter.

Hock, Ron. 1980. *The Social Context of Paul's Ministry*. Minneapolis, Minn.: Fortress.

Kennedy, George. 1998. "Review of Patillon and Bolognesi, *Aelius Théon*: Progymnasmata." *American Journal of Philology* 119: 476–480.

Lampe, Peter. 2003. *From Paul to Valentinus; Christians at Rome in the First Two Centuries*. Translated by Michael Steinhauser. Edited by Marshall Johnson. Minneapolis, Minn.: Fortress Press.

Lanciani, Rodolfo. 1892. *Pagan and Christian Rome*. New York: Houghton, Mifflin & Company.

Lau, O. 1967. "Schuster und Schusterhandwerk in der griechisch-römischen Literature und Kunst." Ph.D. diss., Bonn.

Lovén, Lena Larsson. 2016. "Women, Trade, and Production." Pages 200–221 in *Urban Craftsmen and Traders in the Roman World*. Edited by Andrew Wilson and Miko Flohr. New York: Oxford University Press.

LTUR. *Lexicon Topographicum Urbis Romae*. 1993–2000. Edited by Margareta Steinby. 6 vols. Rome: Quasar.

LTURS. *Lexicon Topographicum Urbis Romae. Suburbium*. 2001–2008. Edited by Adriano La Regina. 5 vols. Rome: Quasar.

Malherbe, Abraham. 1977. *The Cynic Epistles: A Study Edition*. Missoula, Mont.: Scholars Press.

Mattern, Susan. 2013. *The Prince of Medicine: Galen in the Roman Empire*. Oxford: Oxford University Press.

Mayer, Andrew. 2012. *Ancient Middle Classes; Urban Life and Aesthetics in the Roman Empire, 100 BCE–250 CE*. Cambridge: Cambridge University Press.

Origen. 1953. *Contra Celsum*. Edited and translated by Henry Chadwick. Cambridge: Cambridge University Press.

Patillon, Michel and Giancarlo Bolognesi. 1997. *Aelius Théon*: Progymnasmata. Paris: Les Belles Lettres.

Petersen, Lauren Hackworth. 2009. "Clothes Make the Man: Dressing the Roman Freedman Body." Pages 181–214 in *Bodies and Boundaries in Graeco-Roman Antiquity*. Edited by Thorsten Fögen and Mireille M. Lee. Berlin: Walter de Gruyter.

Petersen, Lauren Hackworth. 2015. "Non-elite Patronage." Pages 447–448 in *The Oxford Handbook of Roman Sculpture*. Edited by Elise Friedland, Melanie Sobocinski, and Elaine Gazda. Oxford: Oxford University Press.

Richardson, L. 1992. *A New Topographical Dictionary of Ancient Rome*. Baltimore, Md.: Johns Hopkins University Press.

Sellars, John. 2003. Simon the Shoemaker and the Problem of Socrates. *Classical Philology* 98: 207–216.

Spagnolis, Marisa dé. 2000. *La tomba del calzolaio dalla necropoli monumentale romana di Nocera Superiore*. Studia Archaeologica 106. Rome: "L'Erma" di Bretschneider.

Theon, Aelius. 1997. *Progymnasmata*. Edited by Michel Patillon and Giancarlo Bolognesi. Paris: Les Belles Lettres.

Stobaeus. 1903. *Stoicorum veterum fragmentum* Vol. 1. Edited by Hans von Arnim. Leipzig: Teubner.

Thompson, Dorothy Burr. 1960. "The House of Simon the Shoemaker." *Archaeology* 13: 234–240.

Thorsteinsson, Runar. 2013. Justin's Debate with Crescens the Stoic. *Zeitschrift für Antikes Christentum* 17: 451–478.

Walzer, Richard. 1949. *Galen on Jews and Christians*. Oxford: Oxford University Press.

White, Peter. 2009. Bookshops in the Literary Culture of Rome. Pages 268–287 in *Ancient Literacies*. Edited by William Johnson and Holt Parker. New York: Oxford University Press.

Williams, Frank. 2013. The Panarion *of Epiphanius of Salamis, Books II and III*. De Fide. Nag Hammadi and Manichaean Studies 79. Leiden: Brill.

Author Index

Source Index

Greek and Roman Writings

Quomodo adolescens poetas audire debeat
14b–37b   161n8
De sera numinis vindicta
                       178

Seneca
Epistulae Morales
5   67

Stobaeus
Florilegium
95,21   191n30

Suda [Adler]   48n13

Suetonius
De Vita Caesarum
Augustus
57   198

Julius Caesar
38   200n54

Sybilline Oracles   91, 93, 97

Synesius
Dion
8   171n31

Xenophon
Memorabilia
4.2.1   190n28
4.2.2   186n11

Nag Hammadi Codices (NHC)

Apocryphon of John
(NHC II,*1*; III,*1*; IV,*1*; BG 2)
                       4, 45, 49, 55
1.1–4   46
13.19–21   46n6
22.22–23   46n6
29.6-7   46n6

Gospel of Philip
(NHC II,*3*)   3, 39, 41, 42
55.9–19   39–40
54:13–18   40
60:34–61:5   40n23
62:26–35   40n23
66:23–29   43n23
67:14–18   43n23
69:4–8   43n23
69:8–14   43n23
76:17–22   43n23
80:4–8   43n23

Gospel of Thomas
(NHC II,2)   98
Log. 1   49

Gospel of Truth
(NHC I,*3*; XII,2)   36
19:10–34   34n6

Interpretation of Knowledge
(NHC XI,*1*)   36, 41
5:33-35   34n7
9:17–27   34n6
9:18   34n7

Prayer of the Apostle Paul
(NHC I,*1*)   36n14

Treatise on the Resurrection
(NHC I,*4*)   36, 41

Tripartite Tractate
(NHC I,*5*)   36n15
104:18–25   33n6, 40n24
121:31.37   34n7
123:11–16   33n6
123:12–16   40
123:17–18   34n7
125:4–5   34n7

Printed in the United States
By Bookmasters